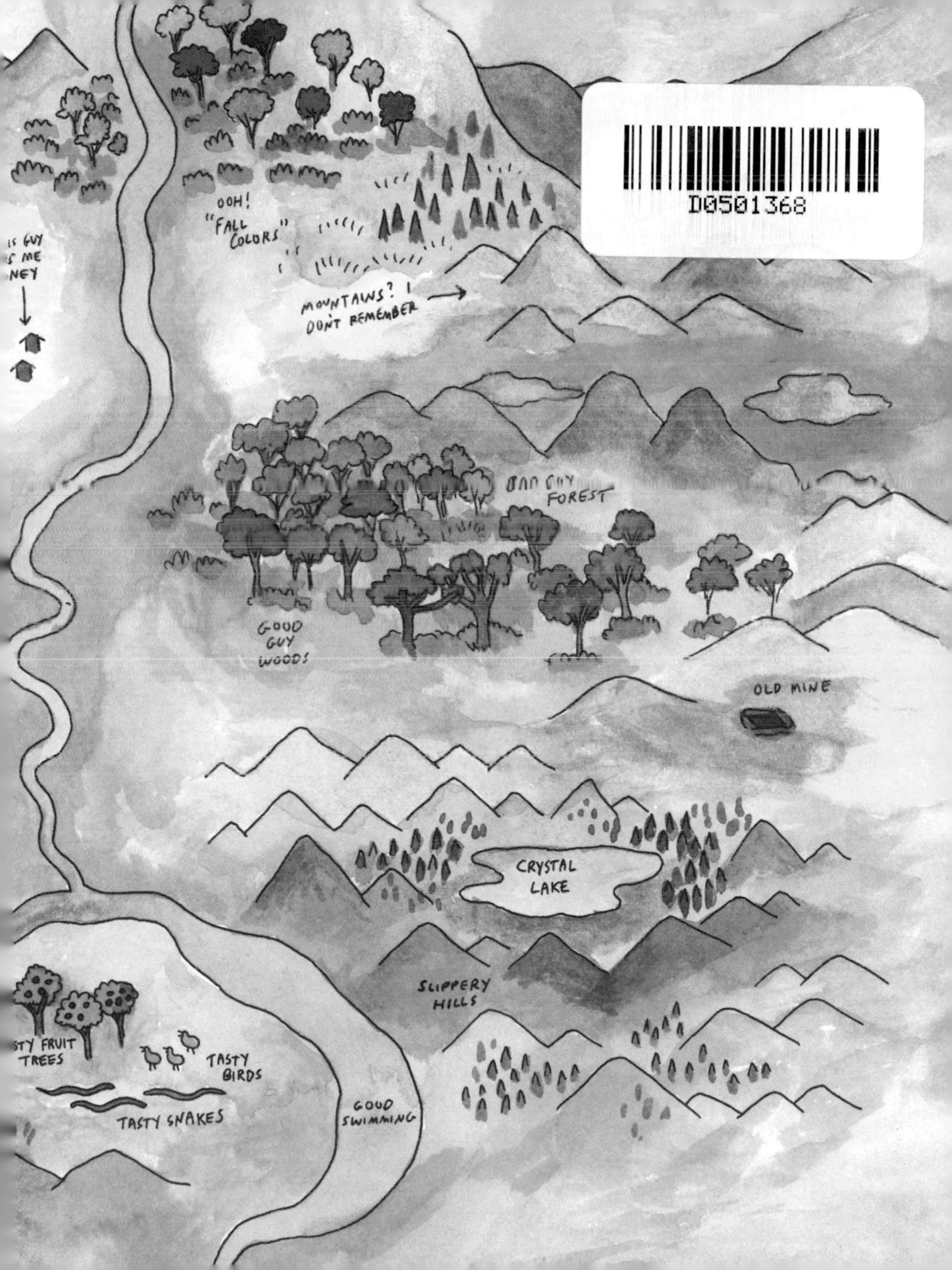
OOH!
"FALL COLORS"
MOUNTAINS? I DON'T REMEMBER
BAD GUY FOREST
GOOD GUY WOODS!
OLD MINE
CRYSTAL LAKE
SLIPPERY HILLS
TREES
TASTY BIRDS
TASTY SNAKES
GOOD SWIMMING

SOME IMPORTANT INFORMATION

PANTS

"COYOTE DOGGIRL"

HALF DOG, HALF COYOTE
WILDERNESS SKILLS: 8/10
INTELLIGENCE: HIGH
ATTITUDE: TOO MUCH

"RED"

Quarterhorse x Mustang mix
Red roan (dominant gene Rn)
Intelligence: Average
Endurance: Excellent
Speed: Very good
Hooves: Great! Great!
Height: 14.2 hh

CROP HALTER TOP

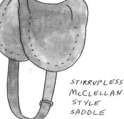

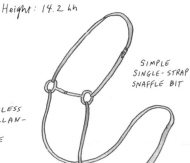

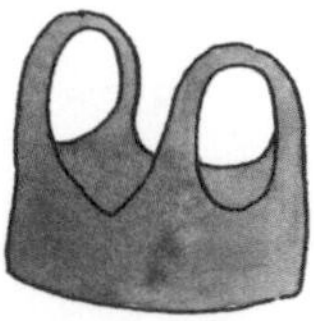

SIMPLE
SINGLE-STRAP
SNAFFLE BIT

STIRRUPLESS
McCLELLAN-
STYLE
SADDLE

ALL TACK DESIGNED AND MADE BY
COYOTE DOGGIRL

OUTFIT
DESIGNED & SEWN BY
COYOTE DOGGIRL

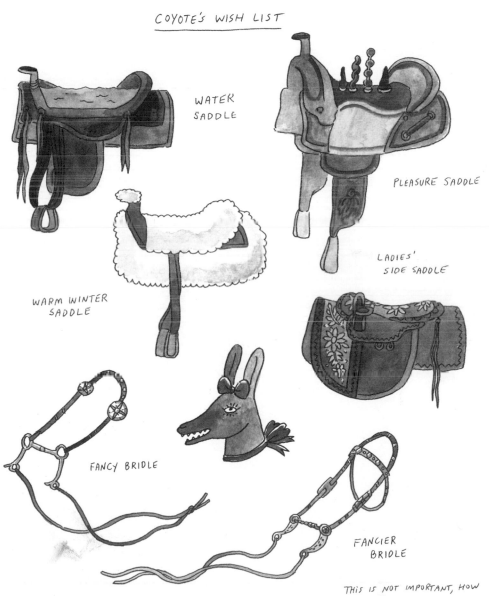

COYOTE'S WISH LIST

WATER SADDLE

PLEASURE SADDLE

LADIES' SIDE SADDLE

WARM WINTER SADDLE

FANCY BRIDLE

FANCIER BRIDLE

THIS IS NOT IMPORTANT, HOW DID THIS GET IN HERE ...

For Adam, my love.

Thank you, horses. All colors, including red.

Much obliged to Mom, Dad, Alex, Ashley, Davee, Raphael, Jaclyn, Meredith, D&Q, ST, & all horse friends.

DRAWNANDQUARTERLY.COM
LISAHANAWALT.COM

First edition: August 2018
Printed in China
10 9 8 7 6 5 4 3 2 1

Cataloguing data available from Library and archives Canada.

Red sky at night, sleep tight;
Red sky in the morning, move your ass!!!

Published in the USA by Drawn & Quarterly, a client publisher of Farrar, Straus and Giroux.
Orders: 888-330-8477
Published in Canada by Drawn & Quarterly, a client publisher of Raincoast Books.
Orders: 800-663-5714
Published in the United Kingdom by Drawn & Quarterly, a client publisher of Publishers Group UK.
Orders: info@PGUK.CO.UK

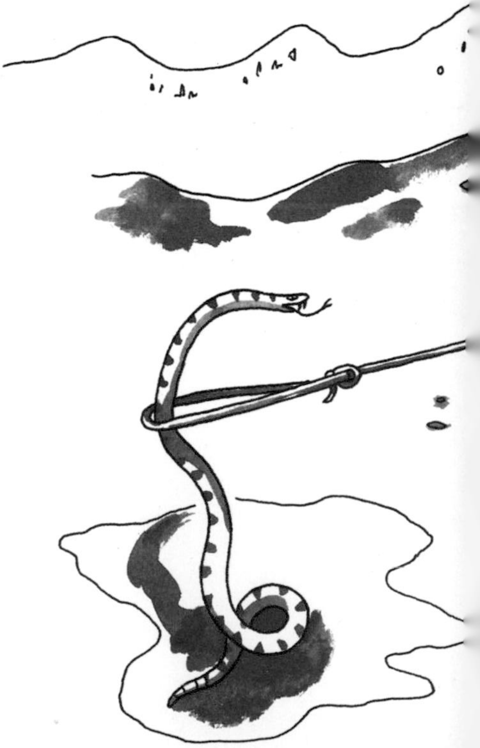

Coyote Doggirl

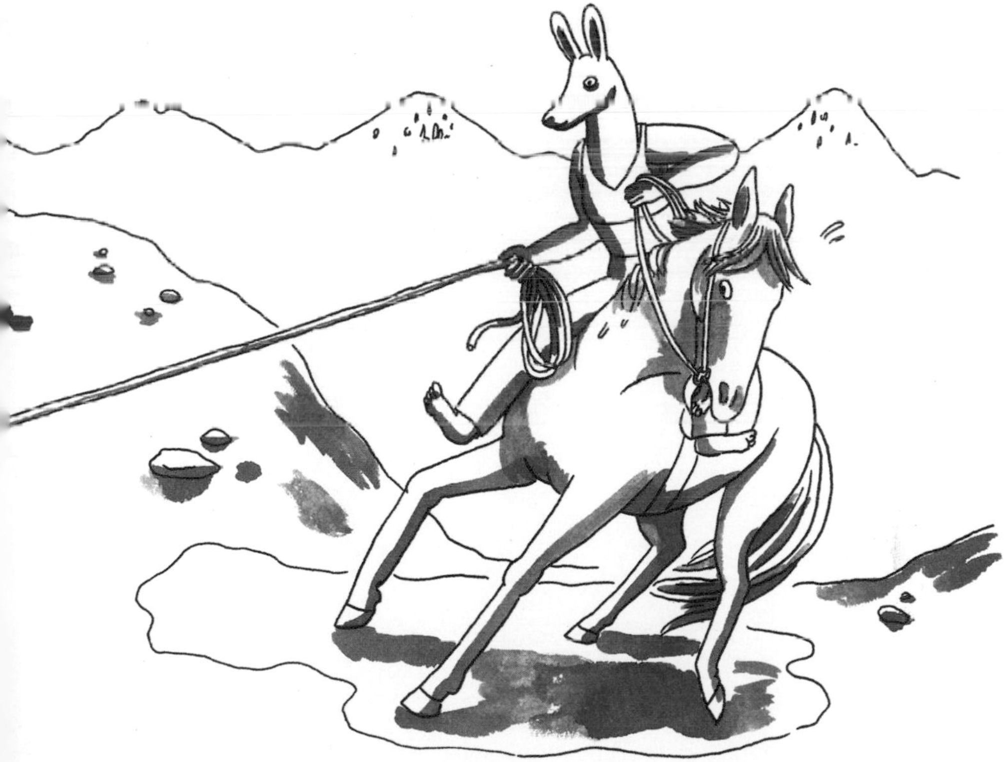

Lisa Hanawalt

DRAWN & QUARTERLY

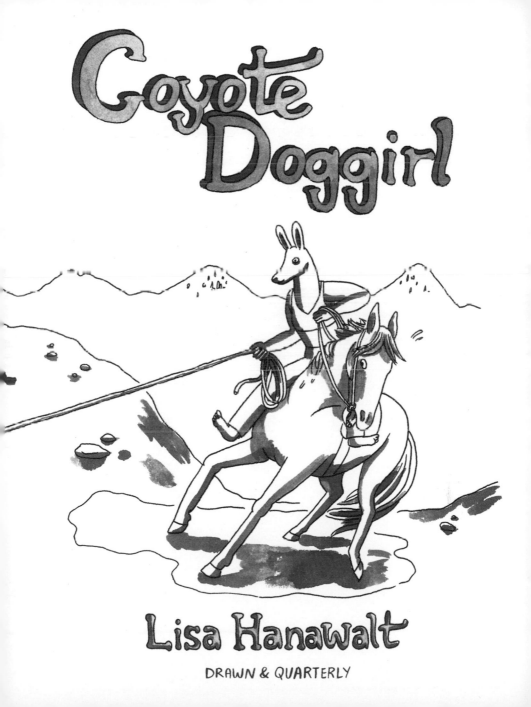

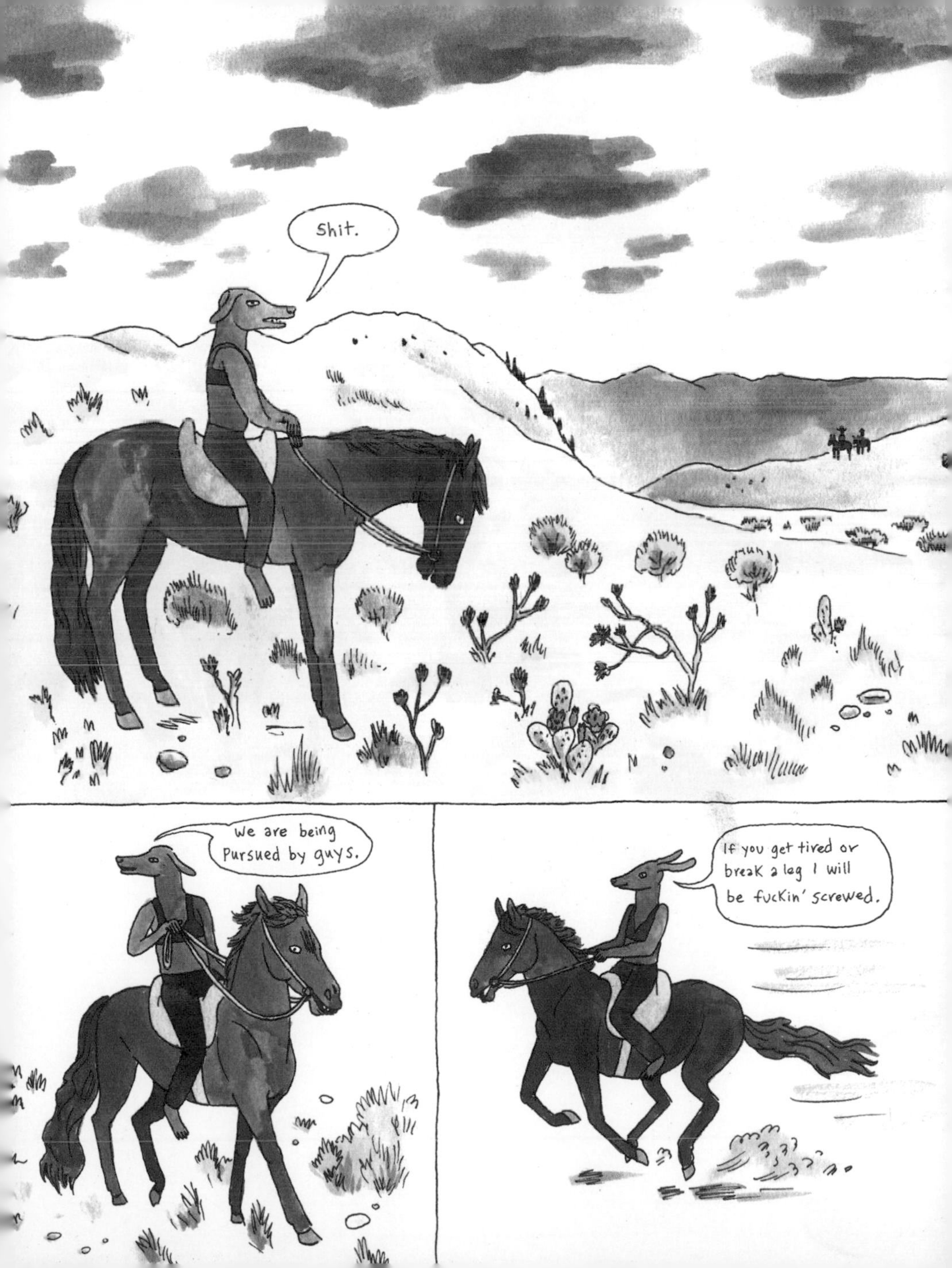
Shit.
We are being Pursued by guys.
If you get tired or break a leg I will be fuckin' screwed.

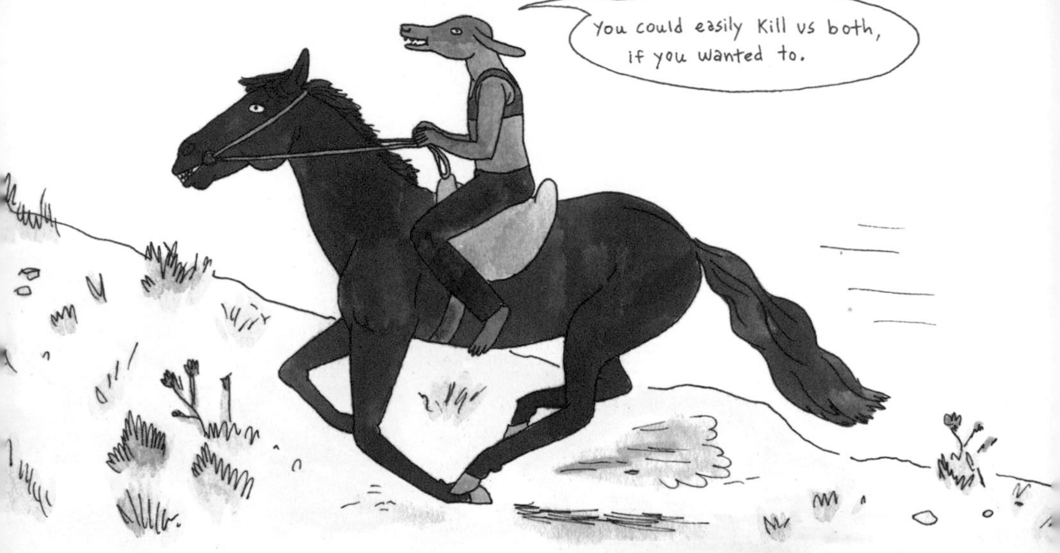
You could easily Kill us both, if you wanted to.

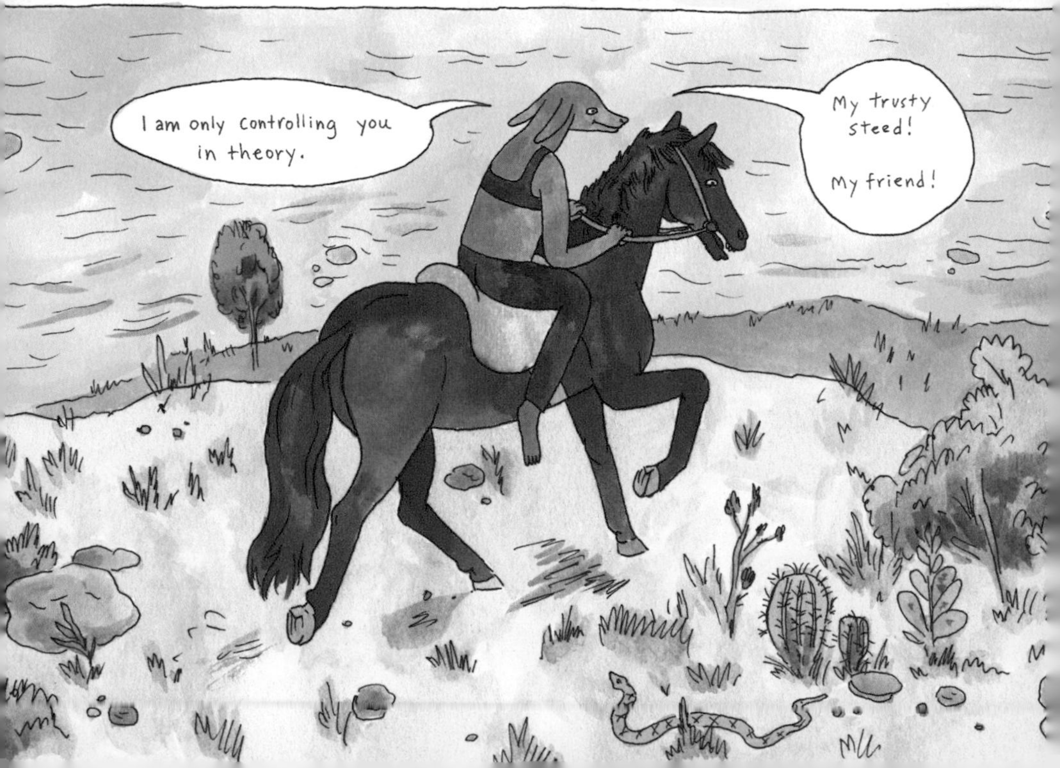
I am only controlling you in theory.
My trusty steed!
My friend!

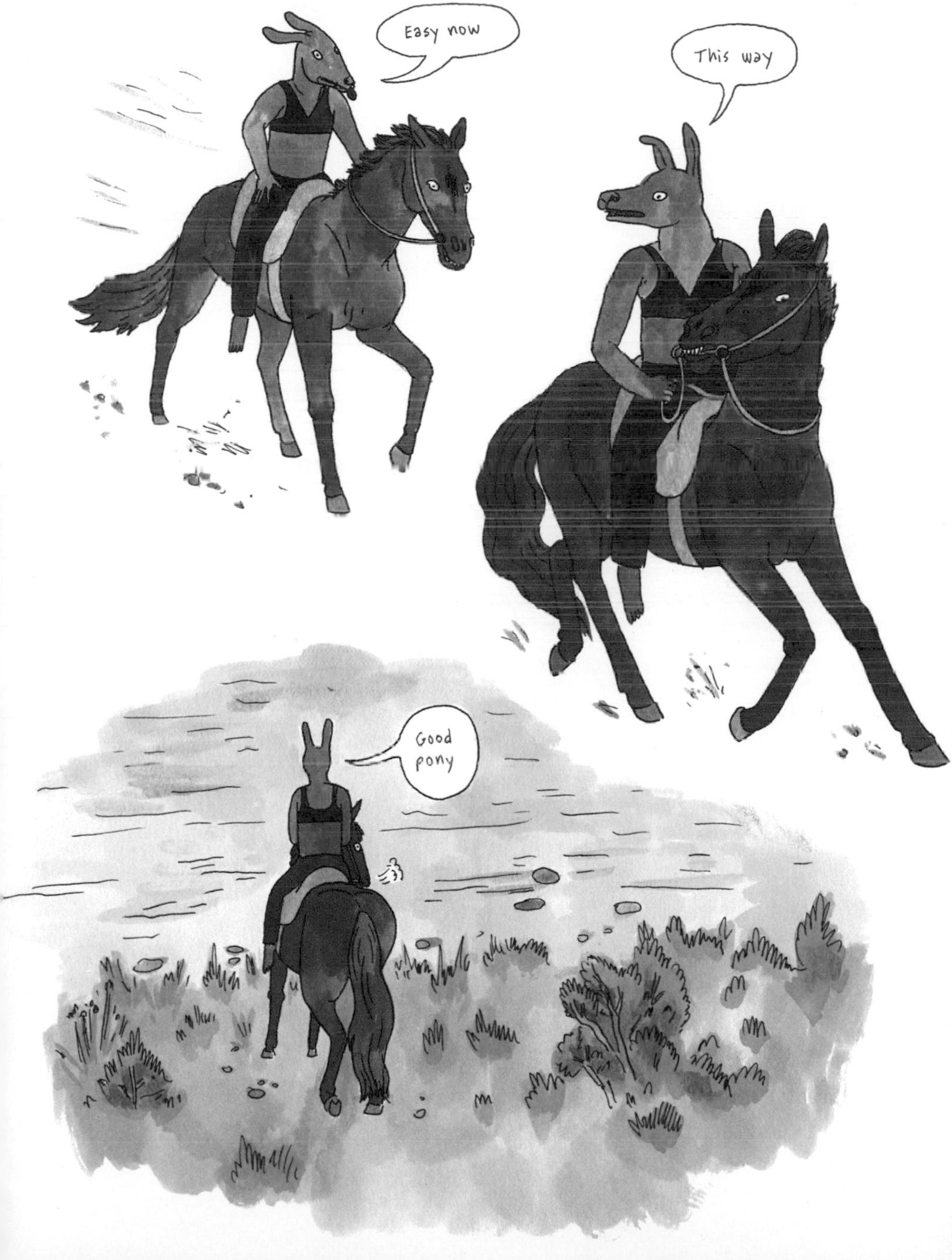
Easy now
This way
Good pony

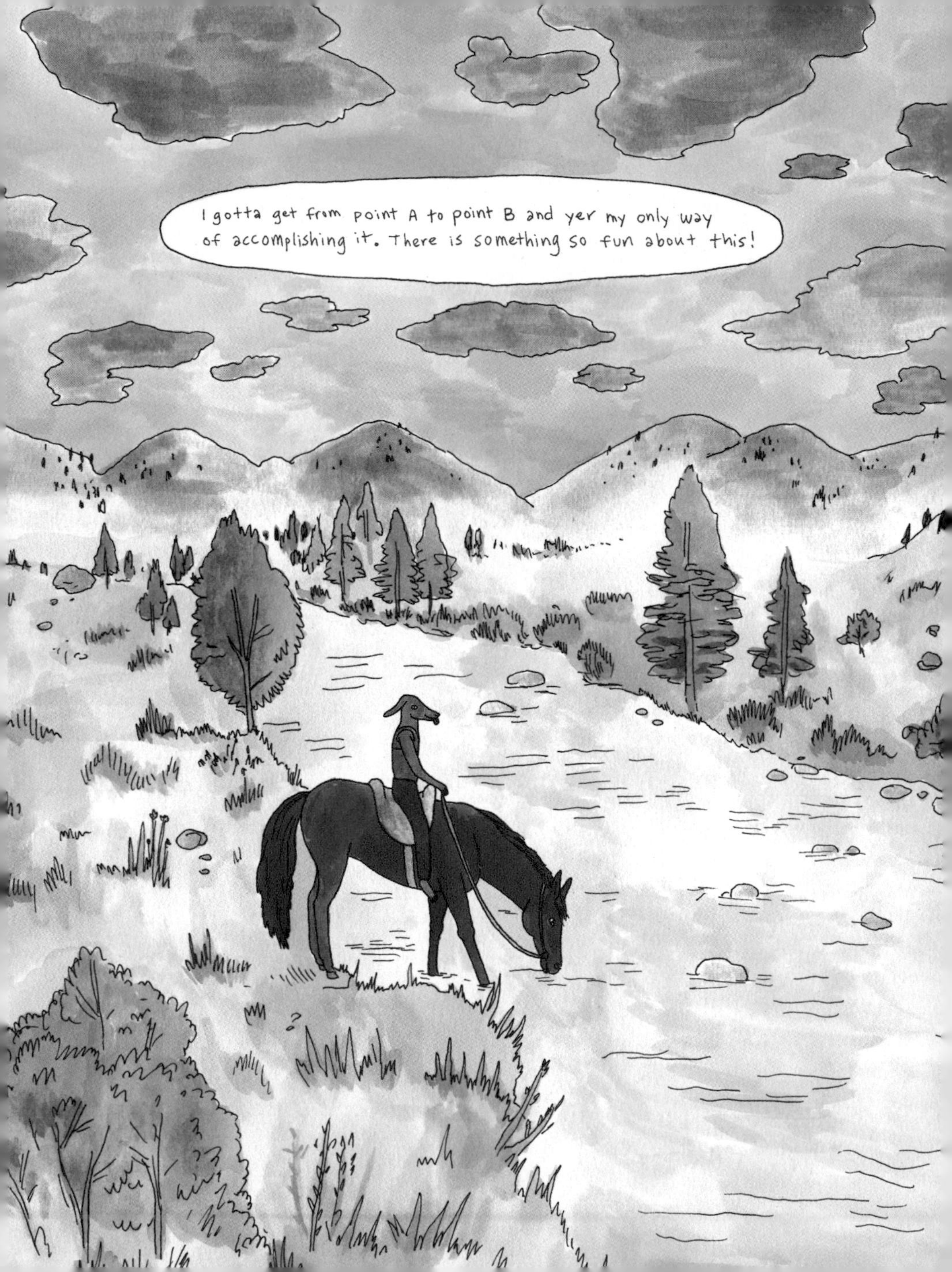
I gotta get from point A to point B and yer my only way of accomplishing it. There is something so fun about this!

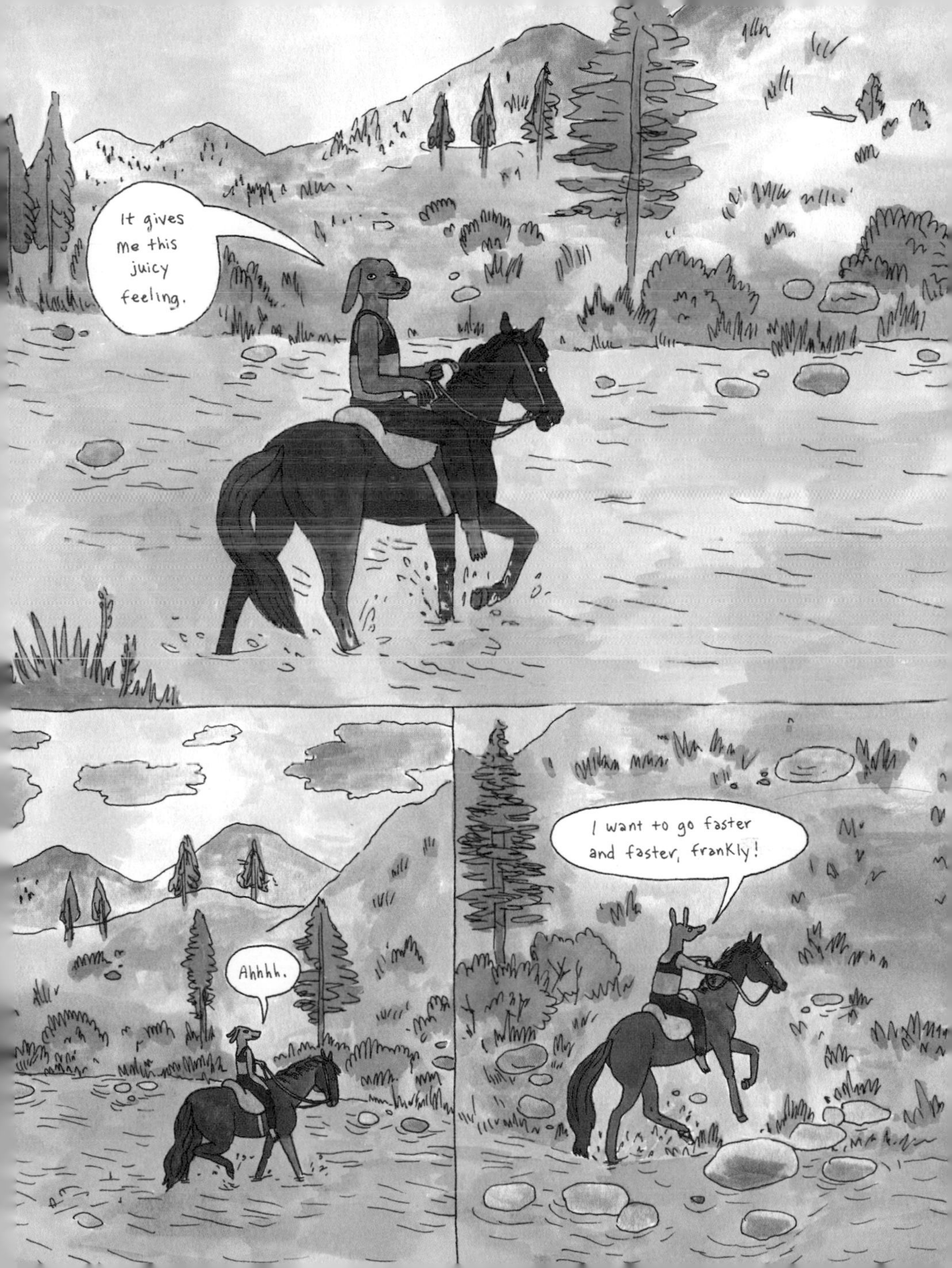
It gives me this juicy feeling.
Ahhhh.
I want to go faster and faster, frankly!

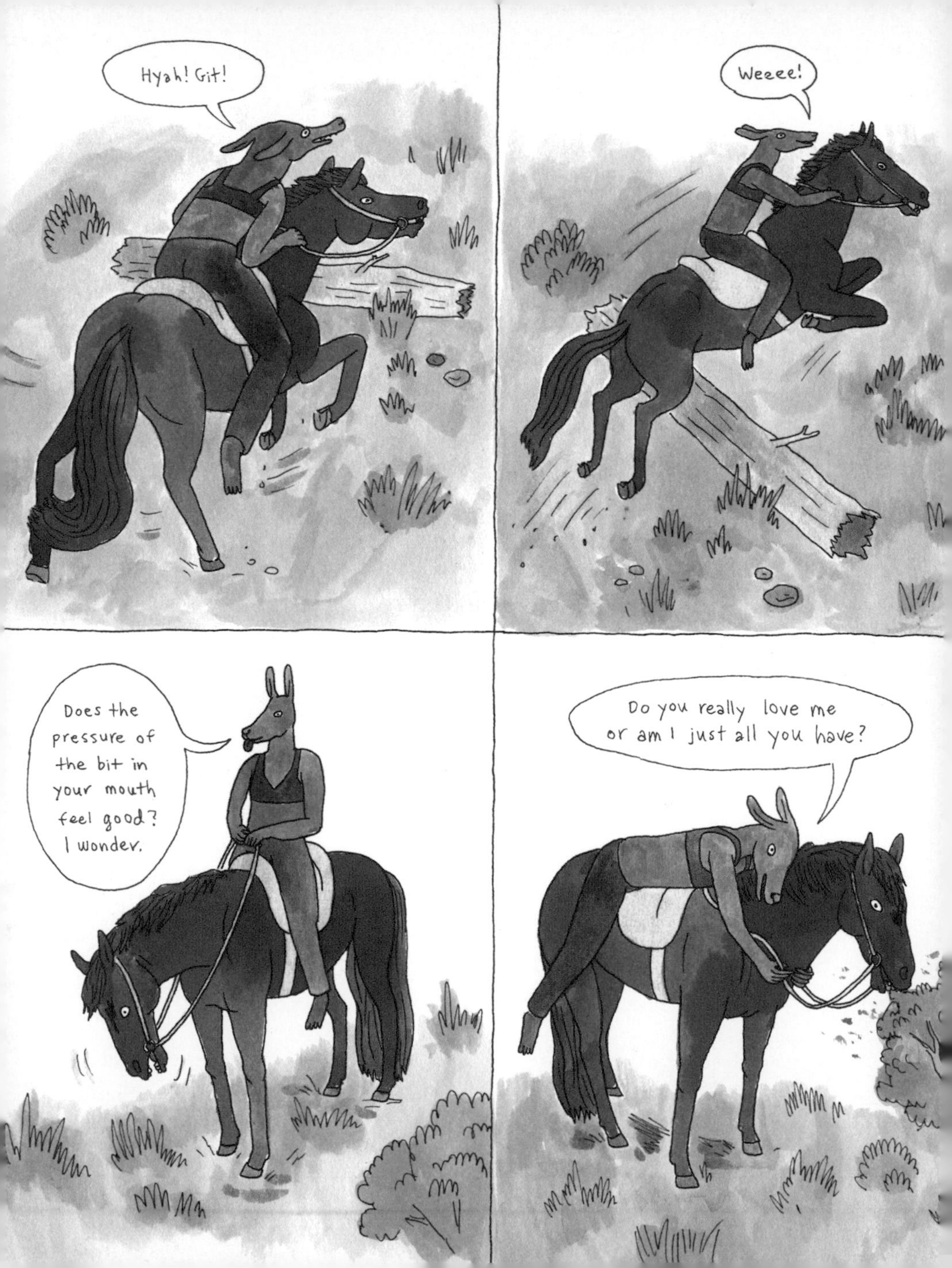

Hyah! Git!
Weeee!
Does the pressure of the bit in your mouth feel good? I wonder.
Do you really love me or am I just all you have?

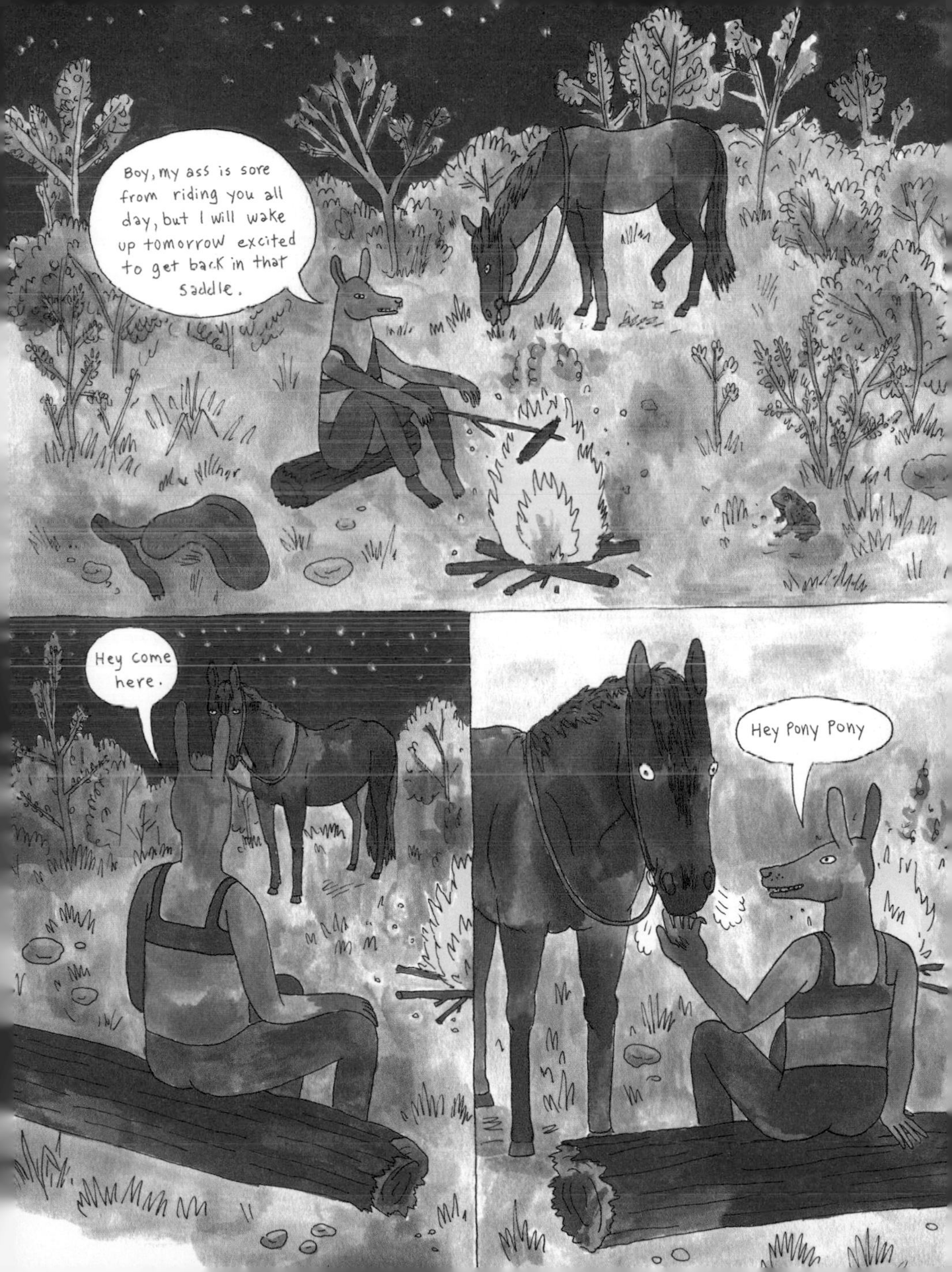
Boy, my ass is sore from riding you all day, but I will wake up tomorrow excited to get back in that saddle.
Hey come here.
Hey Pony Pony

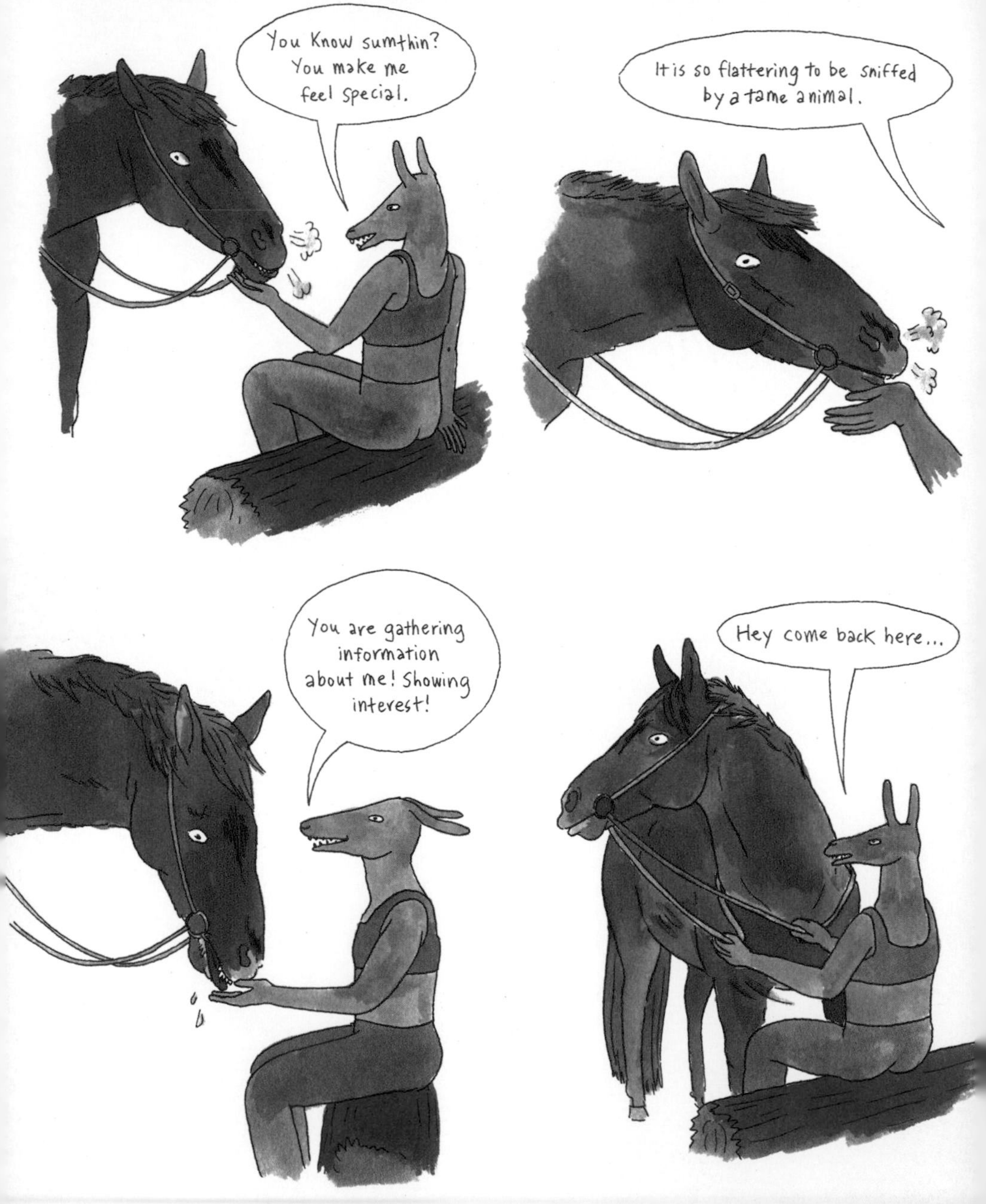
You Know sumthin? You make me feel special.
It is so flattering to be sniffed by a tame animal.
You are gathering information about me! Showing interest!
Hey come back here...

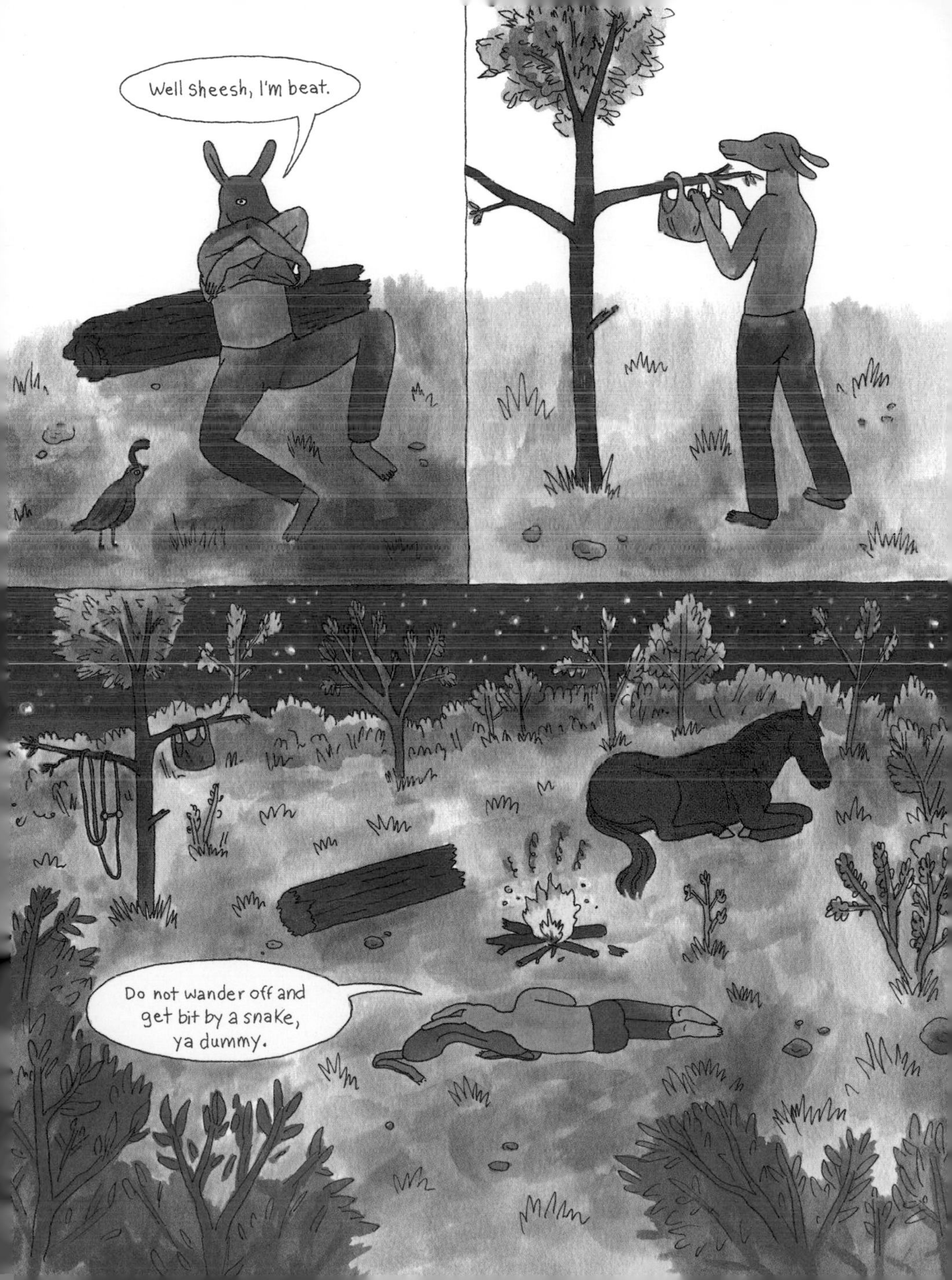
Well sheesh, I'm beat.
Do not wander off and get bit by a snake, ya dummy.

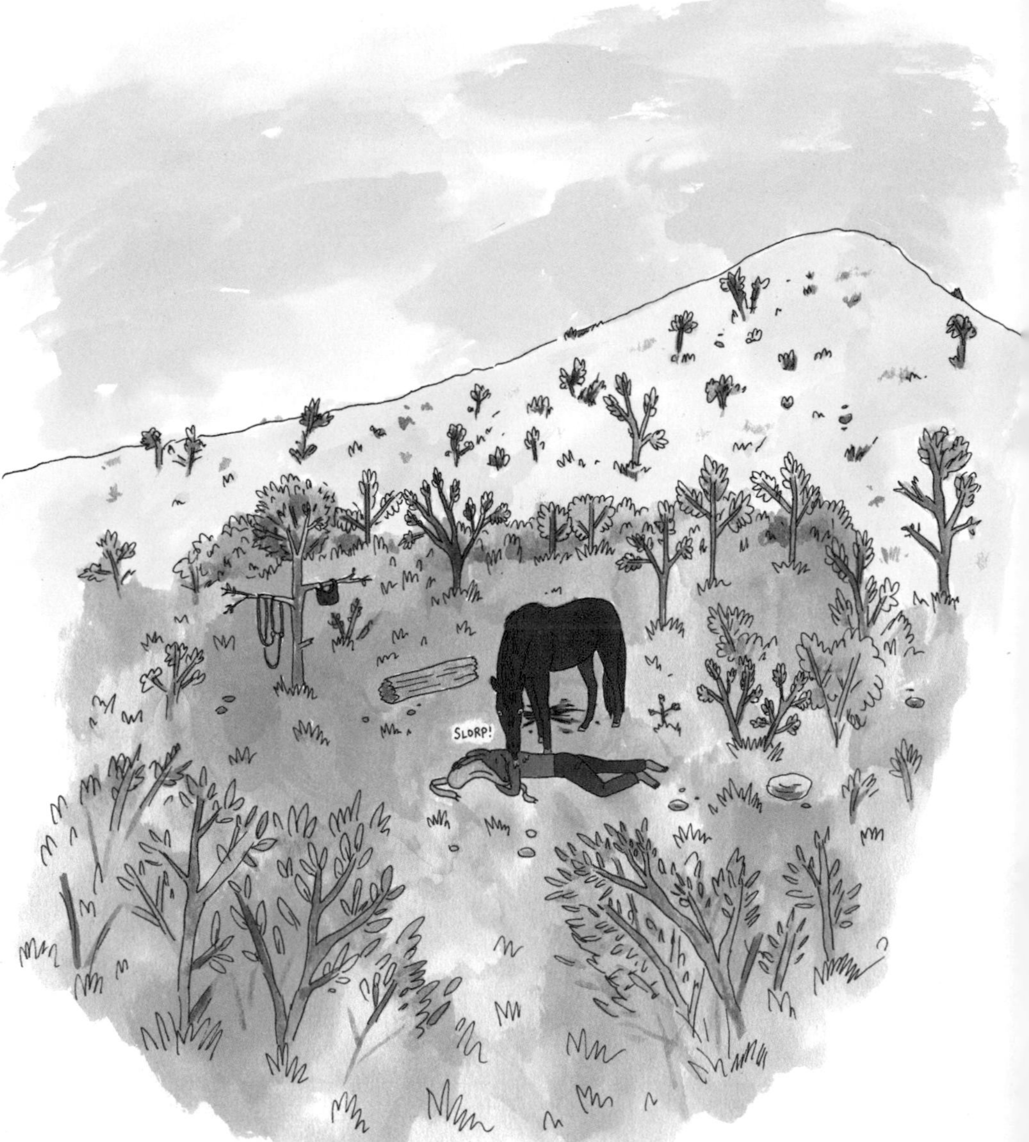
SLORP!

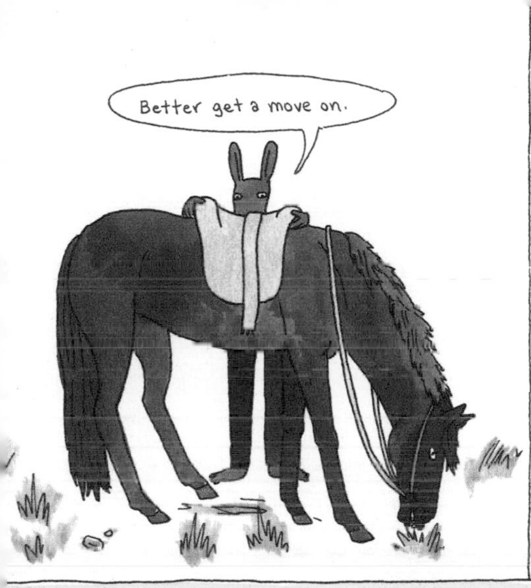
Better get a move on.

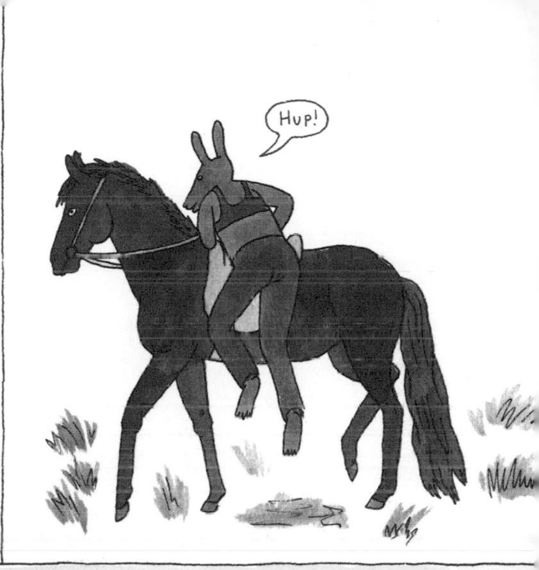
Hup!

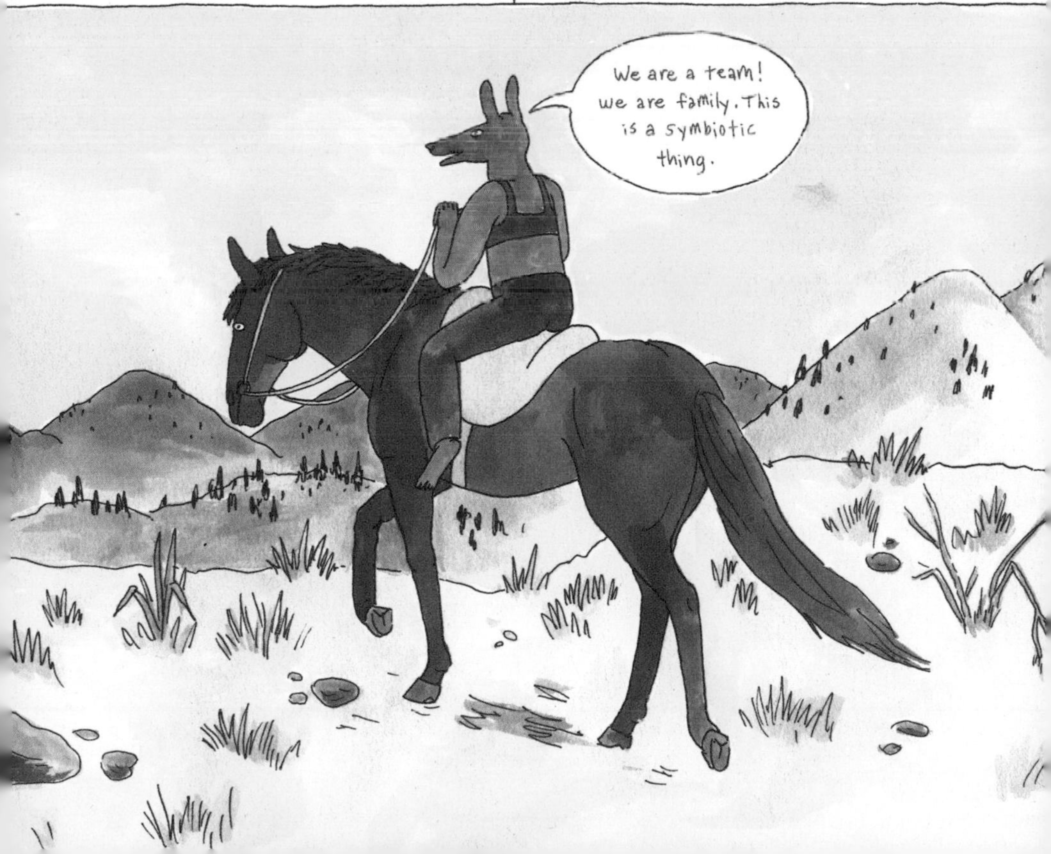
We are a team! we are family. This is a symbiotic thing.

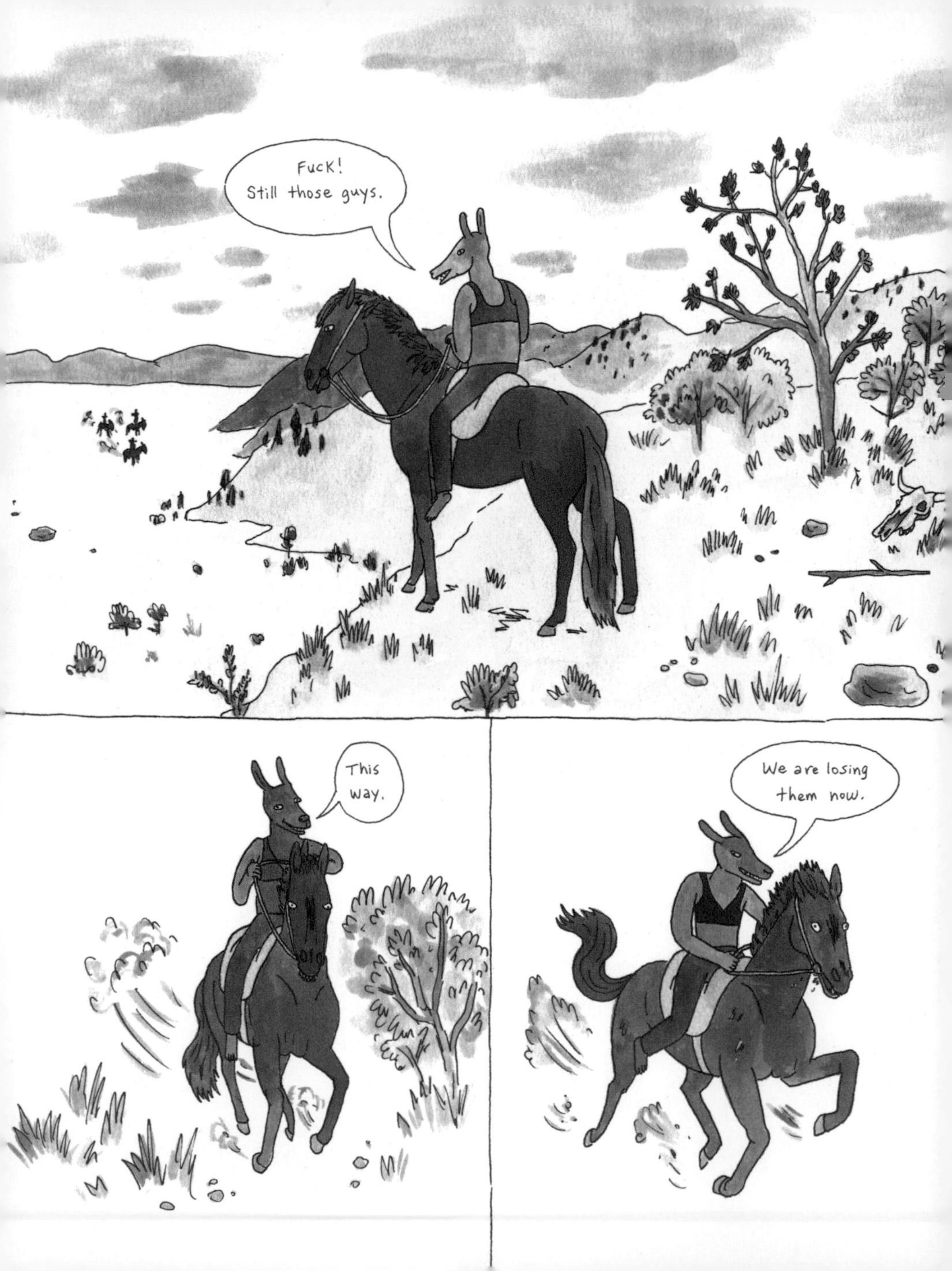
FUCK! Still those guys.
This way.
We are losing them now.

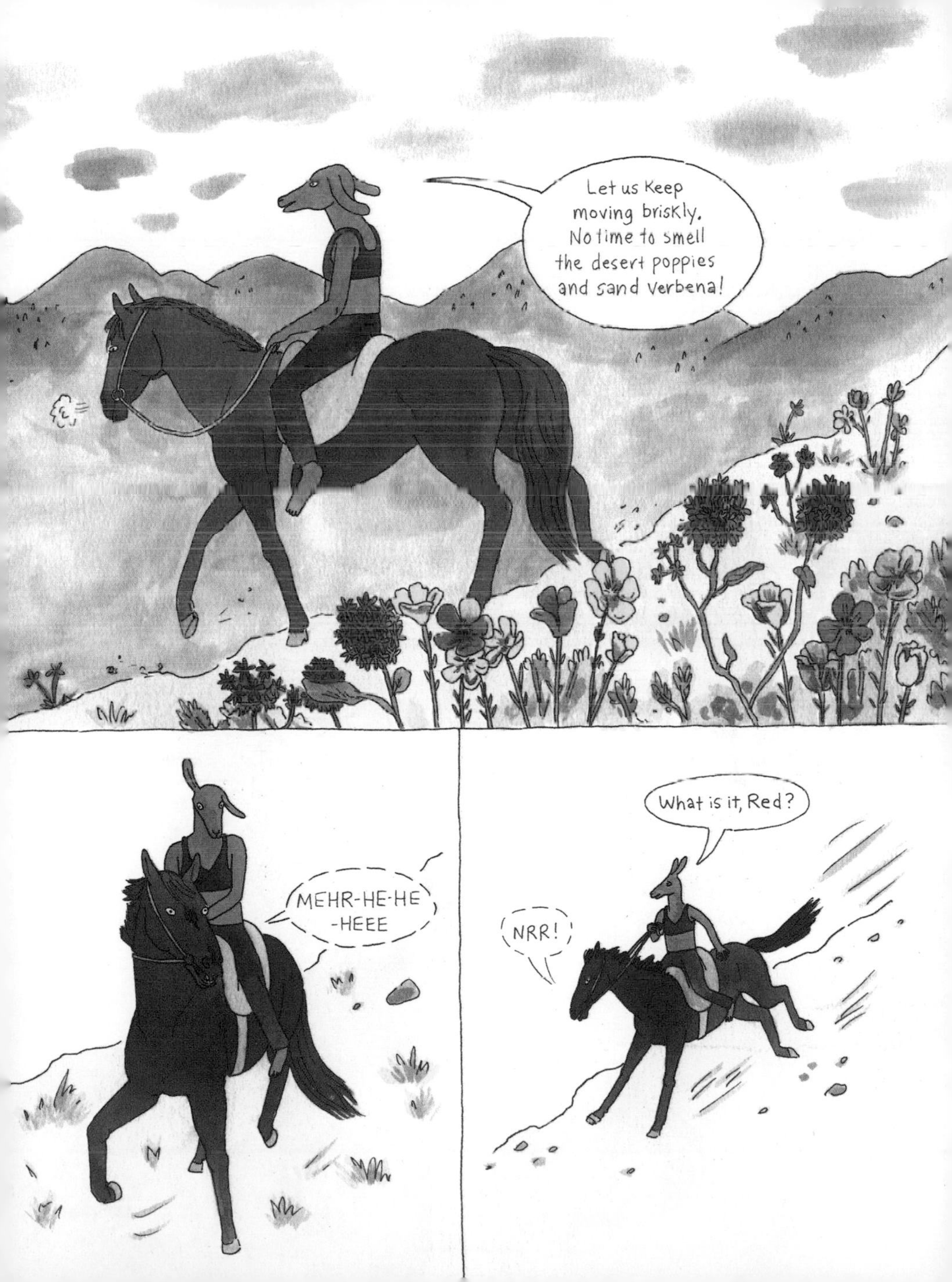
Let us Keep moving brisKly. No time to smell the desert poppies and sand Verbena!
MEHR-HE-HE -HEEE
What is it, Red?
NRR!

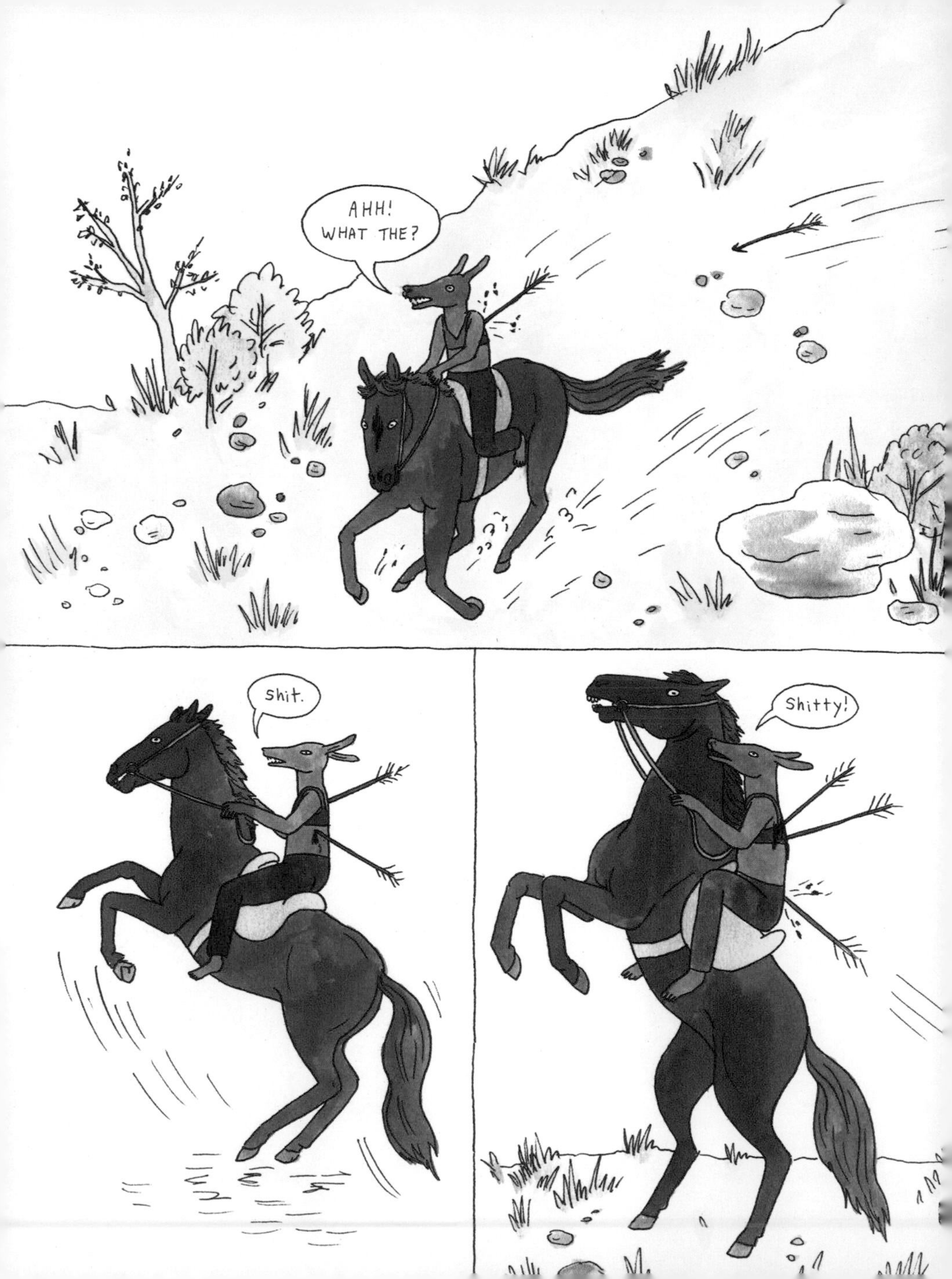
AHH! WHAT THE?
shit.
Shitty!

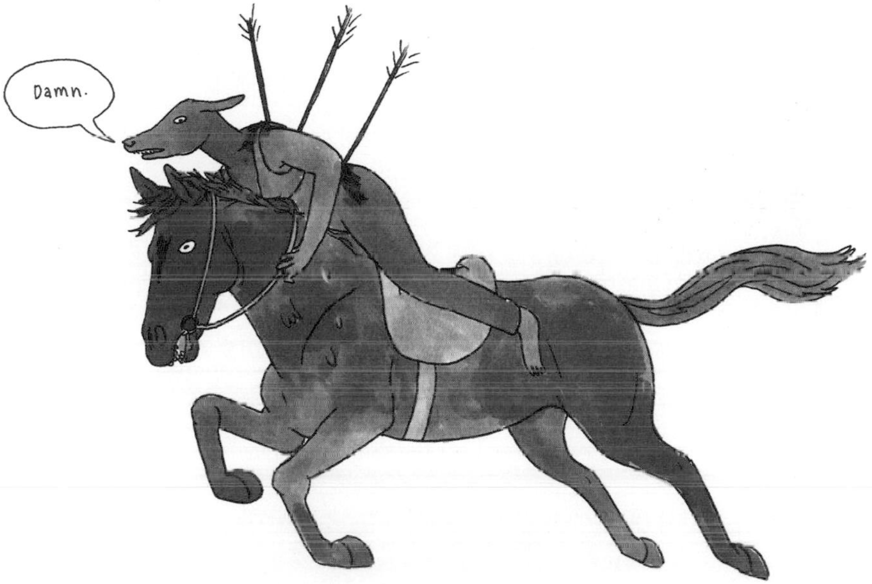
Damn.

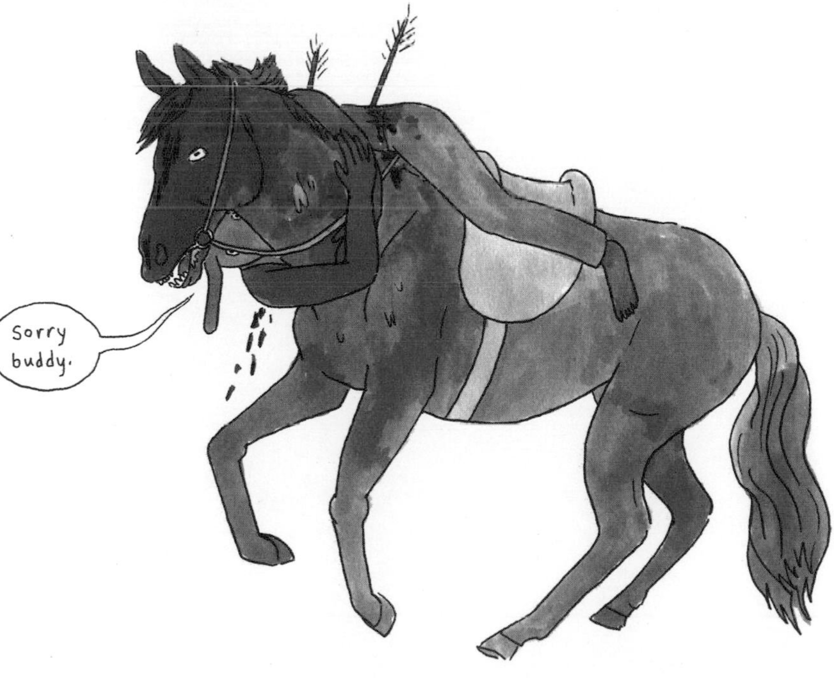
Sorry buddy.

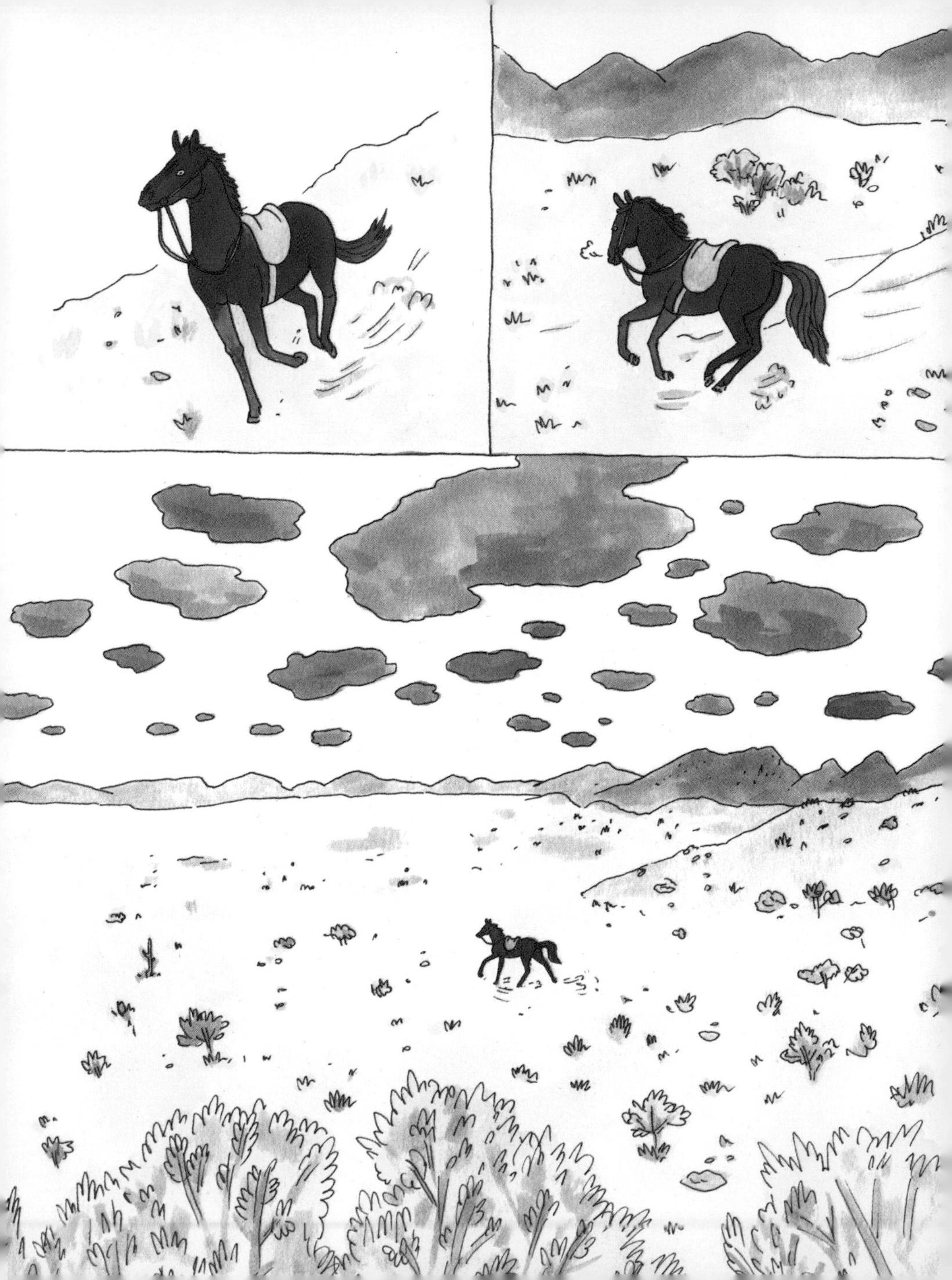

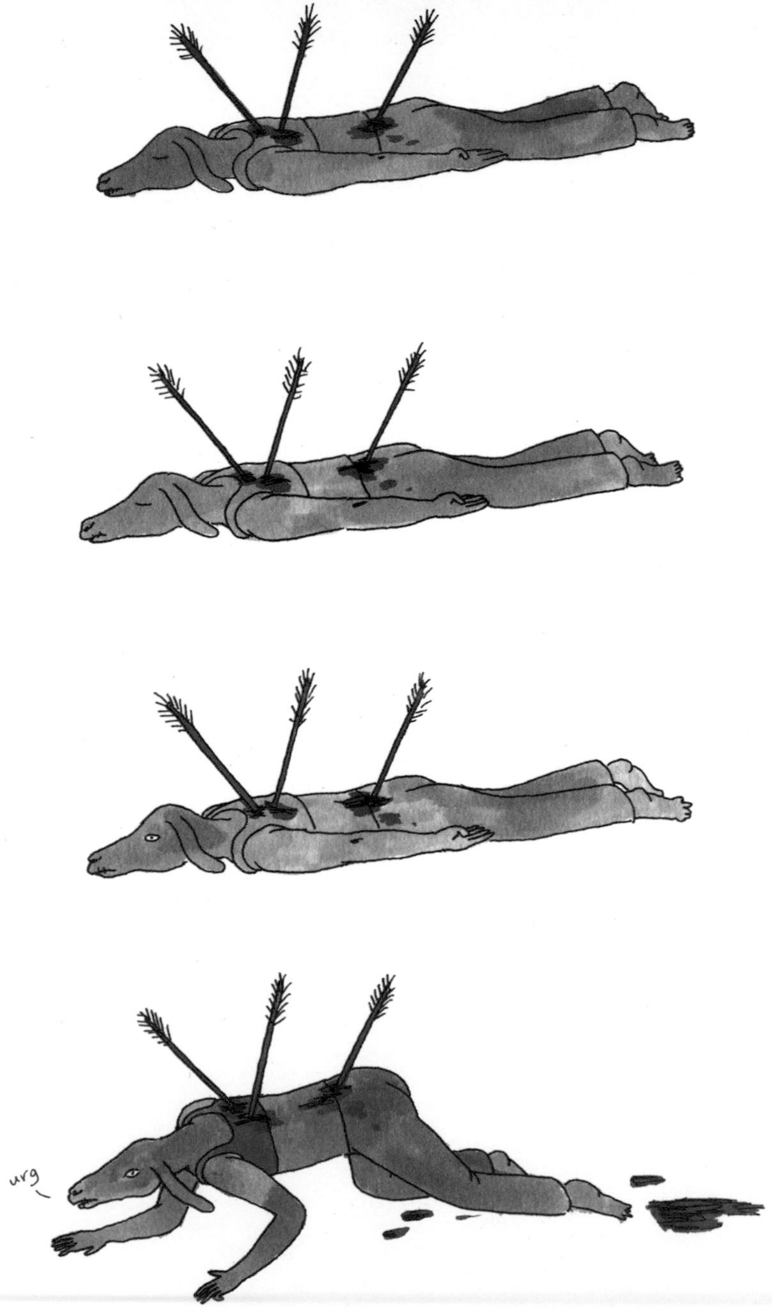
urg

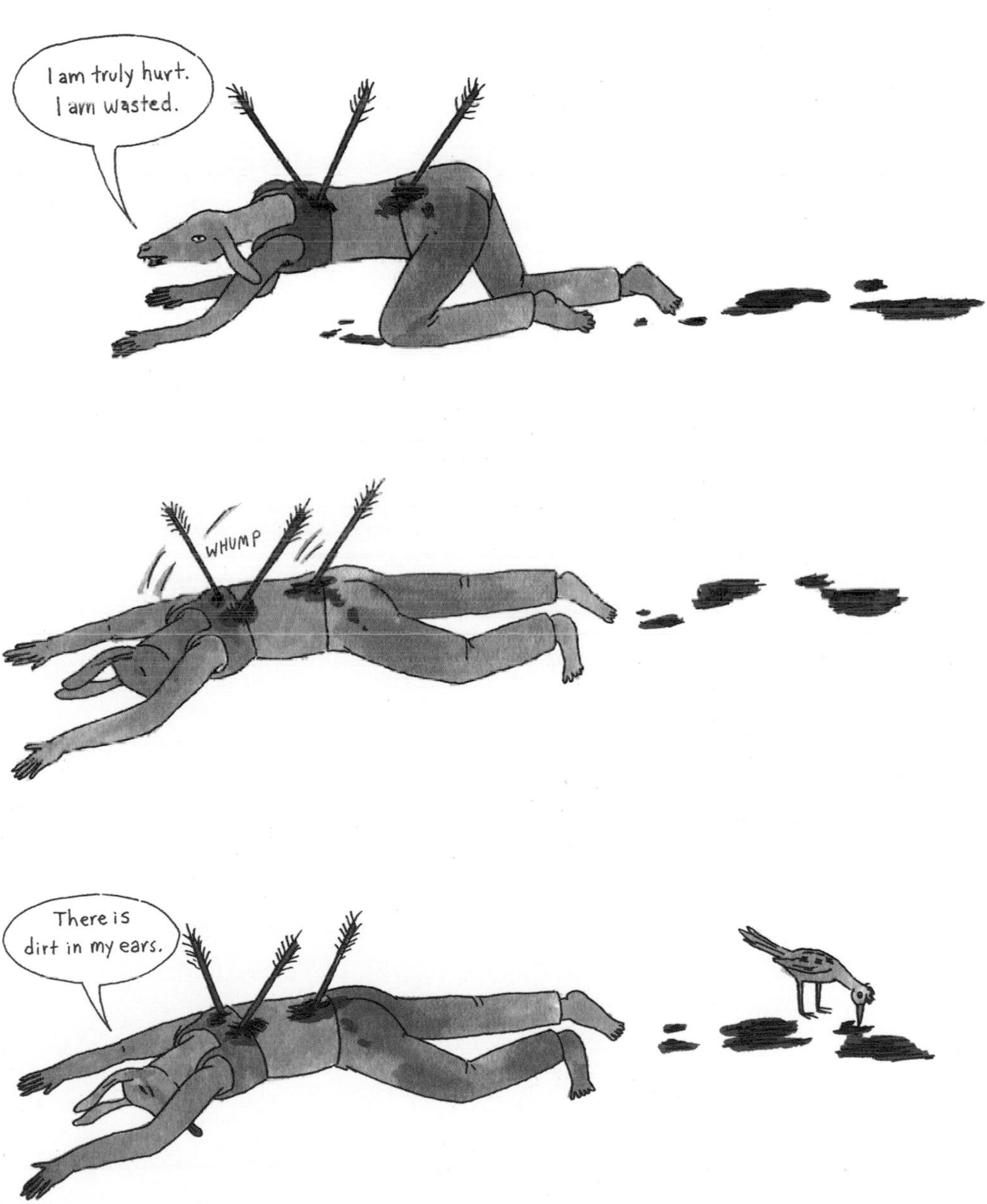
I am truly hurt. I am wasted.
WHUMP
There is dirt in my ears.

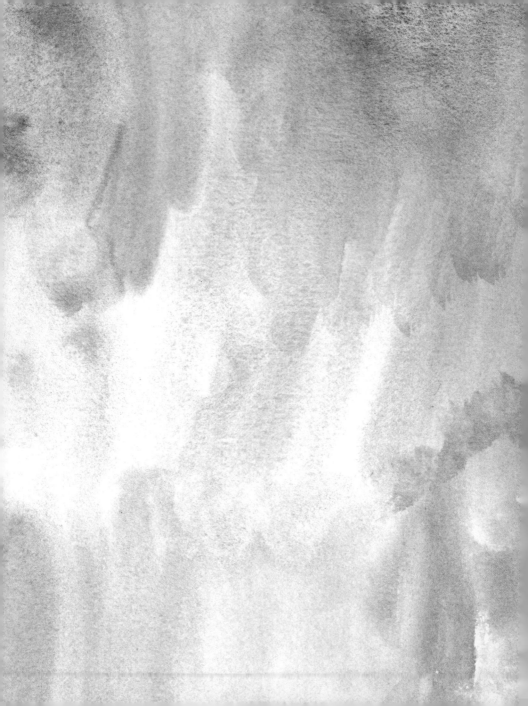

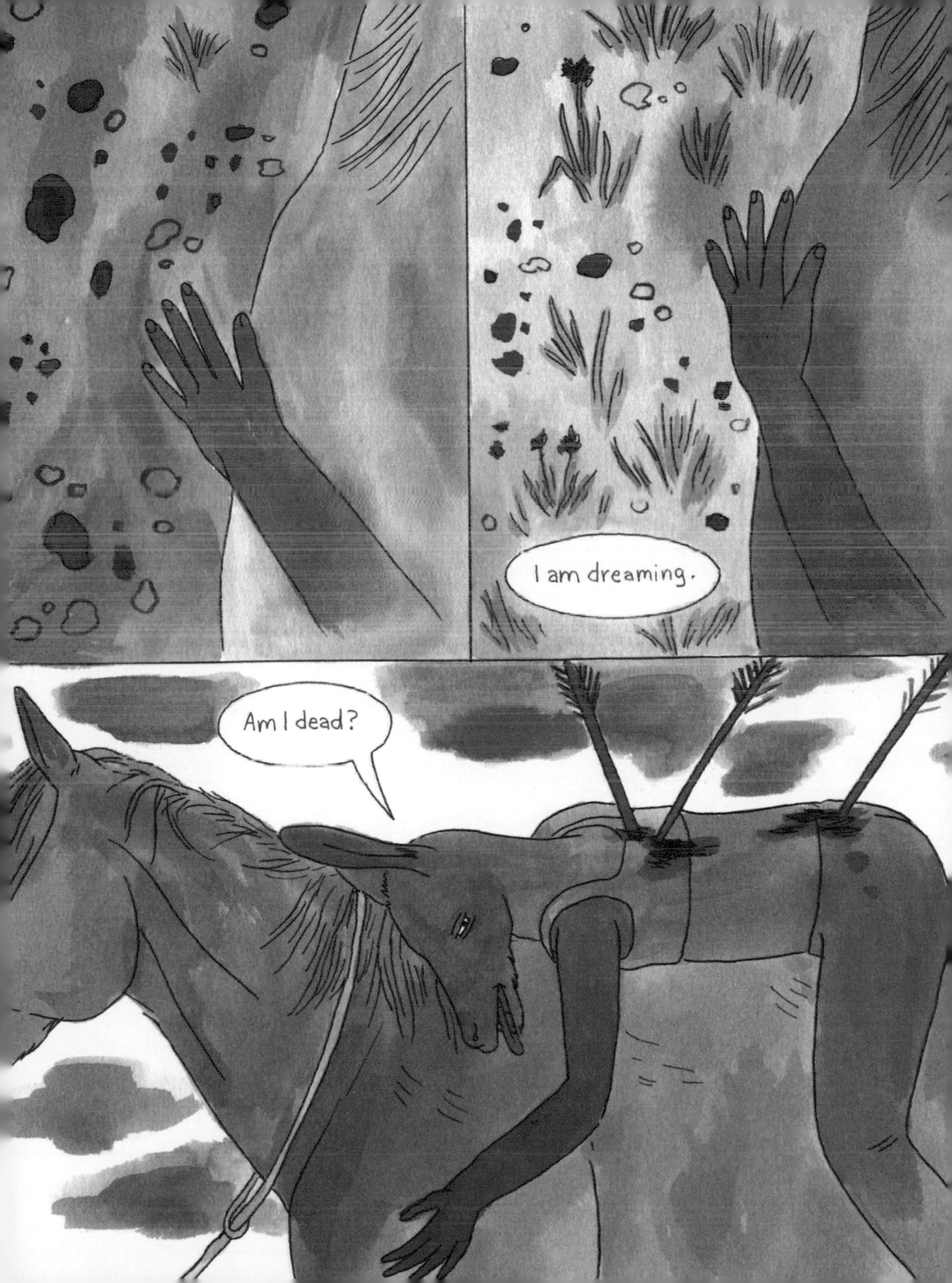
I am dreaming.
Am I dead?

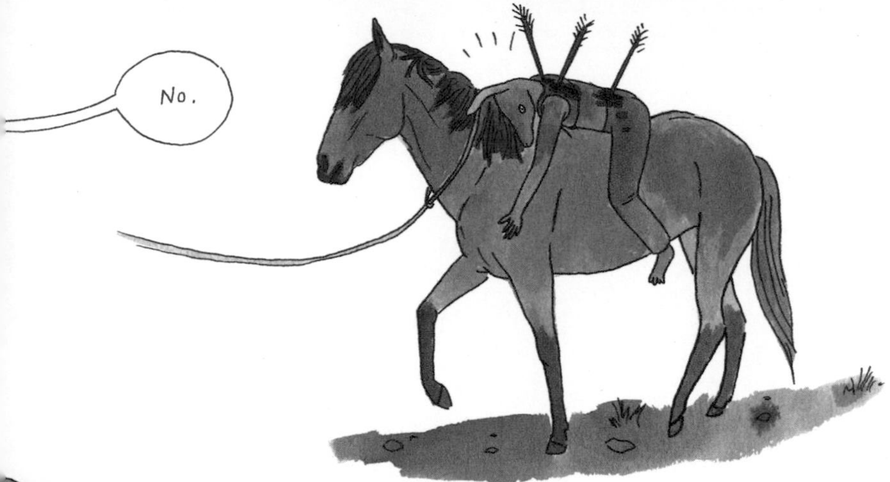
No.

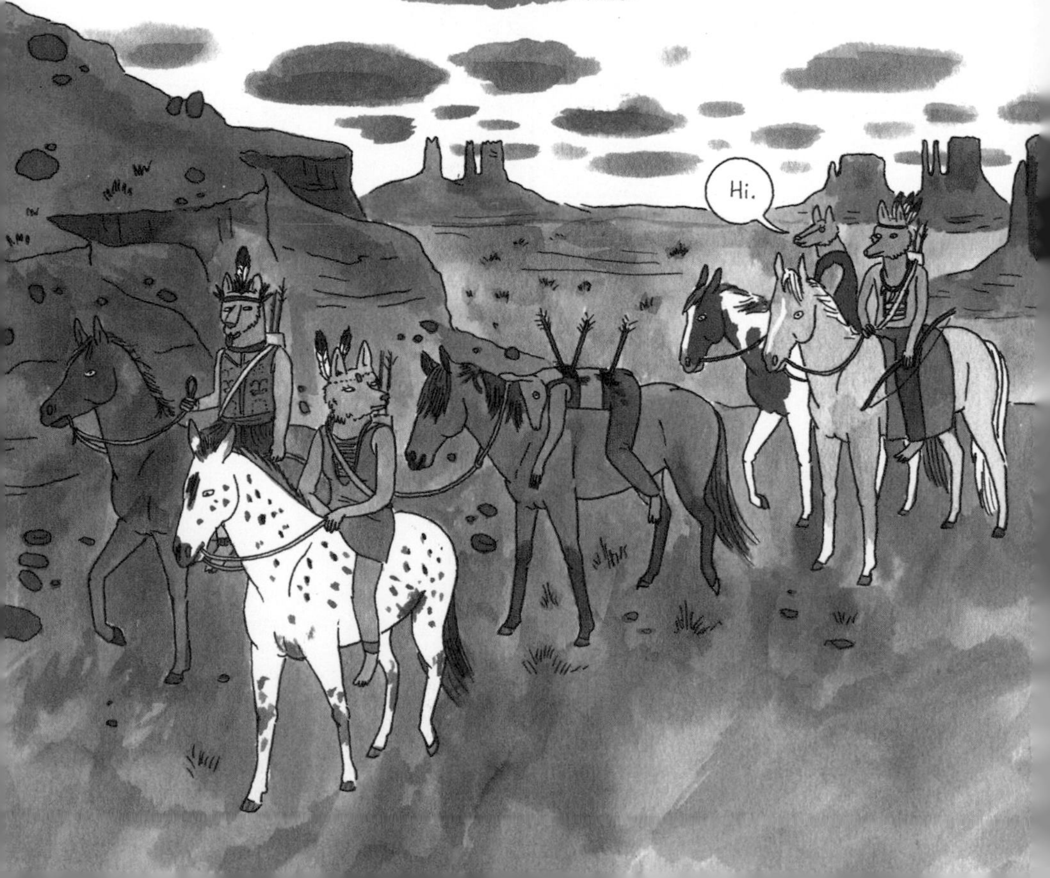
Hi.

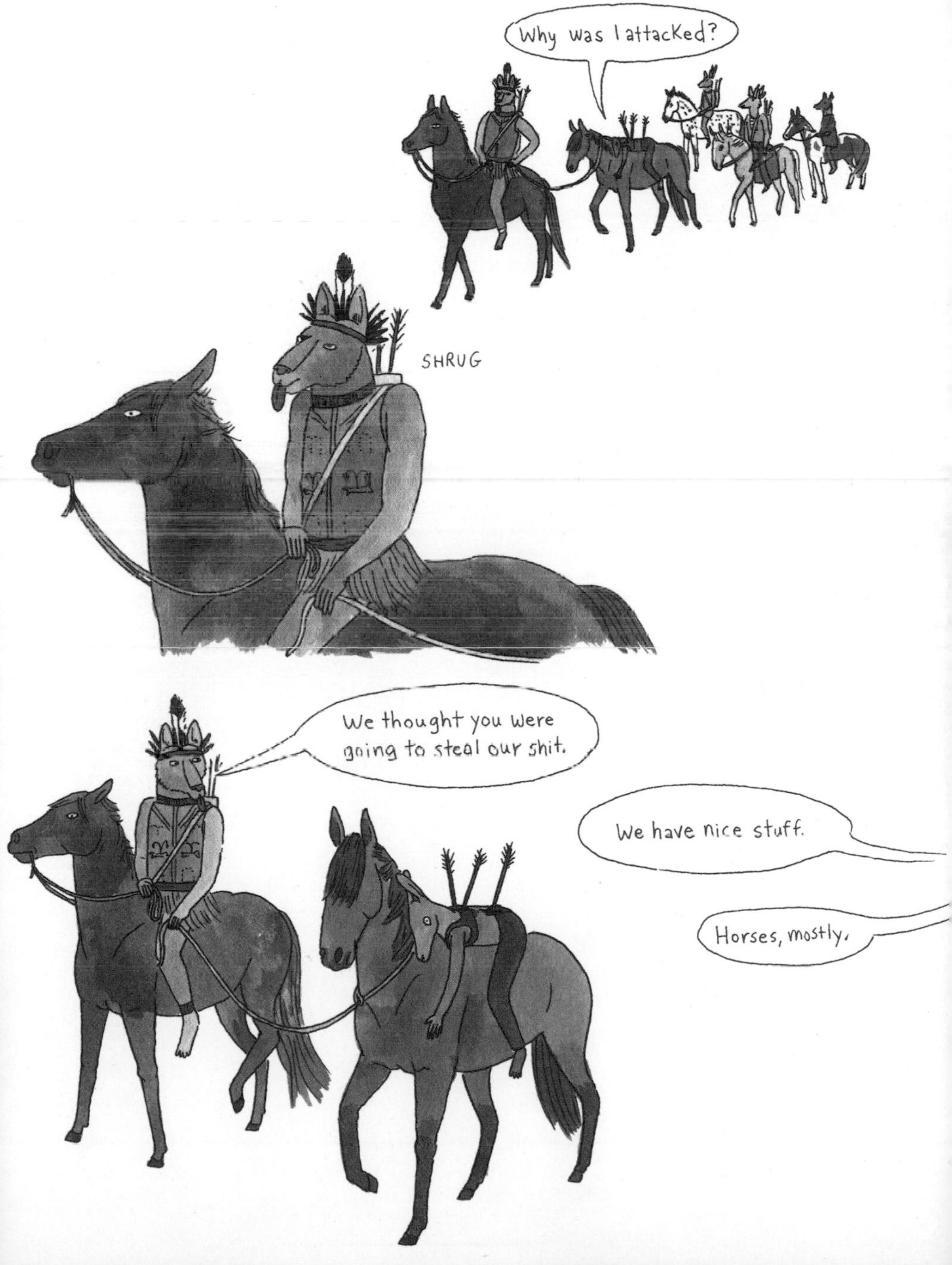
Why was I attacked?
SHRUG
We thought you were going to steal our shit.
We have nice stuff.
Horses, mostly.

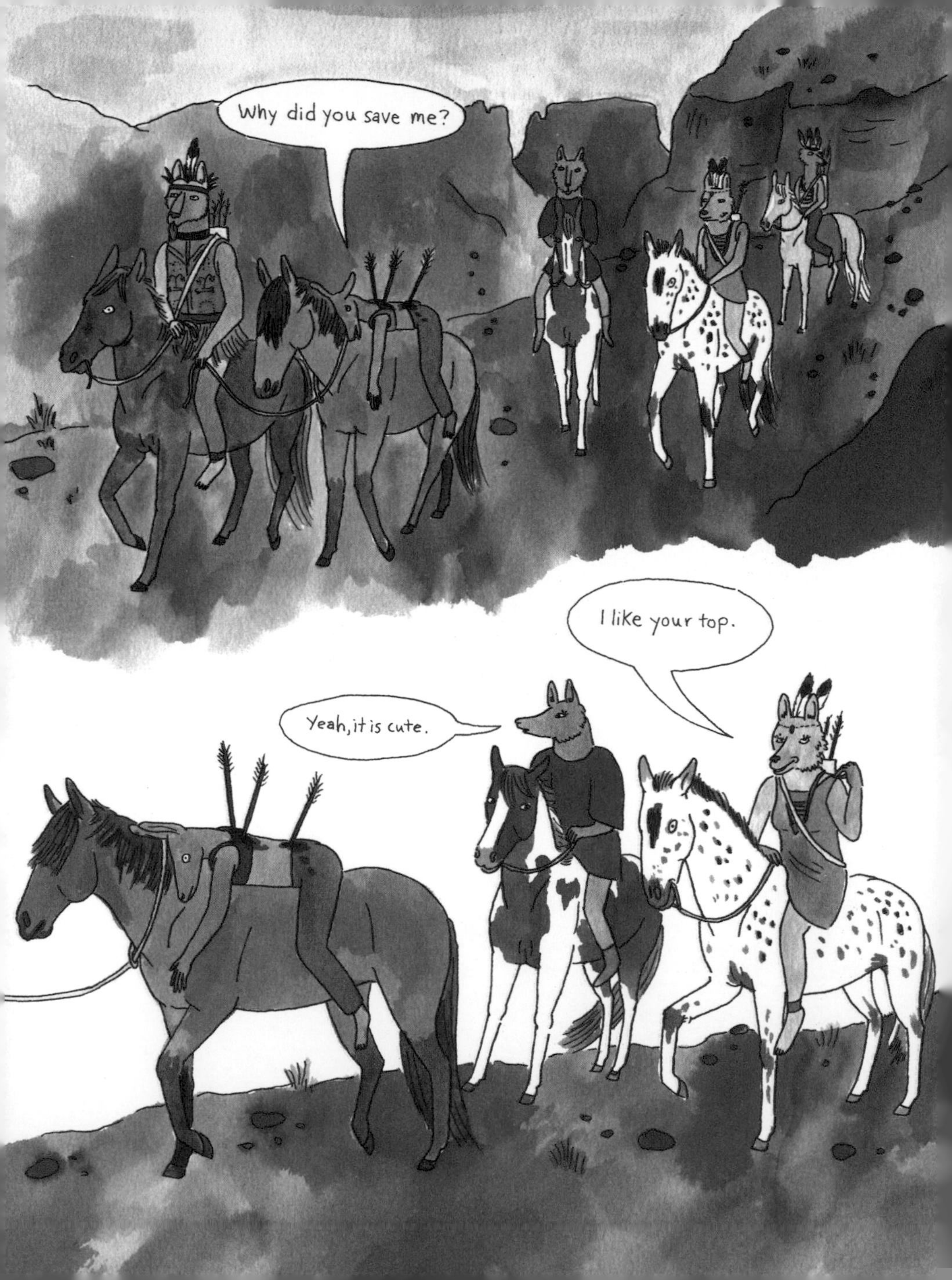
Why did you save me?
I like your top.
Yeah, it is cute.

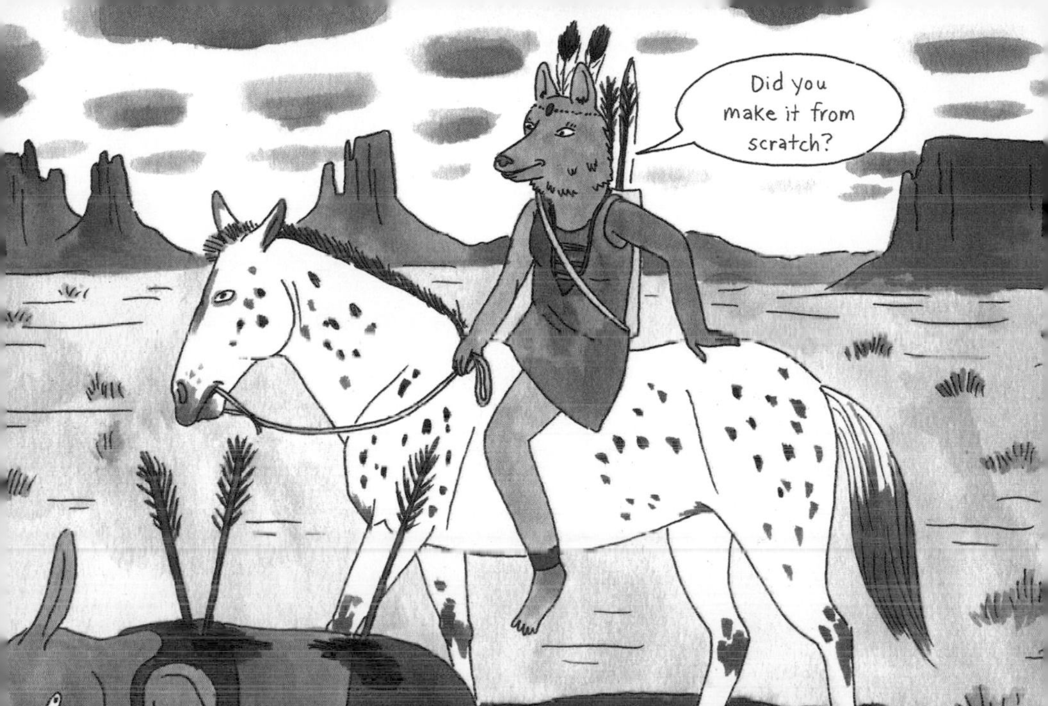
Did you make it from scratch?

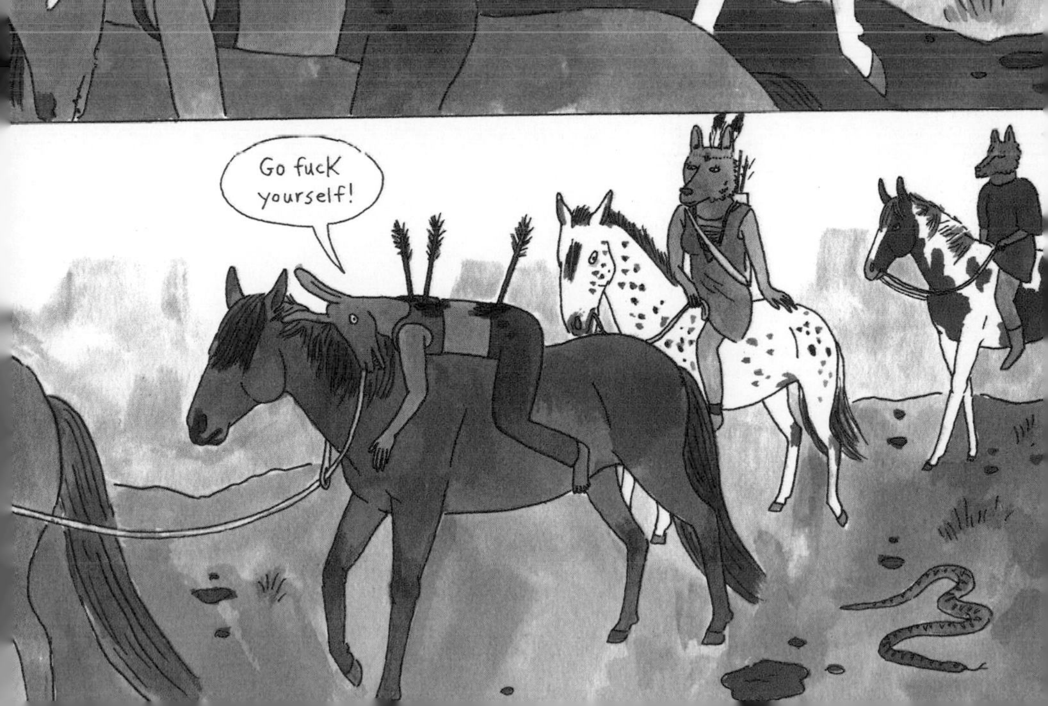
Go fuck yourself!

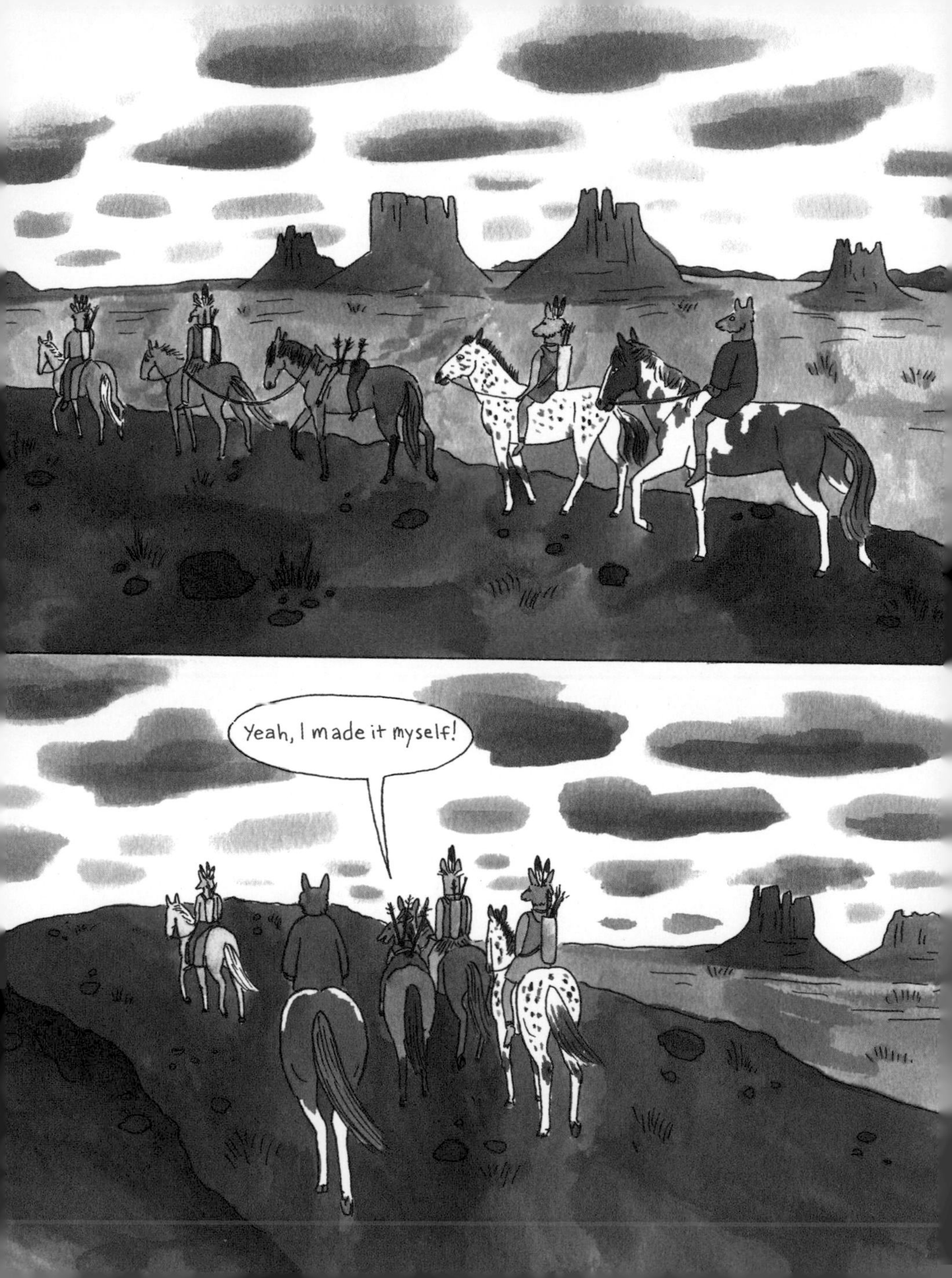
Yeah, I made it myself!

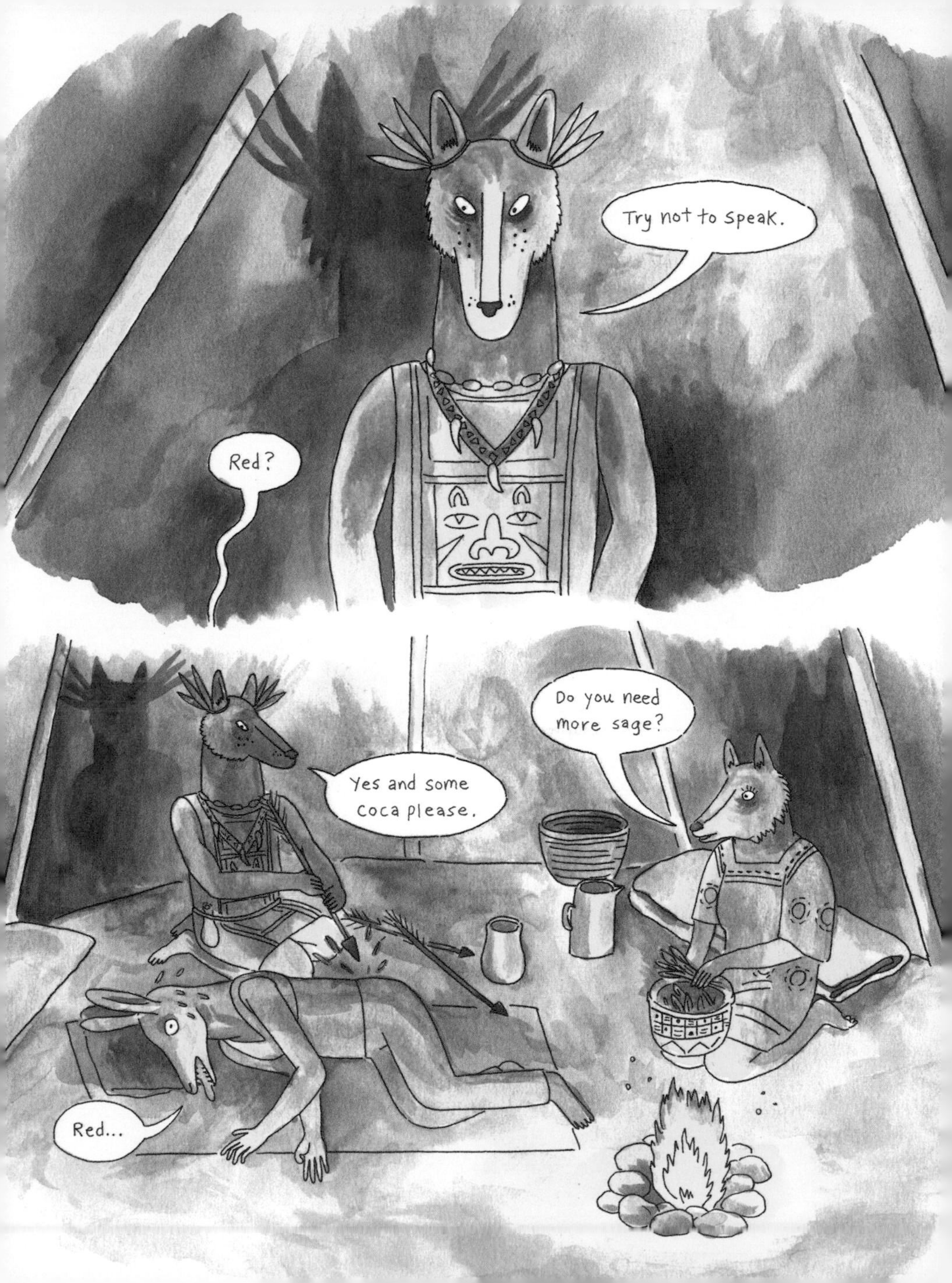
Try not to speak.
Red?
Do you need more sage?
Yes and some coca please.
Red...

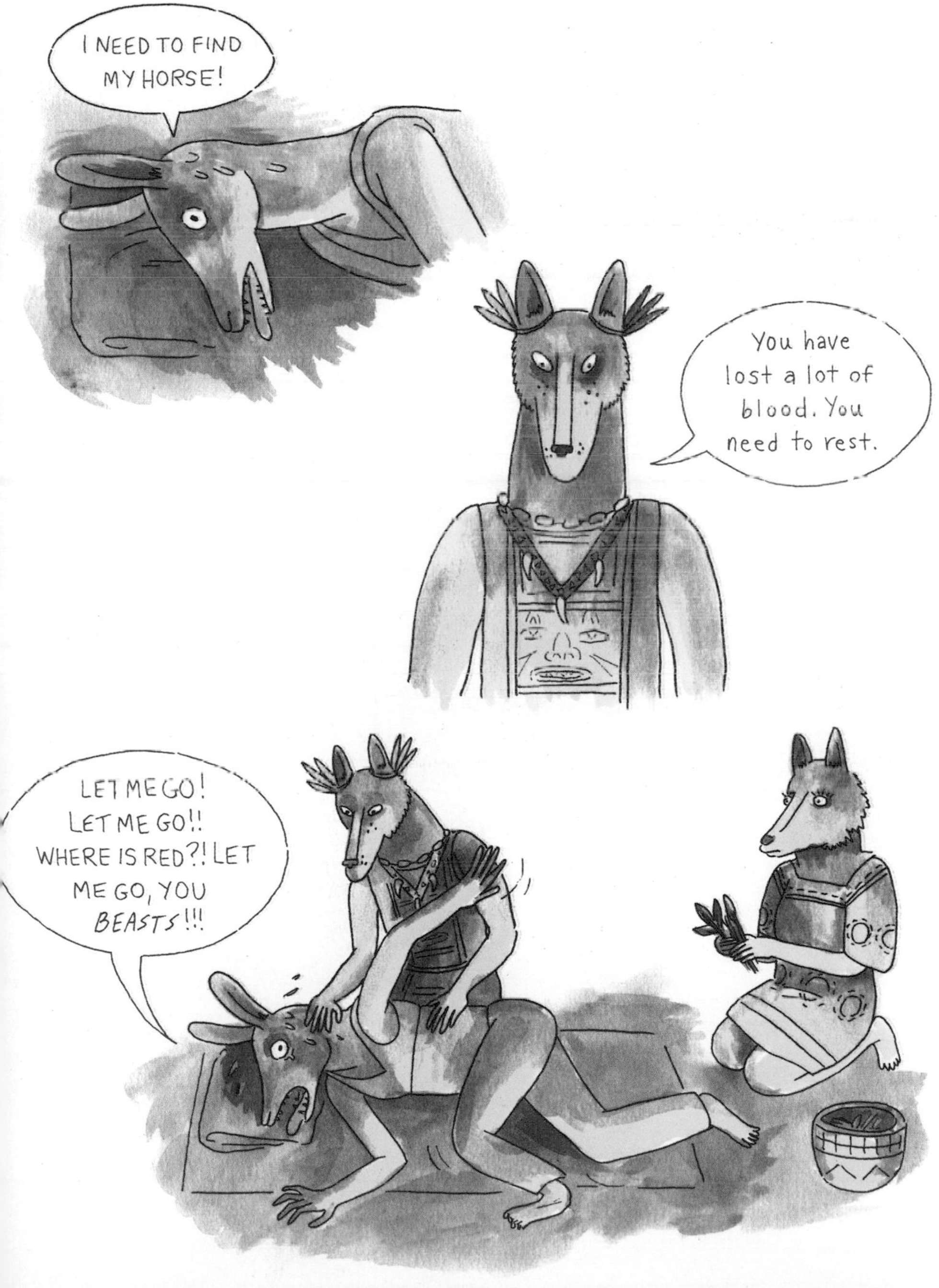
I NEED TO FIND MY HORSE!
You have lost a lot of blood. You need to rest.
LET ME GO! LET ME GO!! WHERE IS RED?! LET ME GO, YOU *BEASTS*!!!

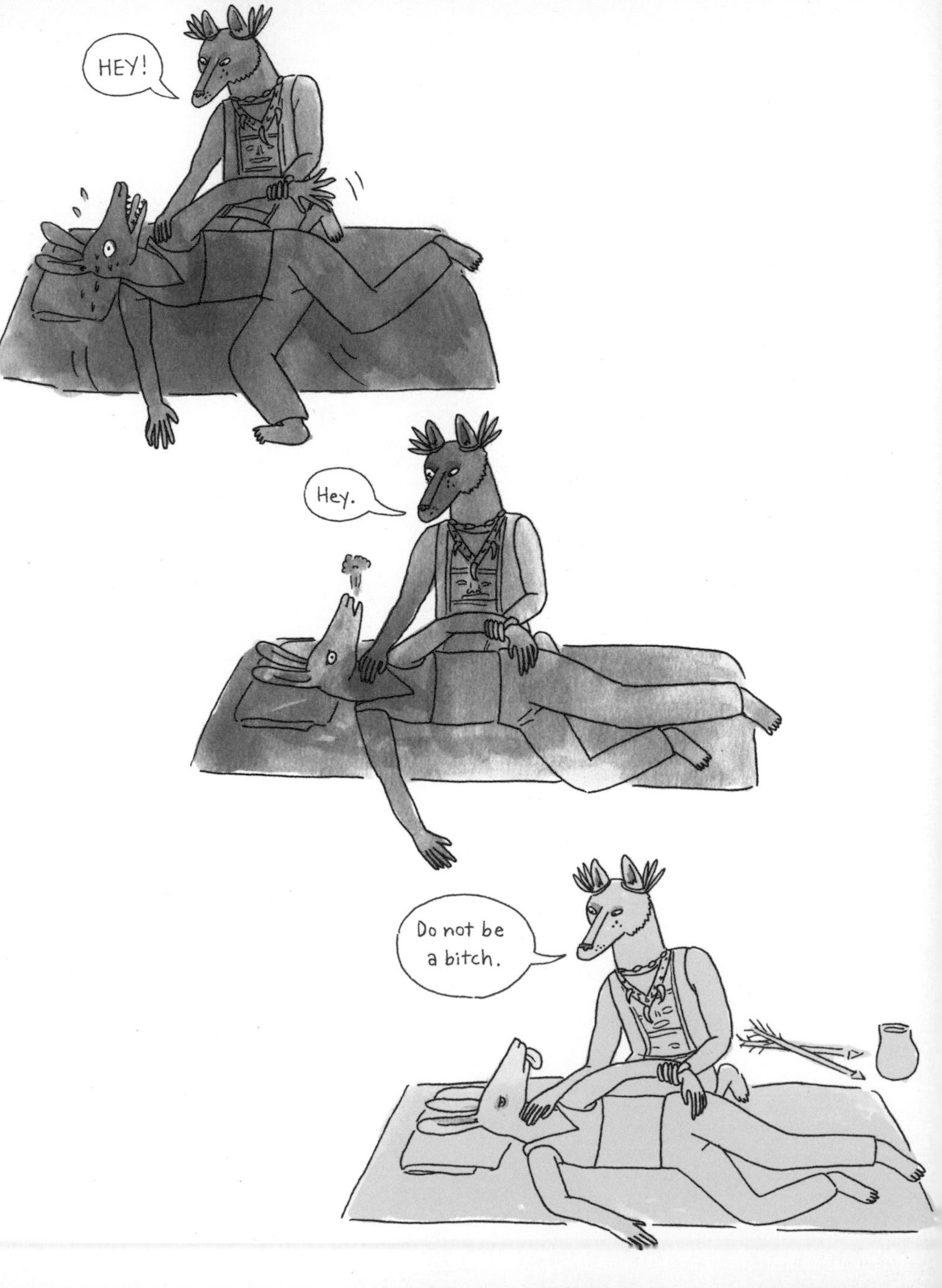
HEY!
Hey.
Do not be a bitch.

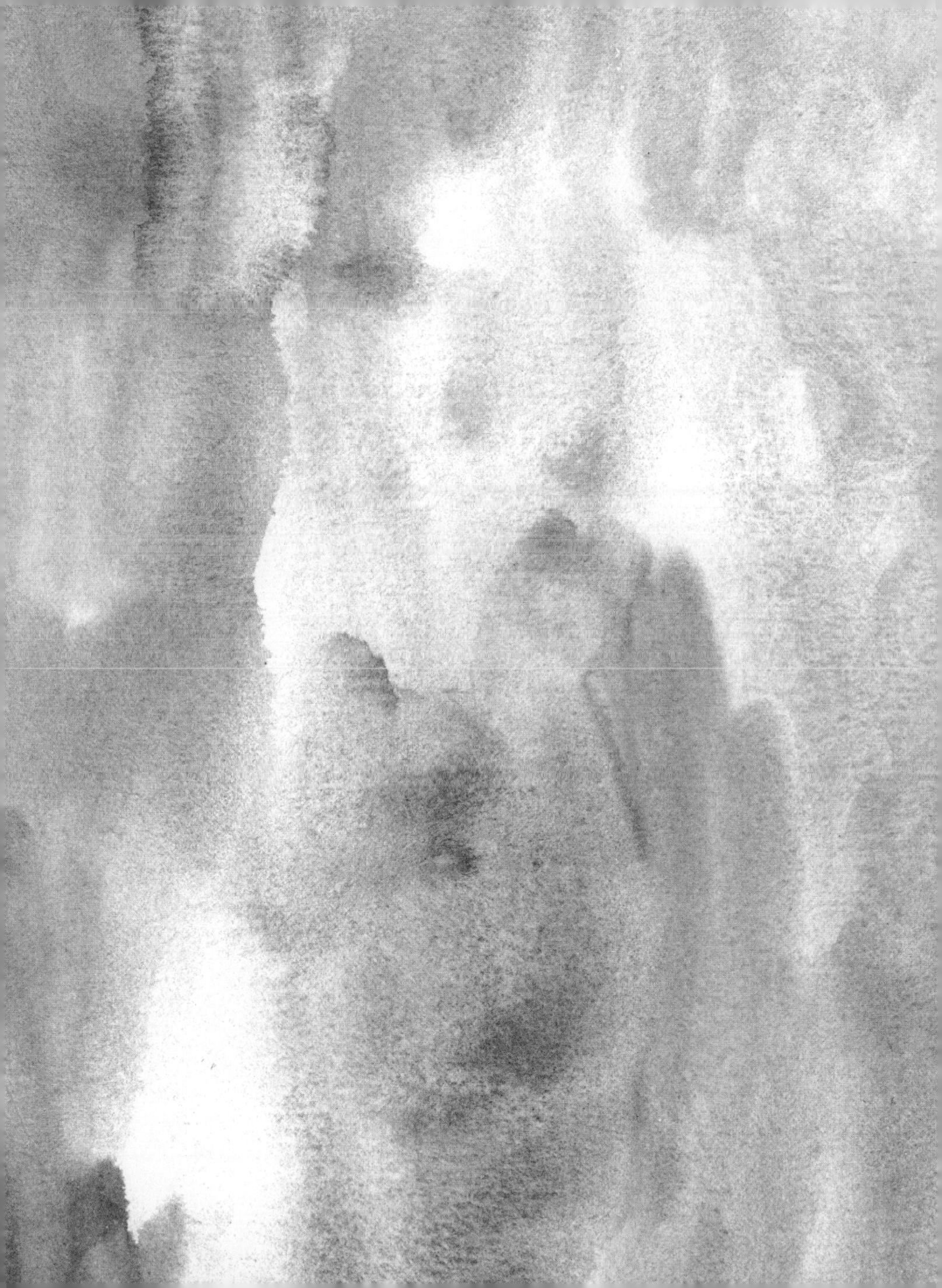

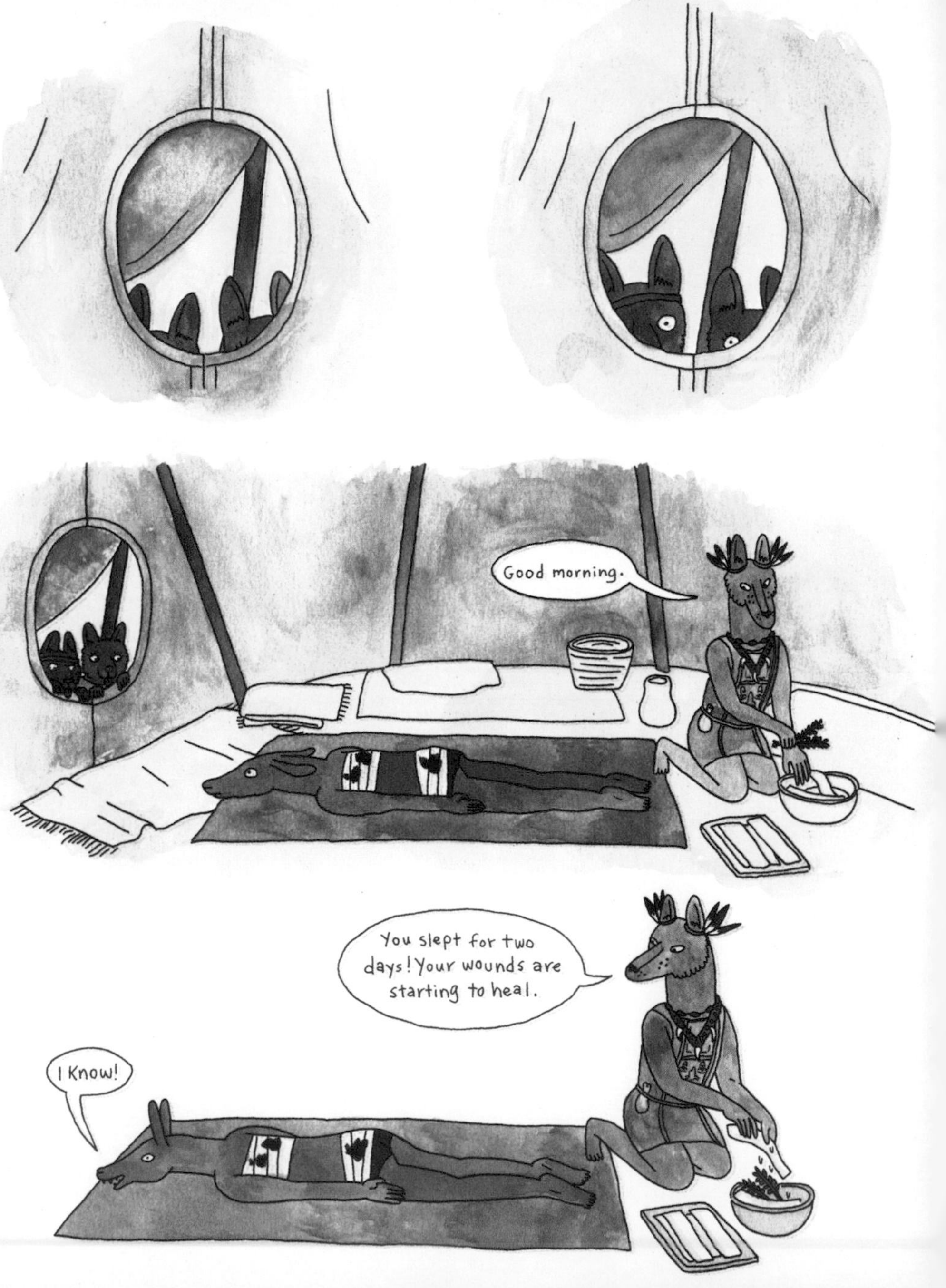

Good morning.
You slept for two days! Your wounds are starting to heal.
I Know!

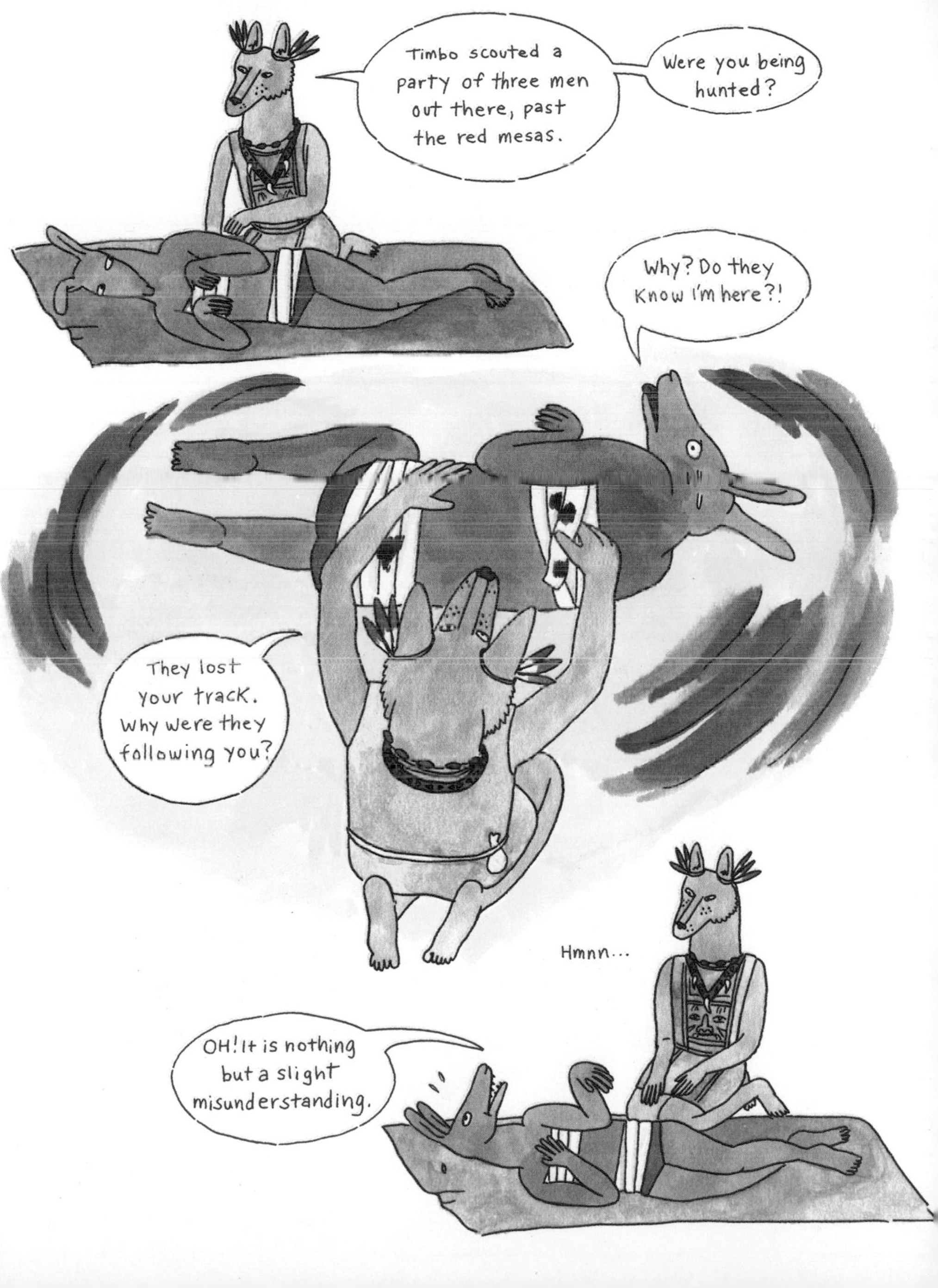

Timbo scouted a party of three men out there, past the red mesas.
Were you being hunted?
Why? Do they know I'm here?!
They lost your track. Why were they following you?
Hmnn...
OH! It is nothing but a slight misunderstanding.

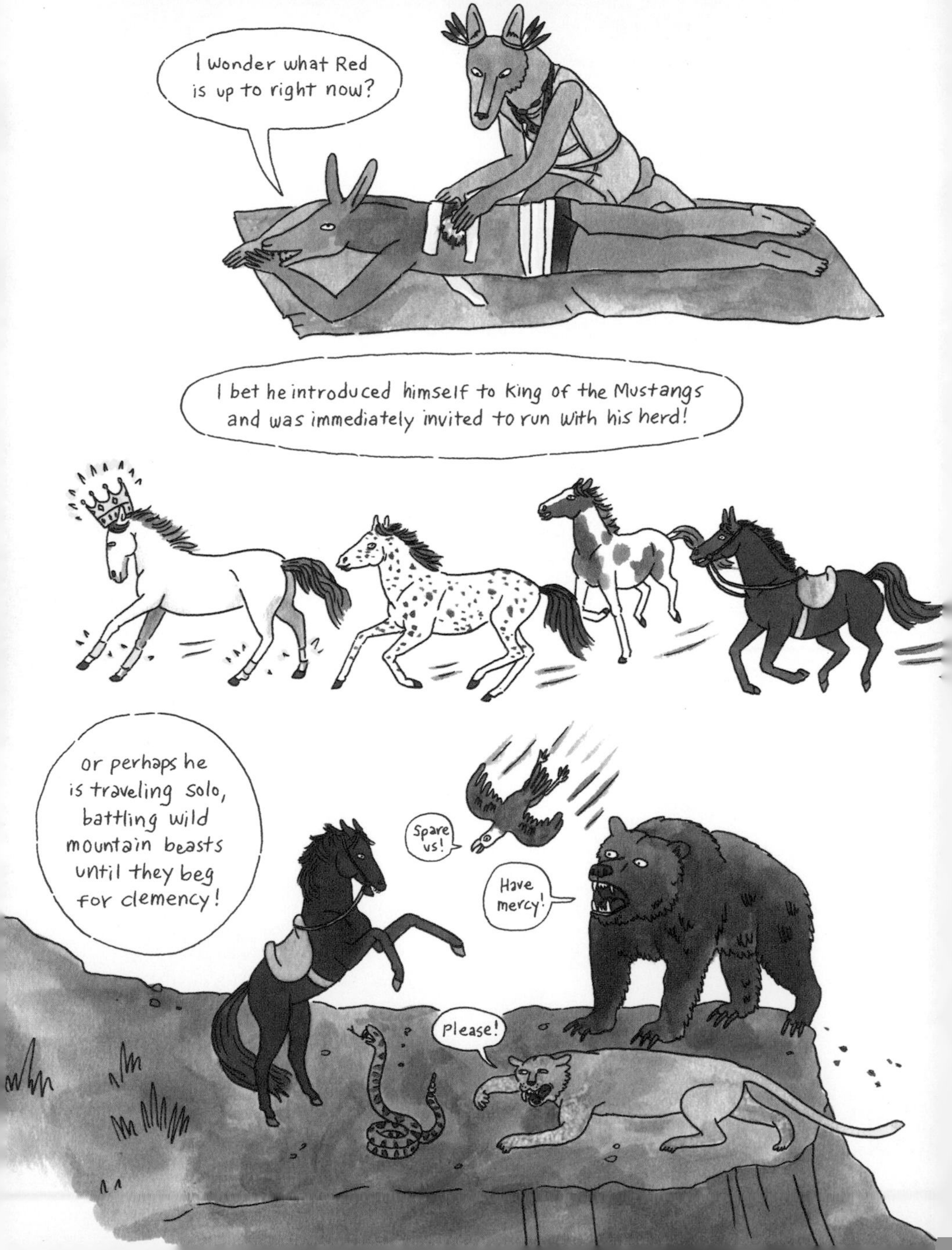
I wonder what Red is up to right now?
I bet he introduced himself to King of the Mustangs and was immediately invited to run with his herd!
or perhaps he is traveling solo, battling wild mountain beasts until they beg for clemency!
Spare us!
Have mercy!
Please!

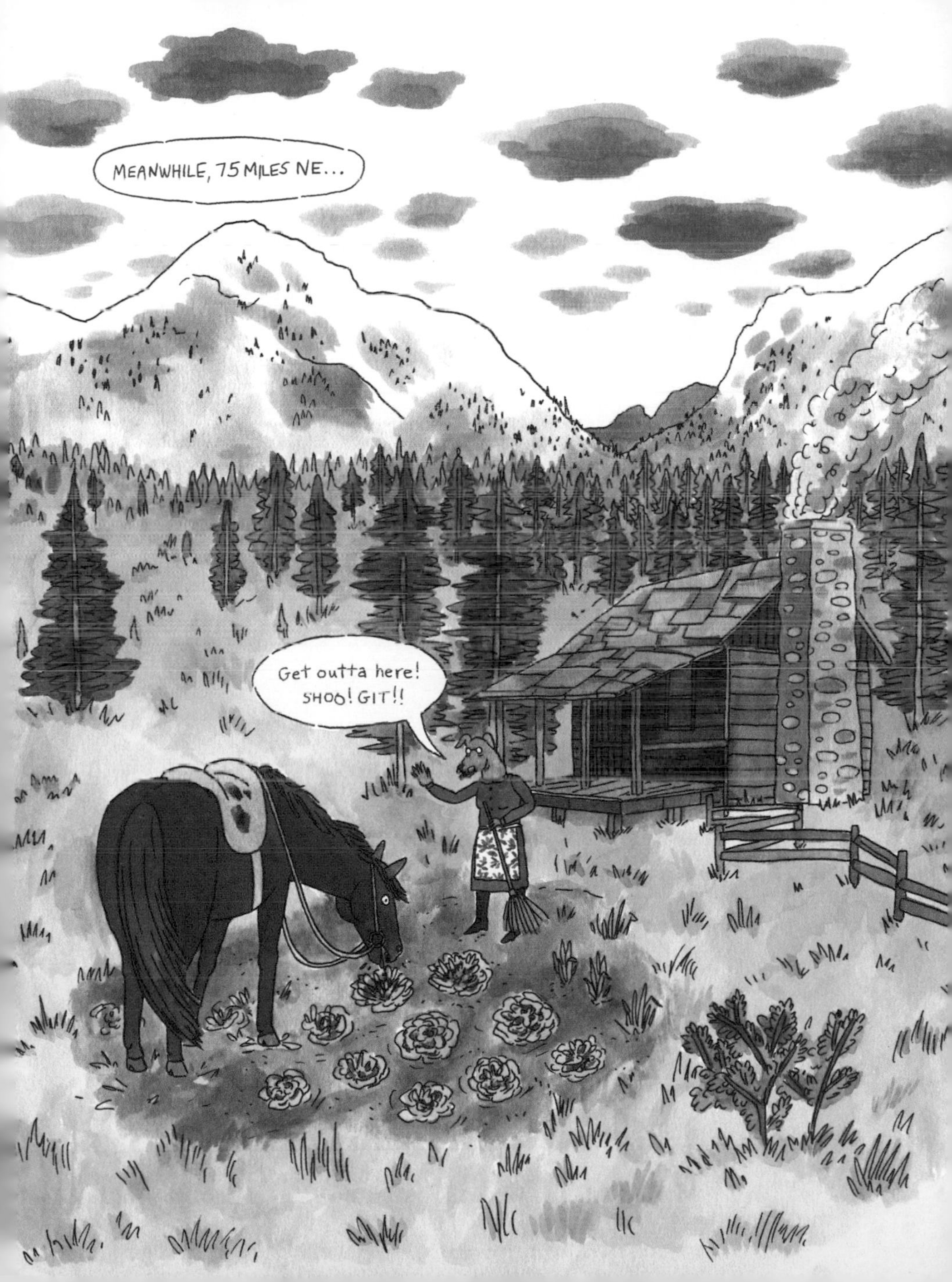
MEANWHILE, 75 MILES NE...
Get outta here! SHOO! GIT!!

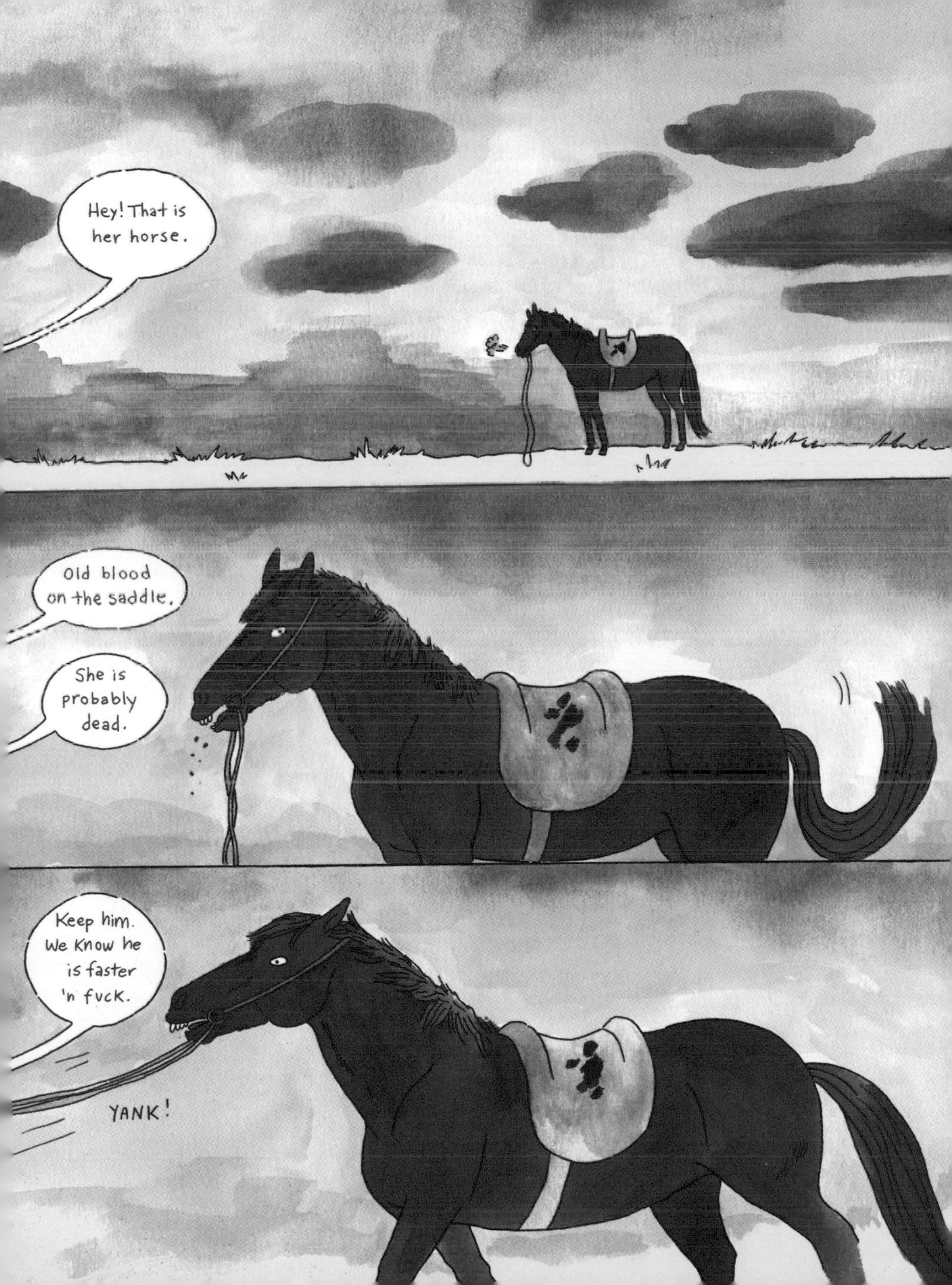

Hey! That is her horse.
Old blood on the saddle.
She is probably dead.
Keep him. We know he is faster 'n fuck.
YANK!

What if she is still out there, boss?
I will not be satisfied until I see her body roasting over a spit.

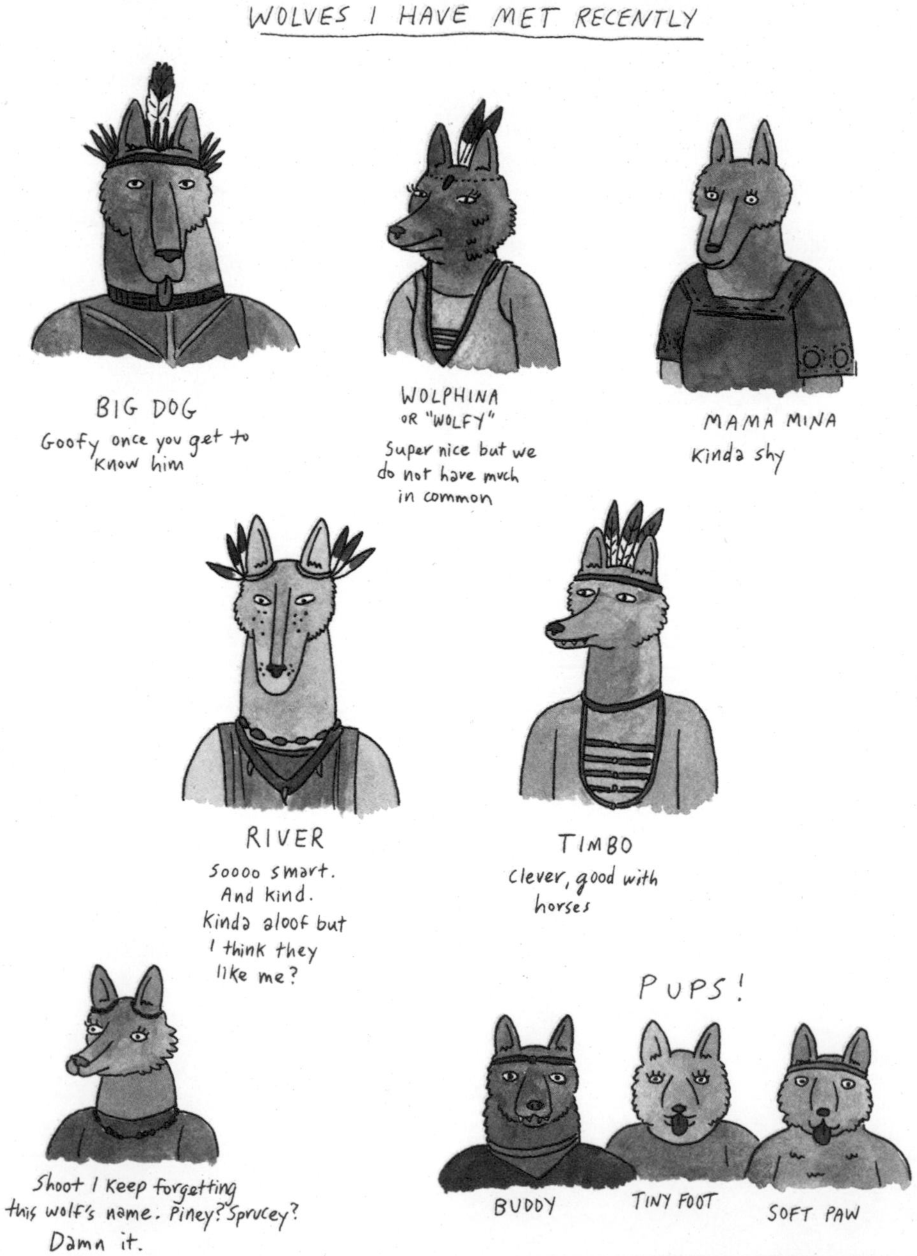
WOLVES I HAVE MET RECENTLY
BIG DOG
Goofy once you get to know him
WOLPHINA
OR "WOLFY"
Super nice but we do not have much in common
MAMA MINA
Kinda shy
RIVER
Soooo smart. And kind. Kinda aloof but I think they like me?
TIMBO
Clever, good with horses
PUPS!
Shoot I keep forgetting this wolf's name. Piney? Sprucey? Damn it.
BUDDY
TINY FOOT
SOFT PAW

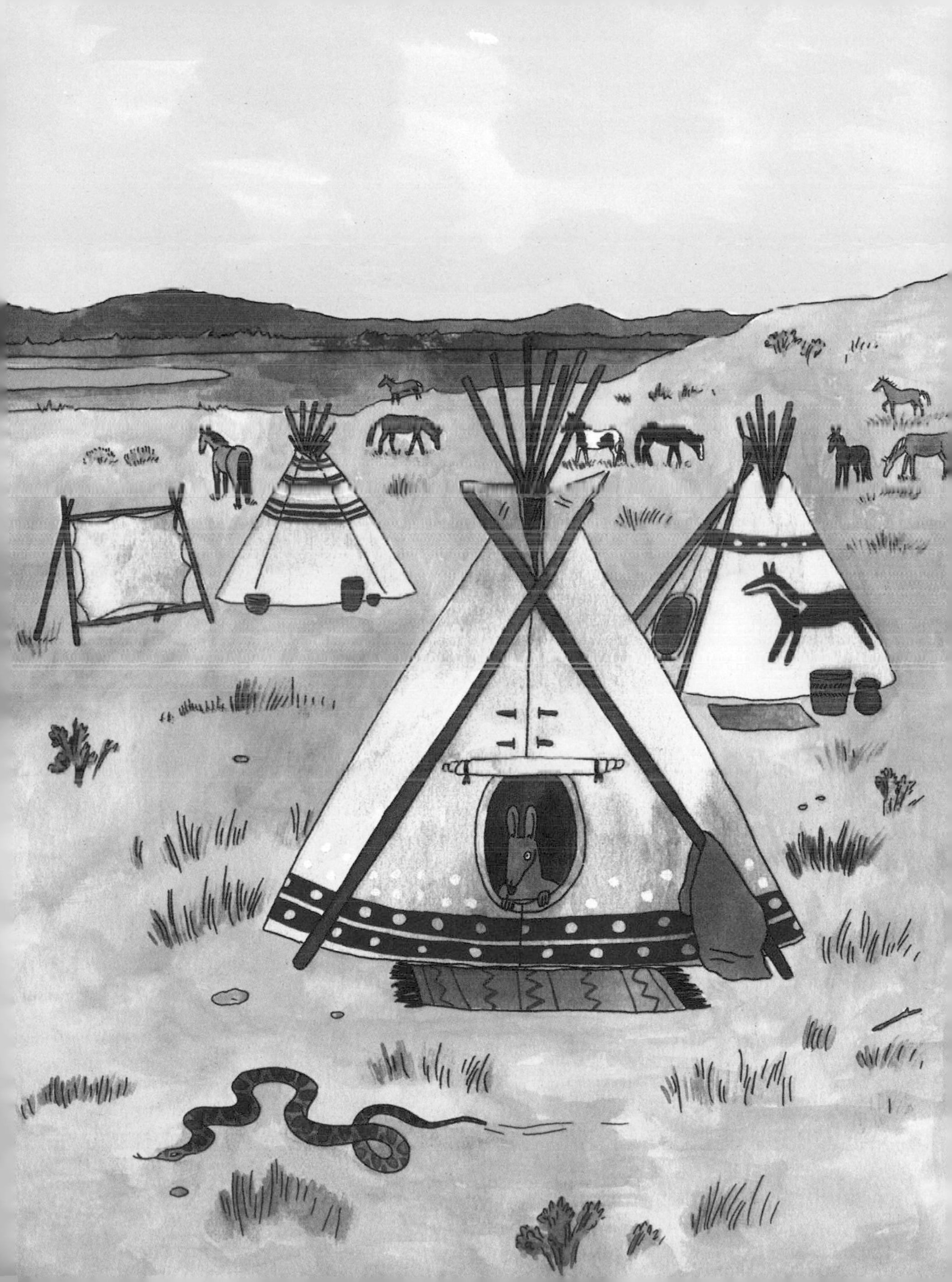

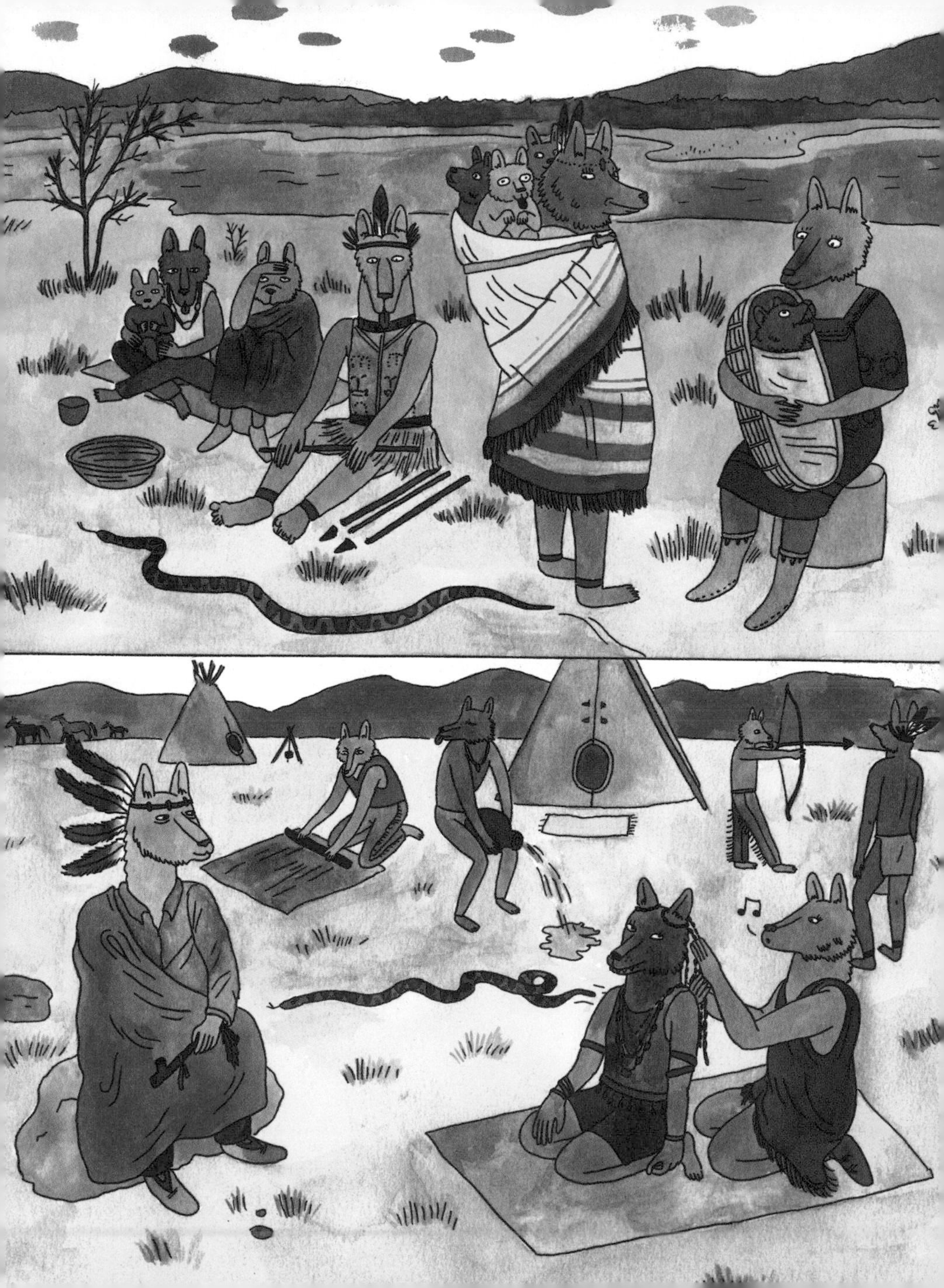

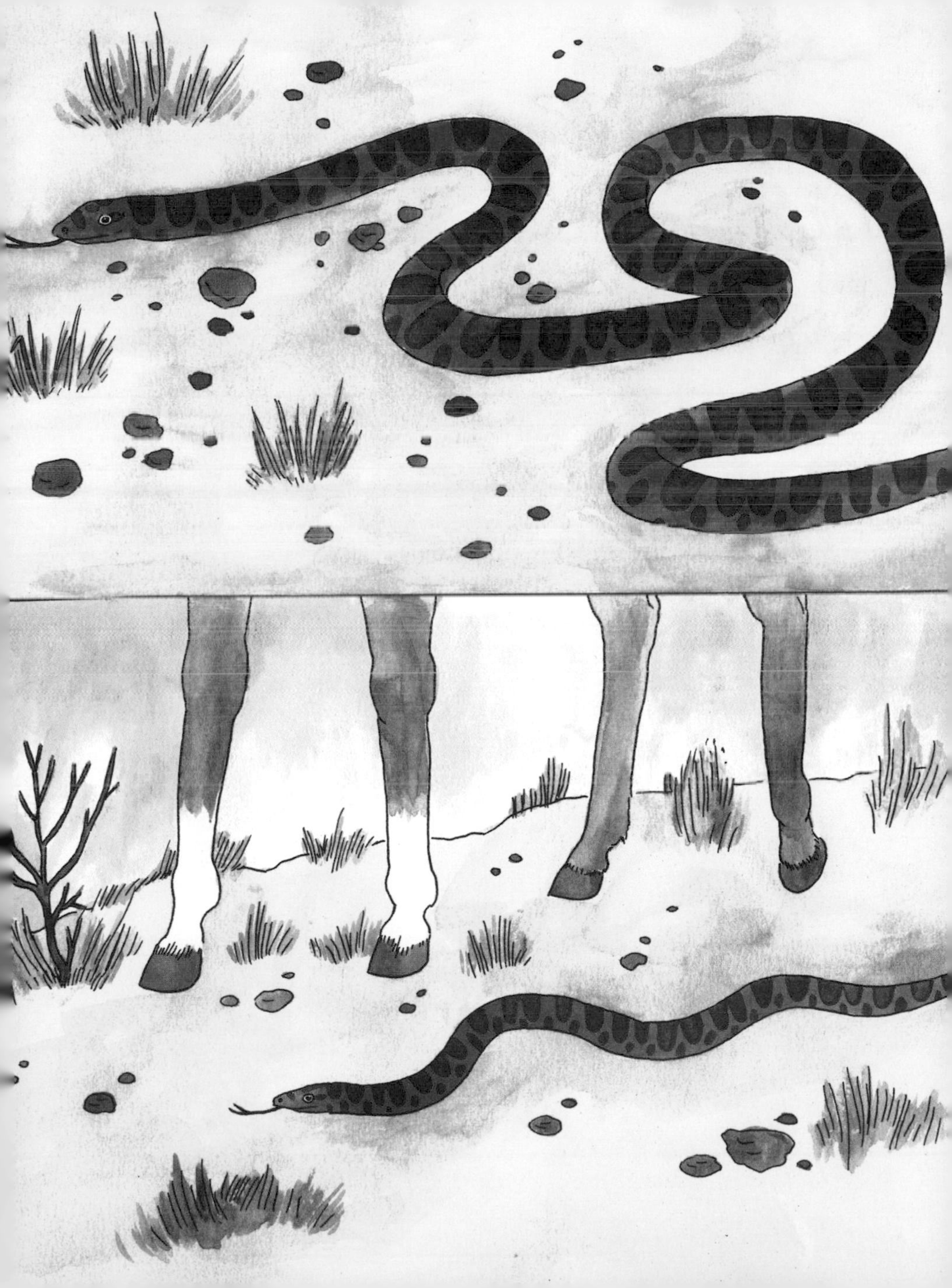

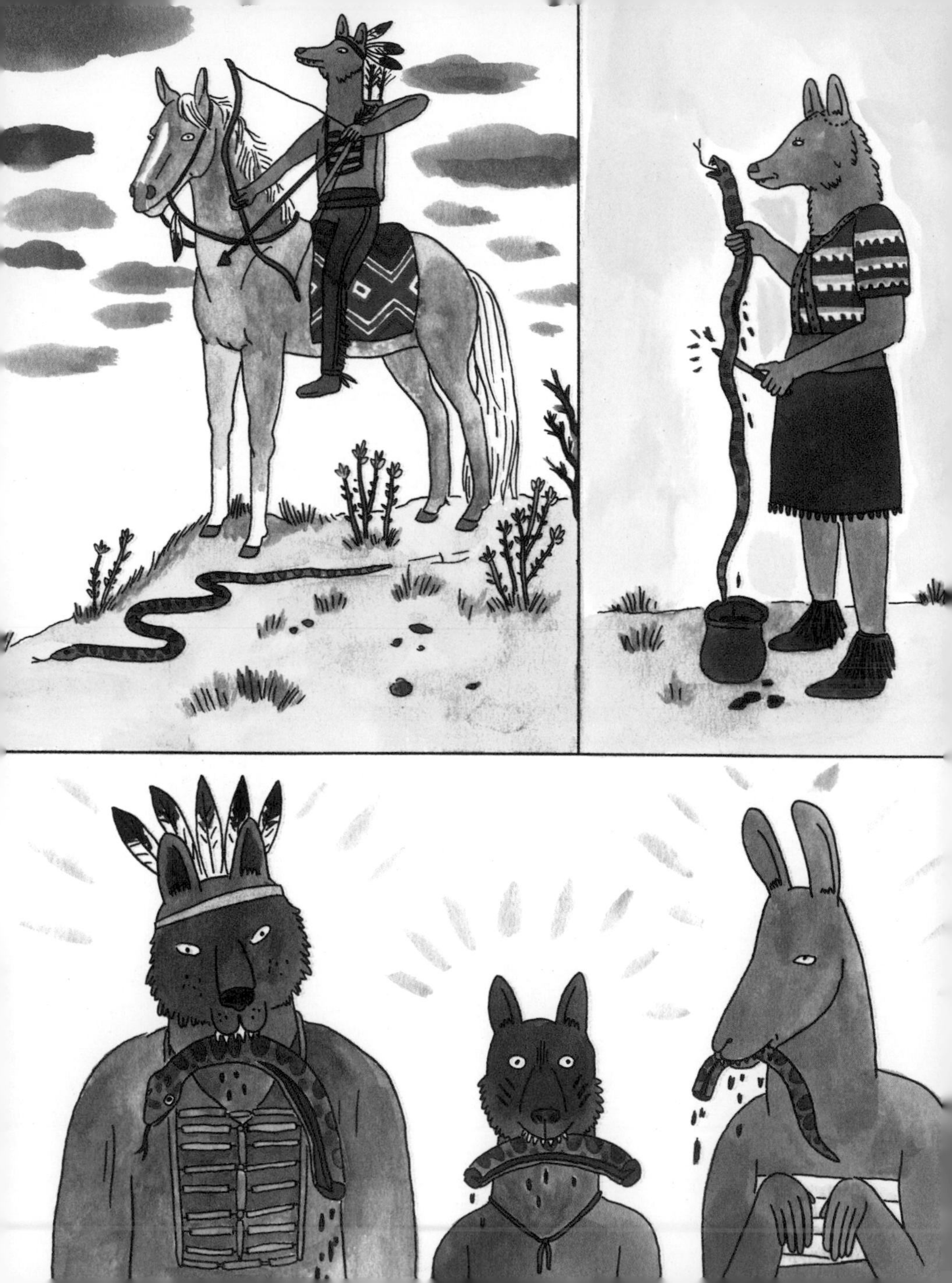

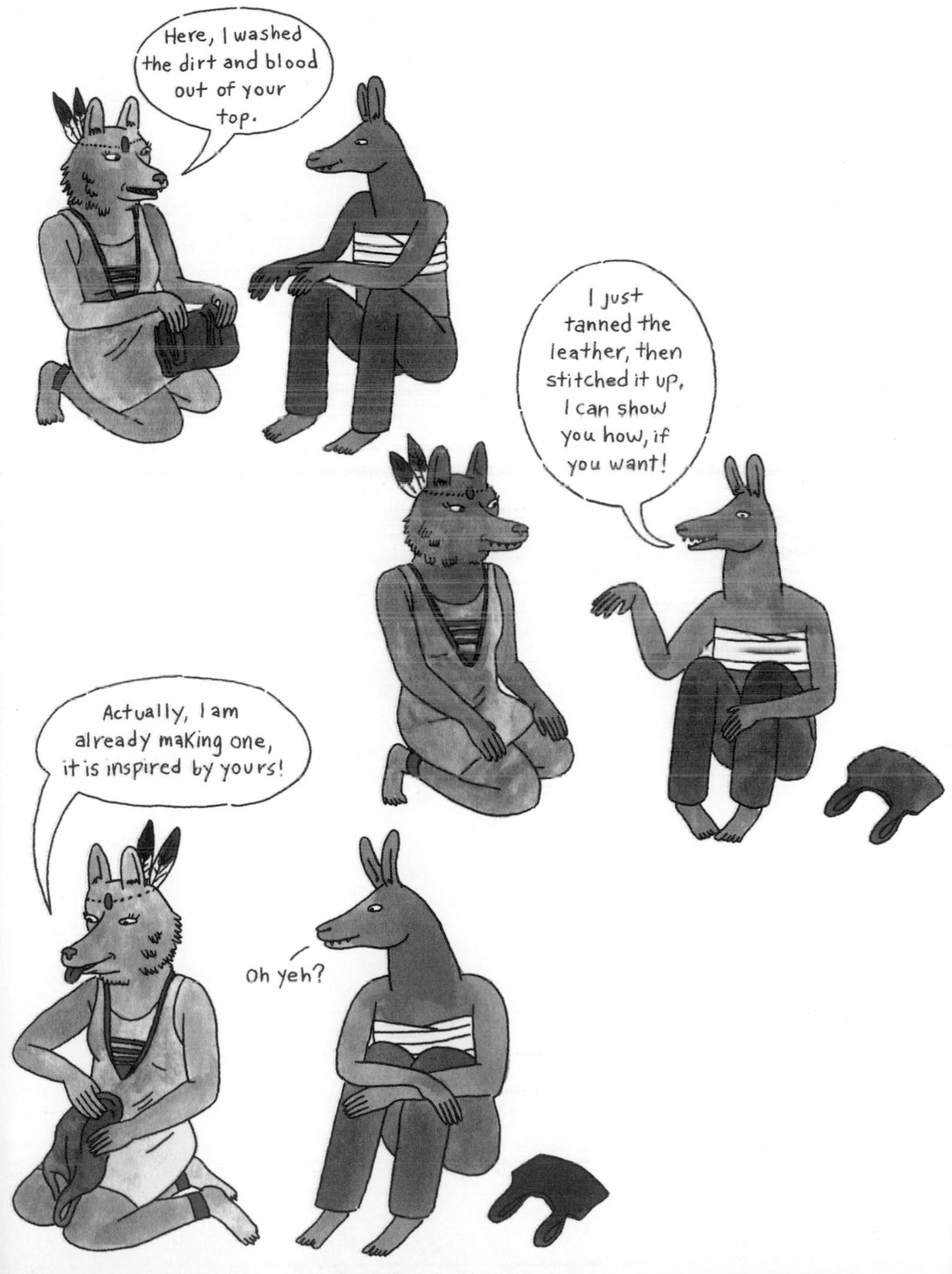
Here, I washed the dirt and blood out of your top.
I just tanned the leather, then stitched it up, I can show you how, if you want!
Actually, I am already making one, it is inspired by yours!
Oh yeh?

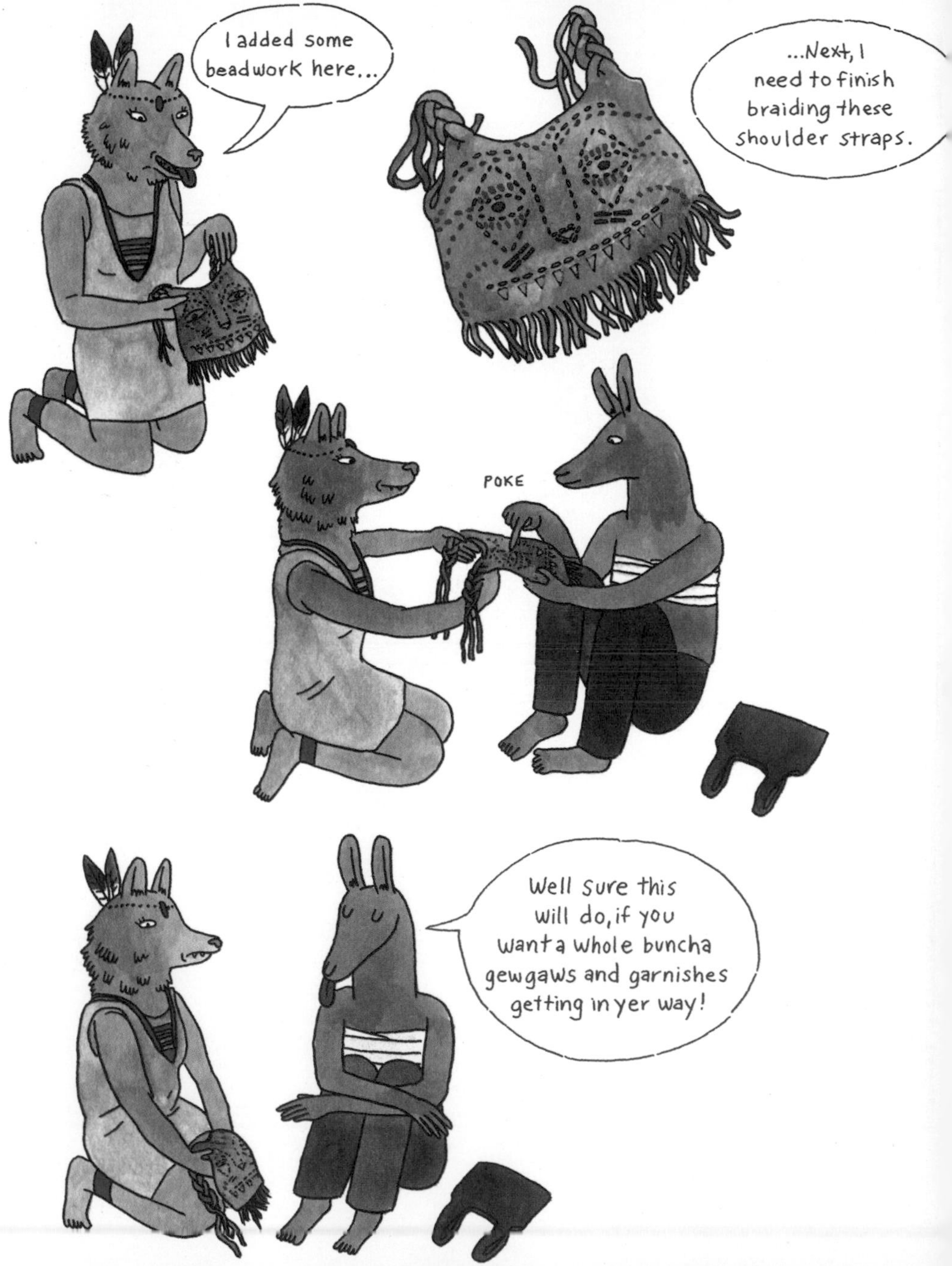
I added some beadwork here...
...Next, I need to finish braiding these shoulder straps.
POKE
Well sure this will do, if you want a whole buncha gewgaws and garnishes getting in yer way!

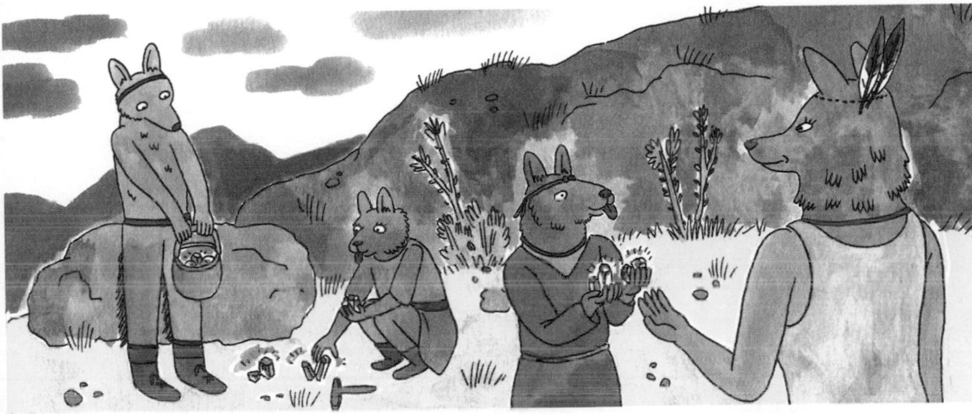

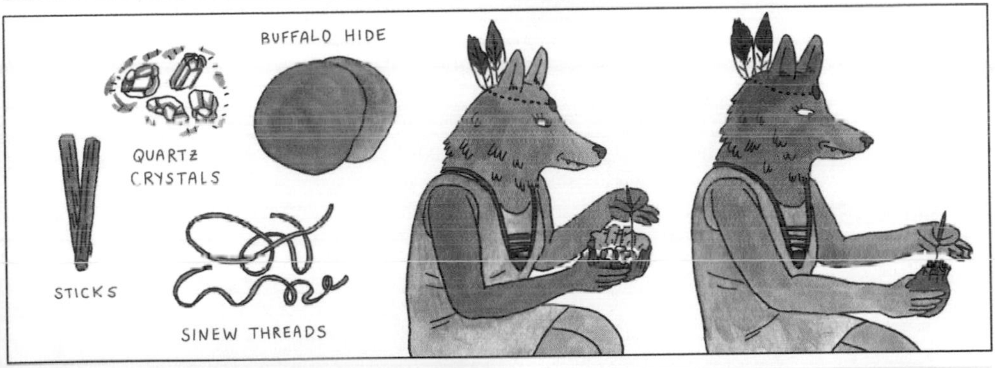
BUFFALO HIDE
QUARTZ CRYSTALS
STICKS
SINEW THREADS

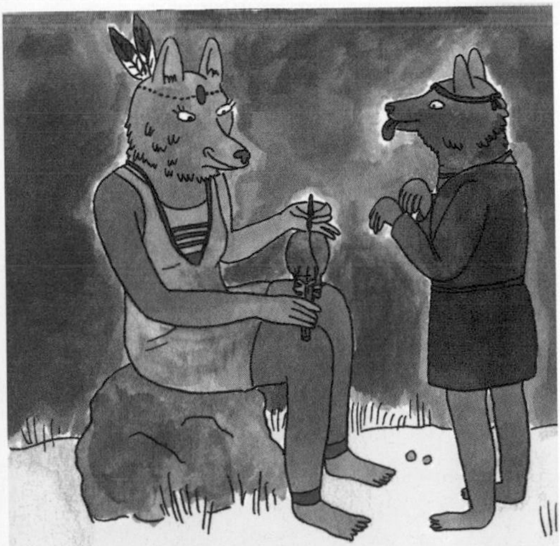

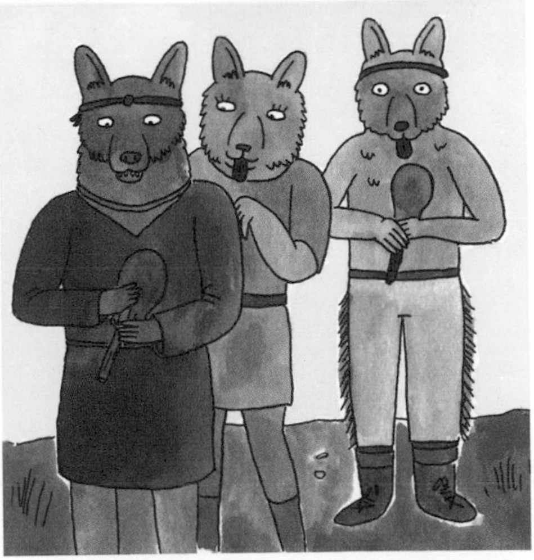

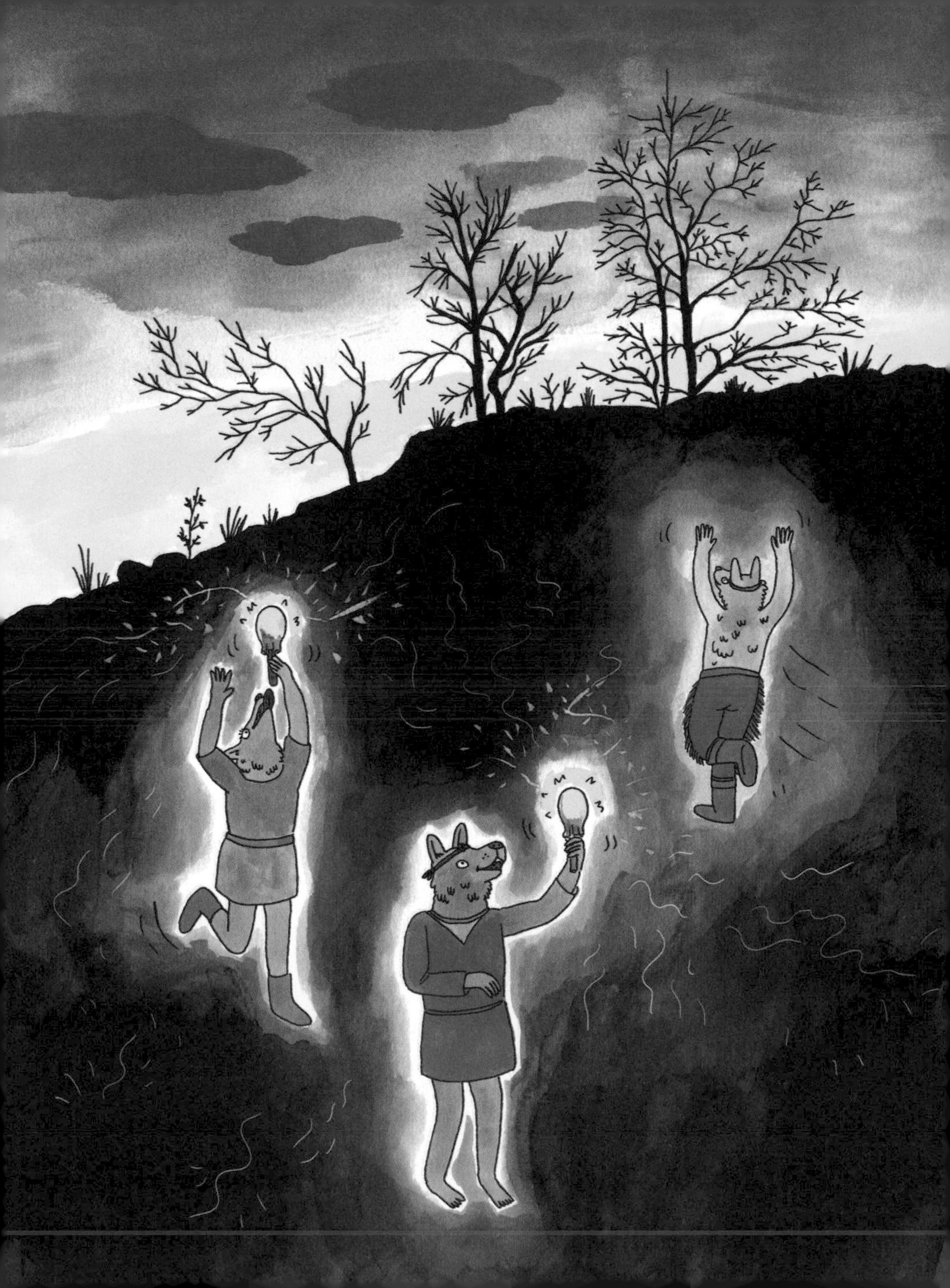

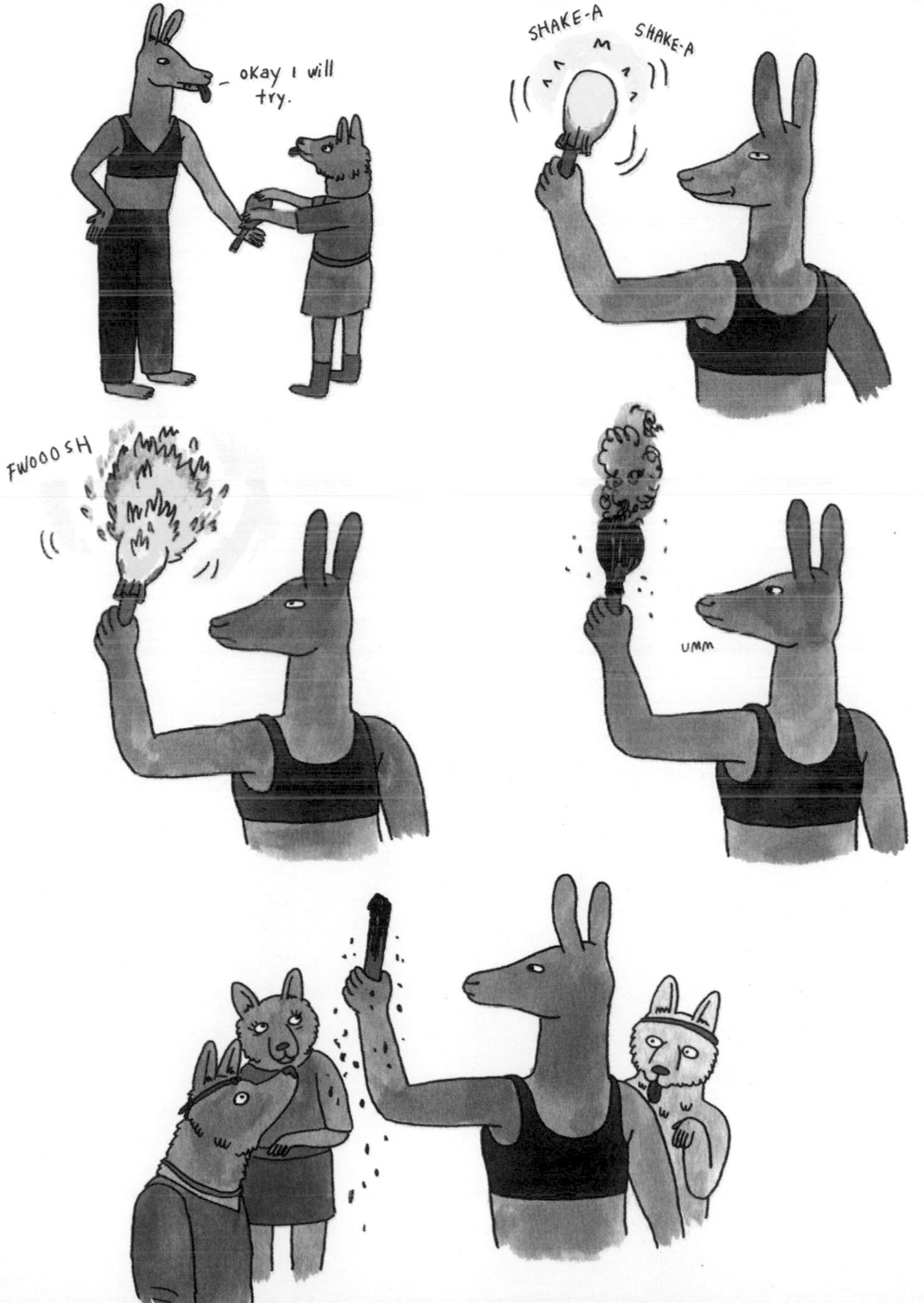
okay I will try.
SHAKE-A
SHAKE-A
FWOOOSH
UMM

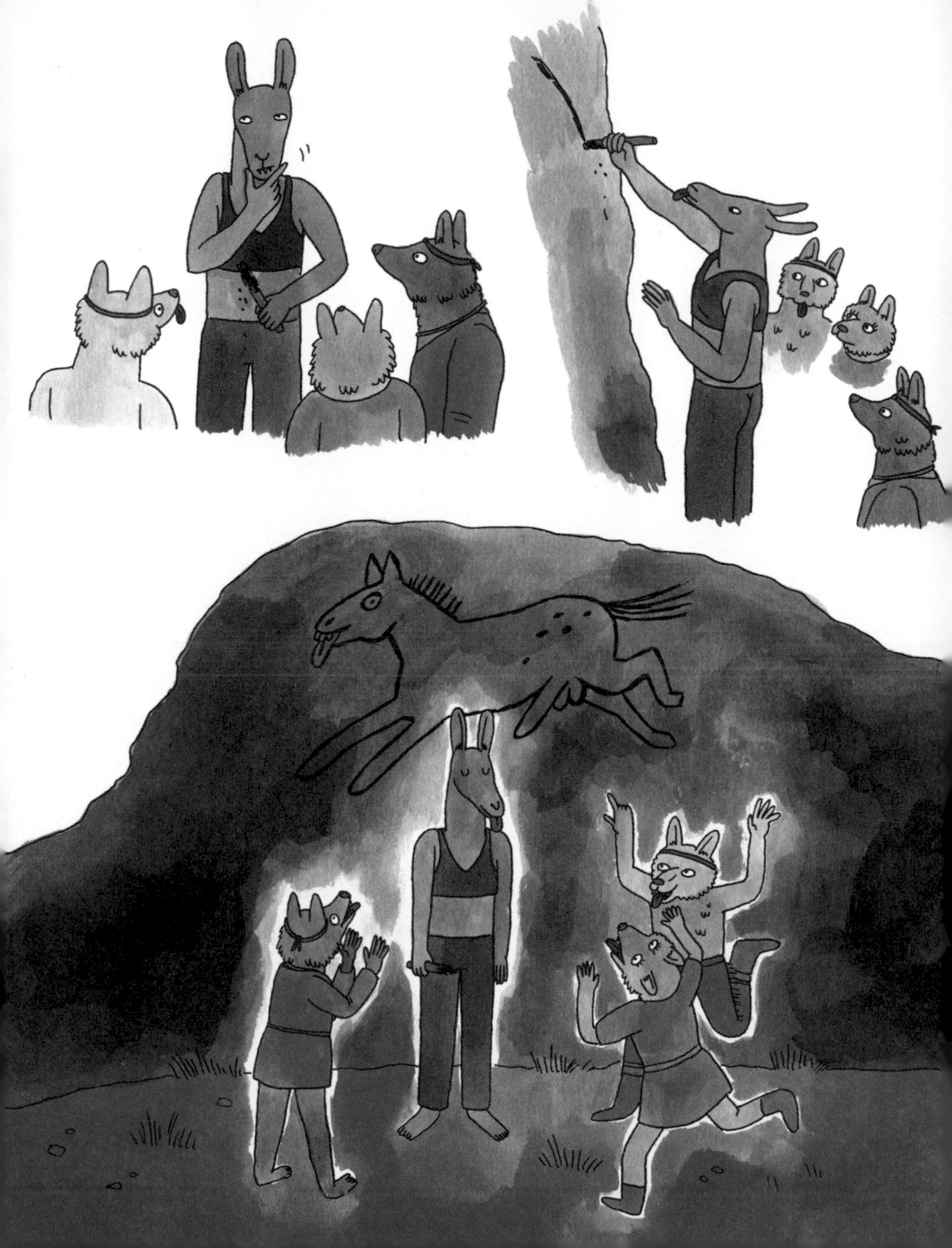

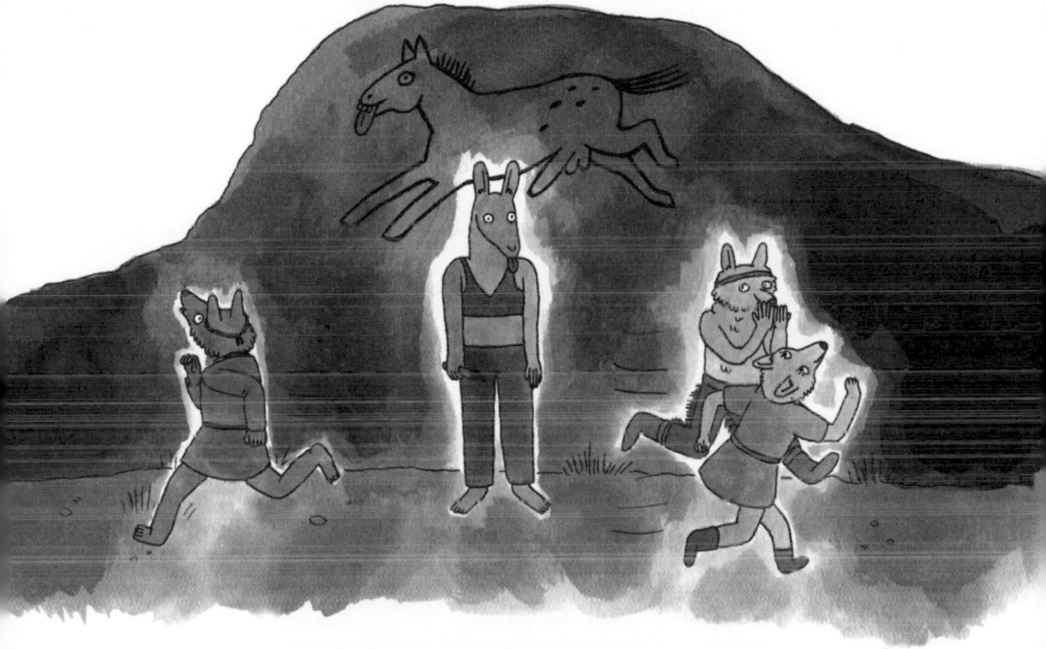

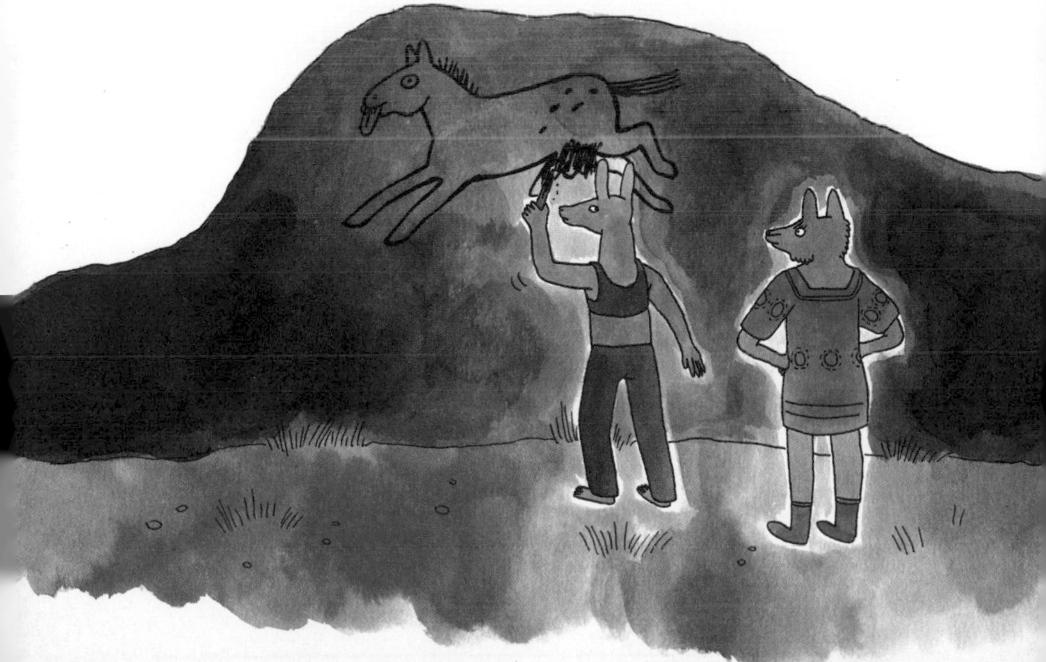

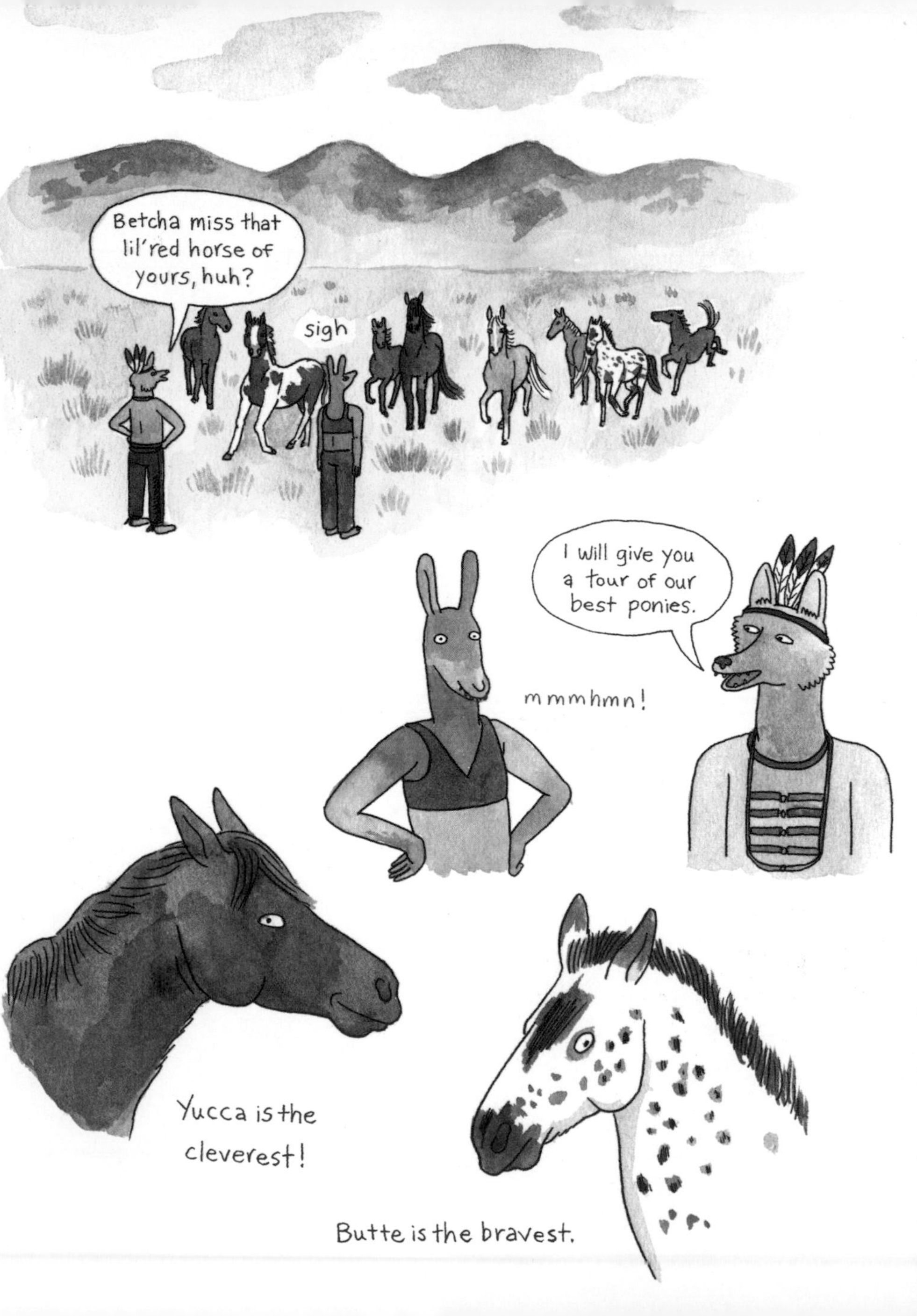
Betcha miss that lil'red horse of yours, huh?
sigh
I will give you a tour of our best ponies.
mmmhmn!
Yucca is the cleverest!
Butte is the bravest.

Soot is the smoothest ride.

Sweetie Face is fastest.

SnaKey is fast AND sneaKy.

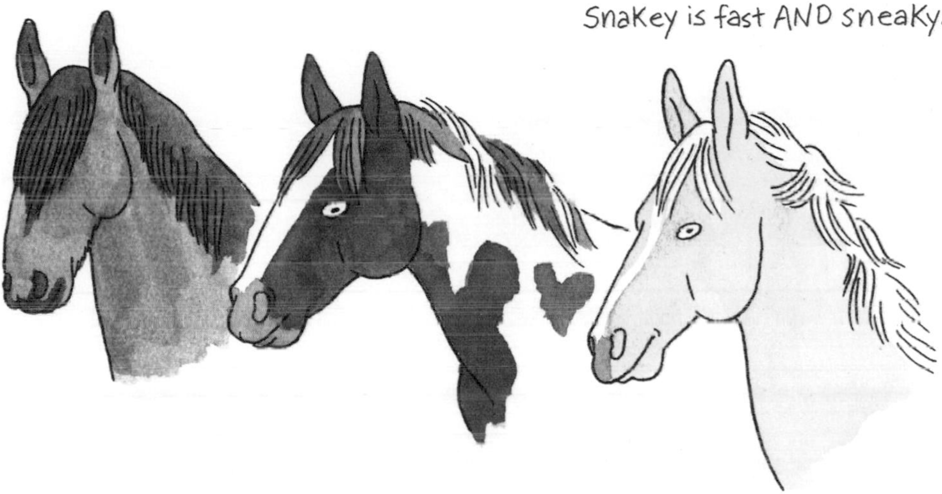

TomTom's personality... is pretty similar to Soot's. Y'Know, they are both horses.

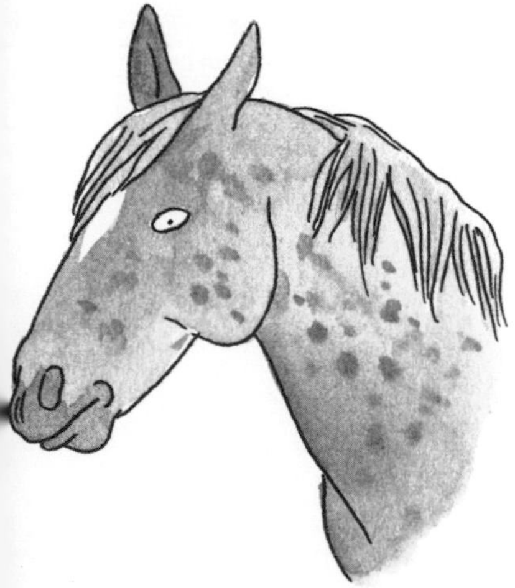

Honey has magical powers.

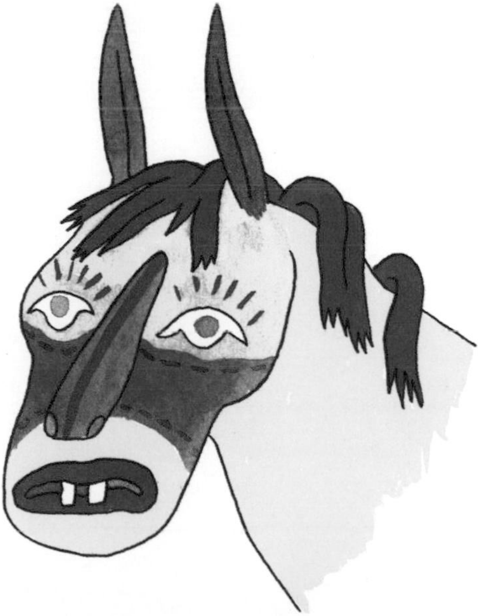

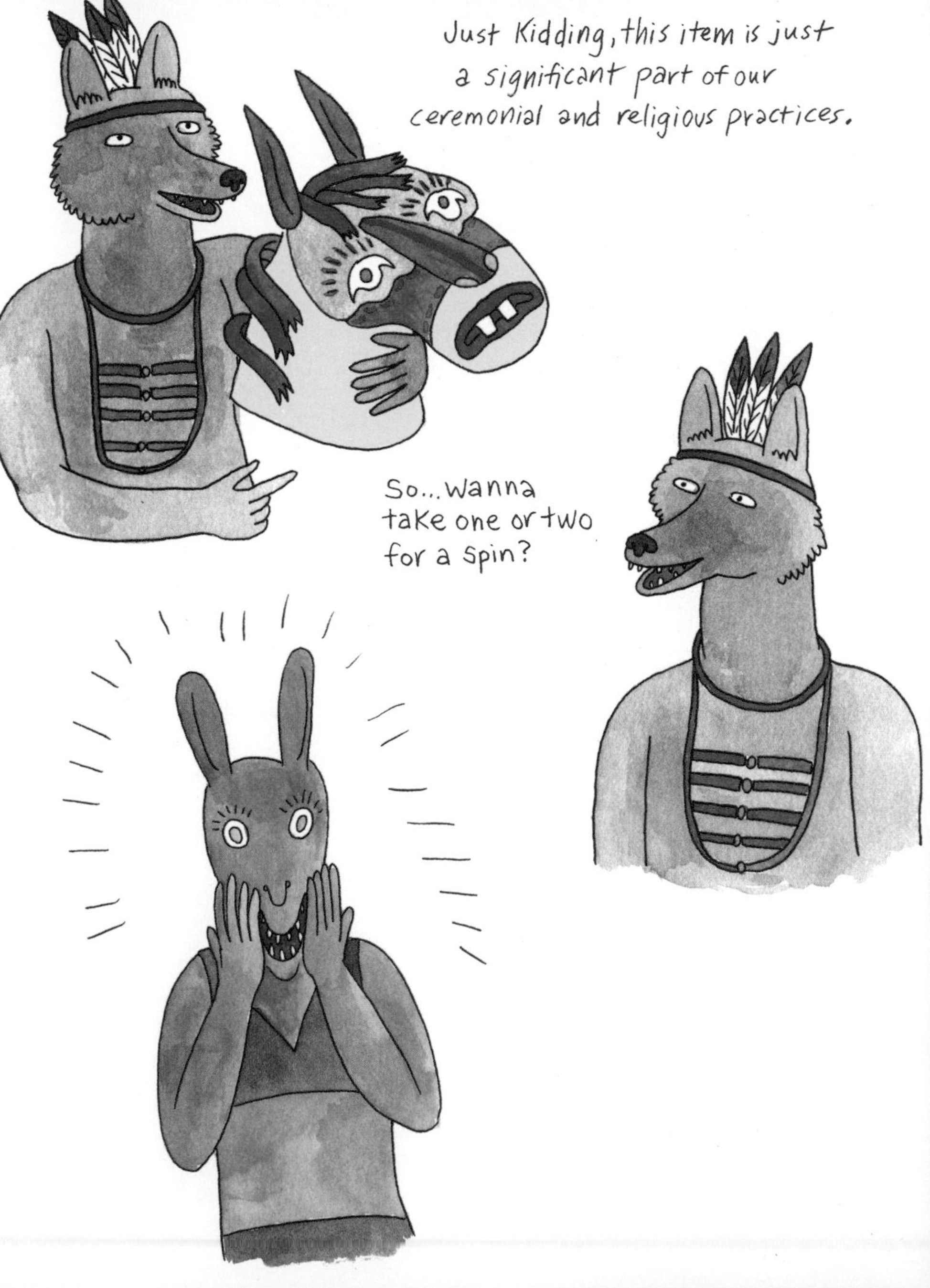
Just Kidding, this item is just a significant part of our ceremonial and religious practices.
So... wanna take one or two for a spin?

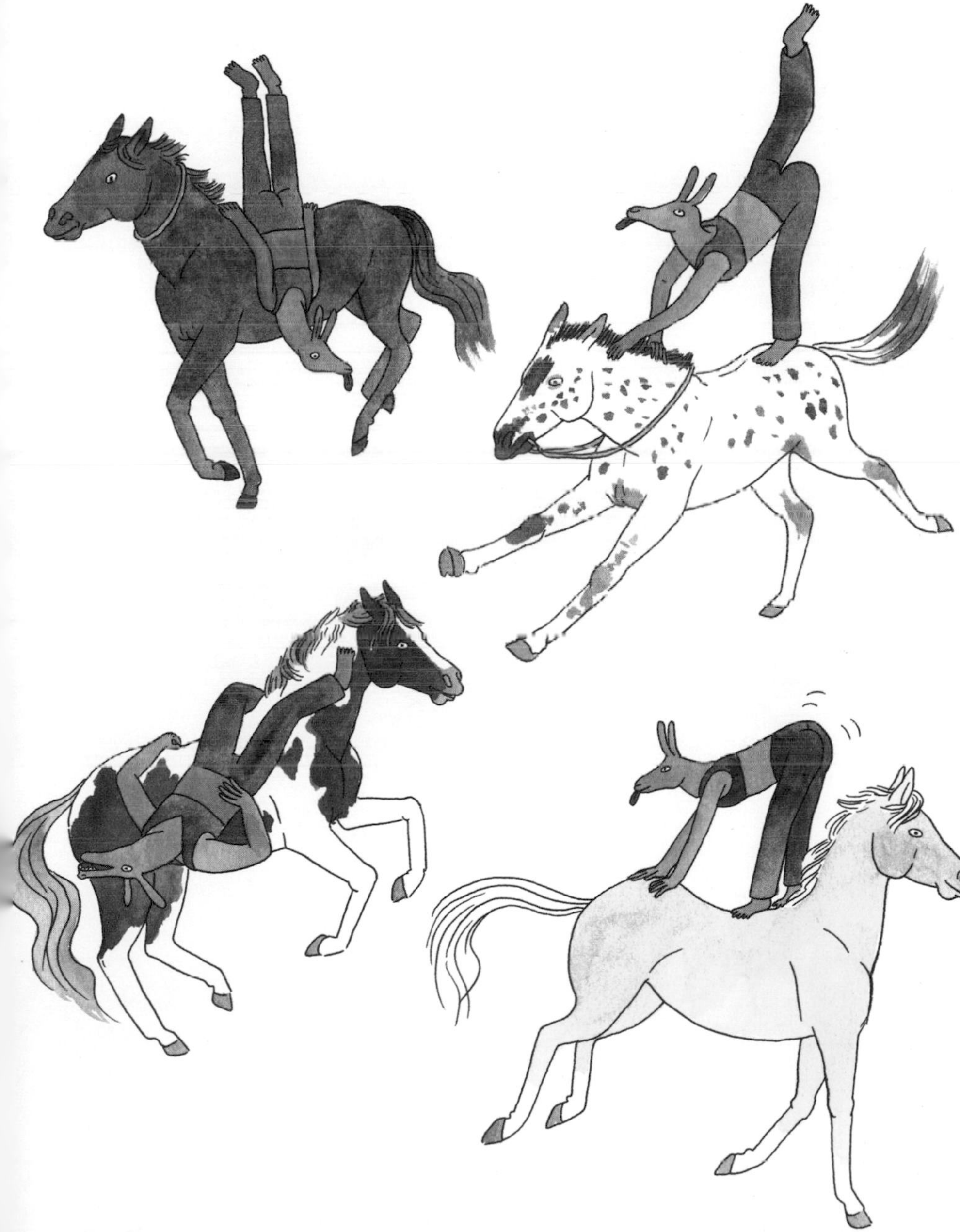

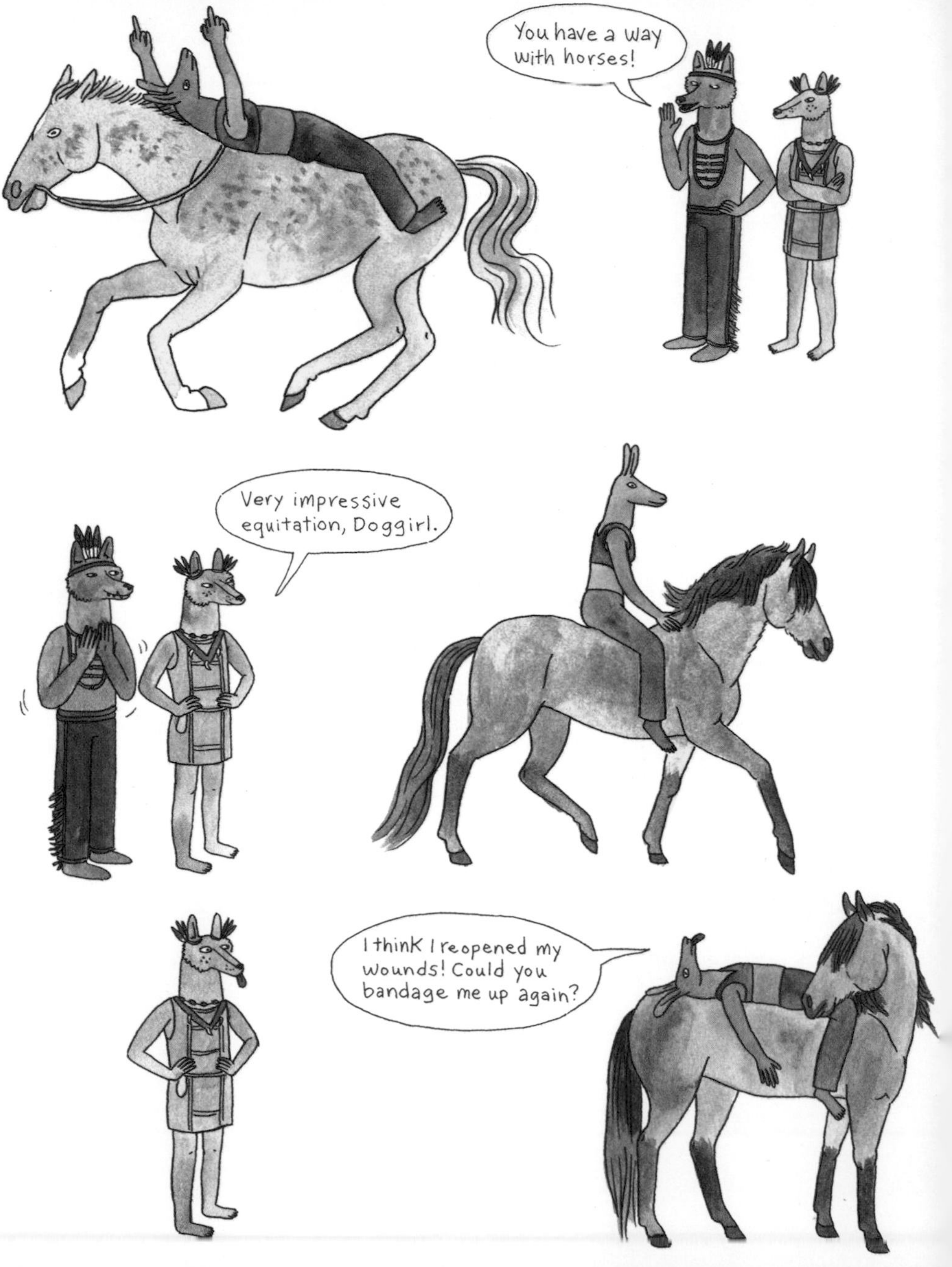

You have a way with horses!
Very impressive equitation, Doggirl.
I think I reopened my wounds! Could you bandage me up again?

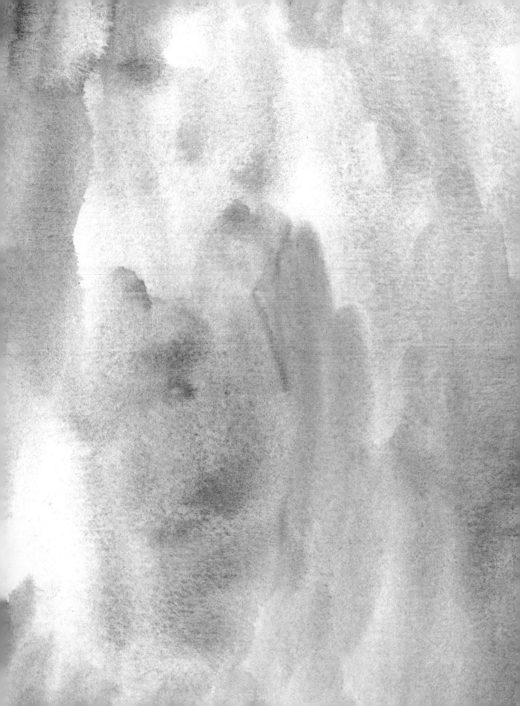

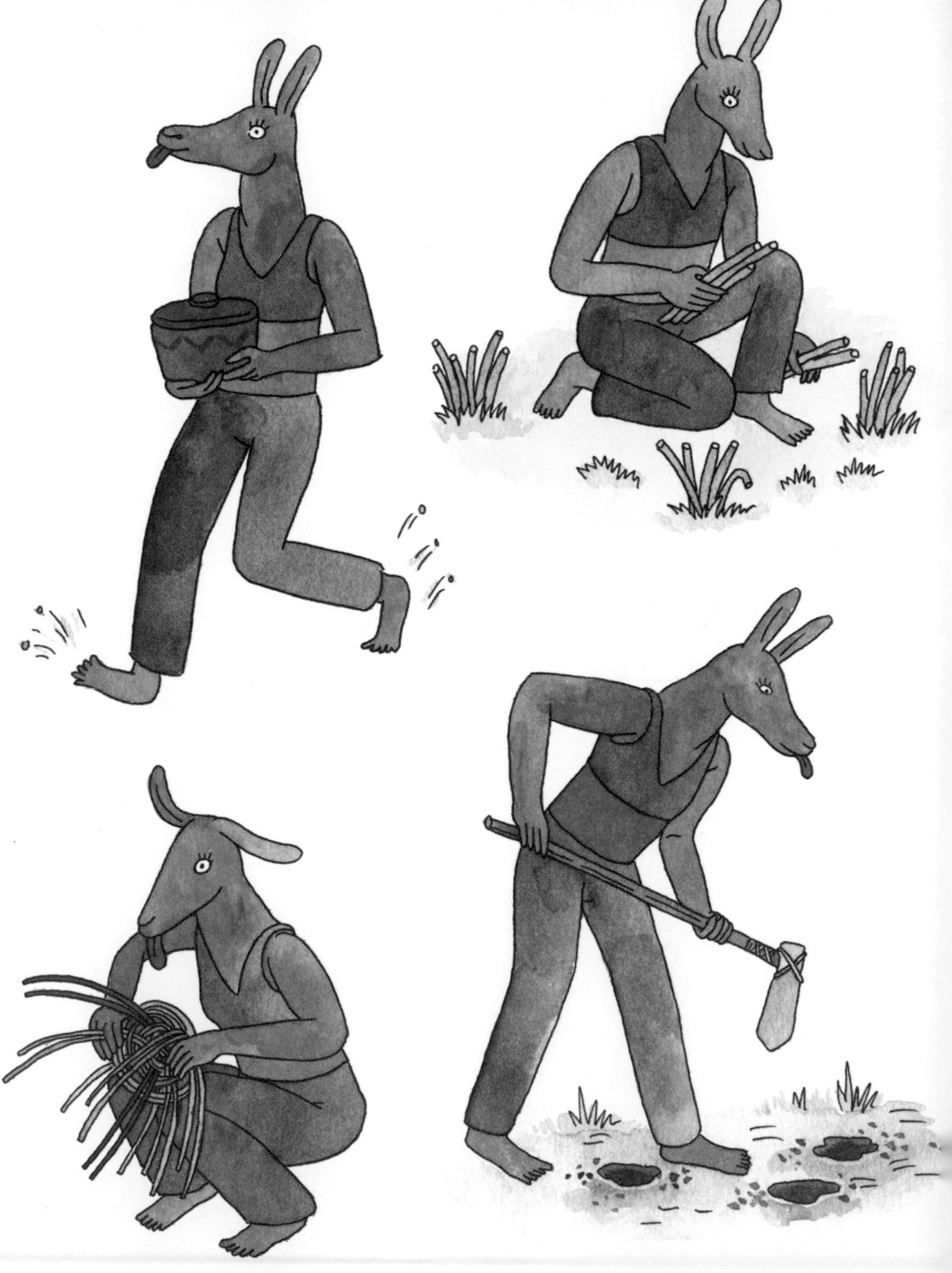

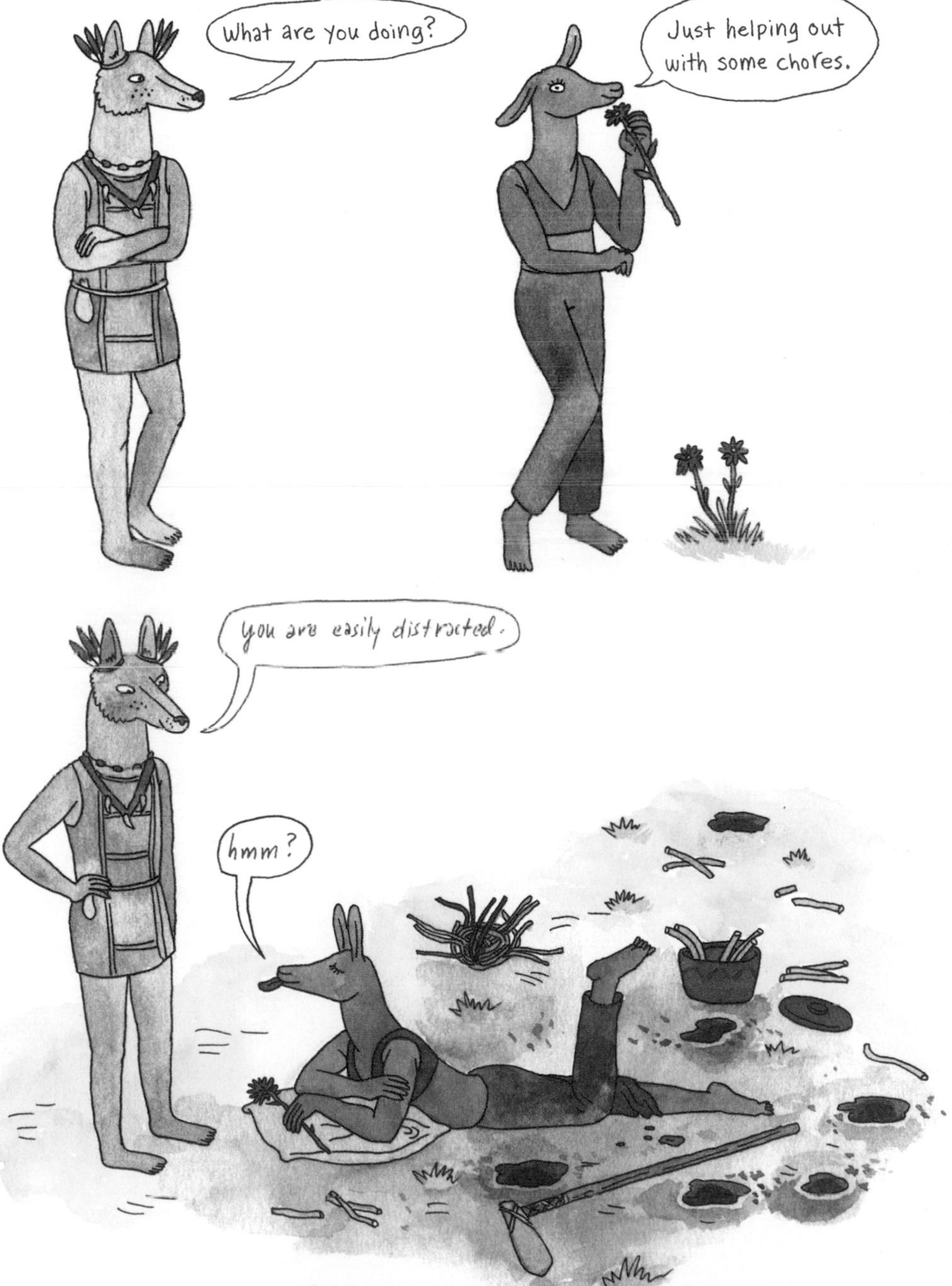
What are you doing?
Just helping out with some chores.
you are easily distracted.
hmm?

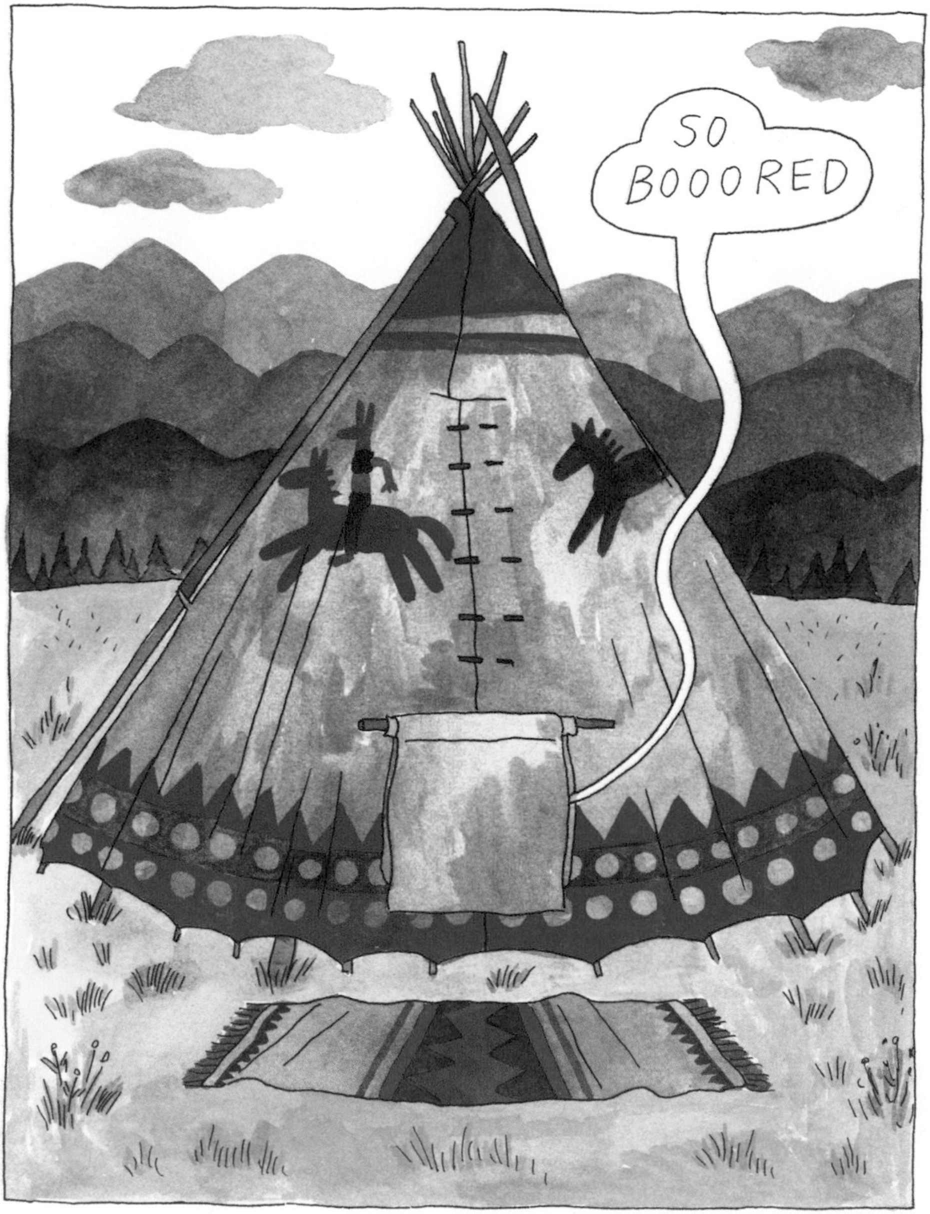
SO BOOORED

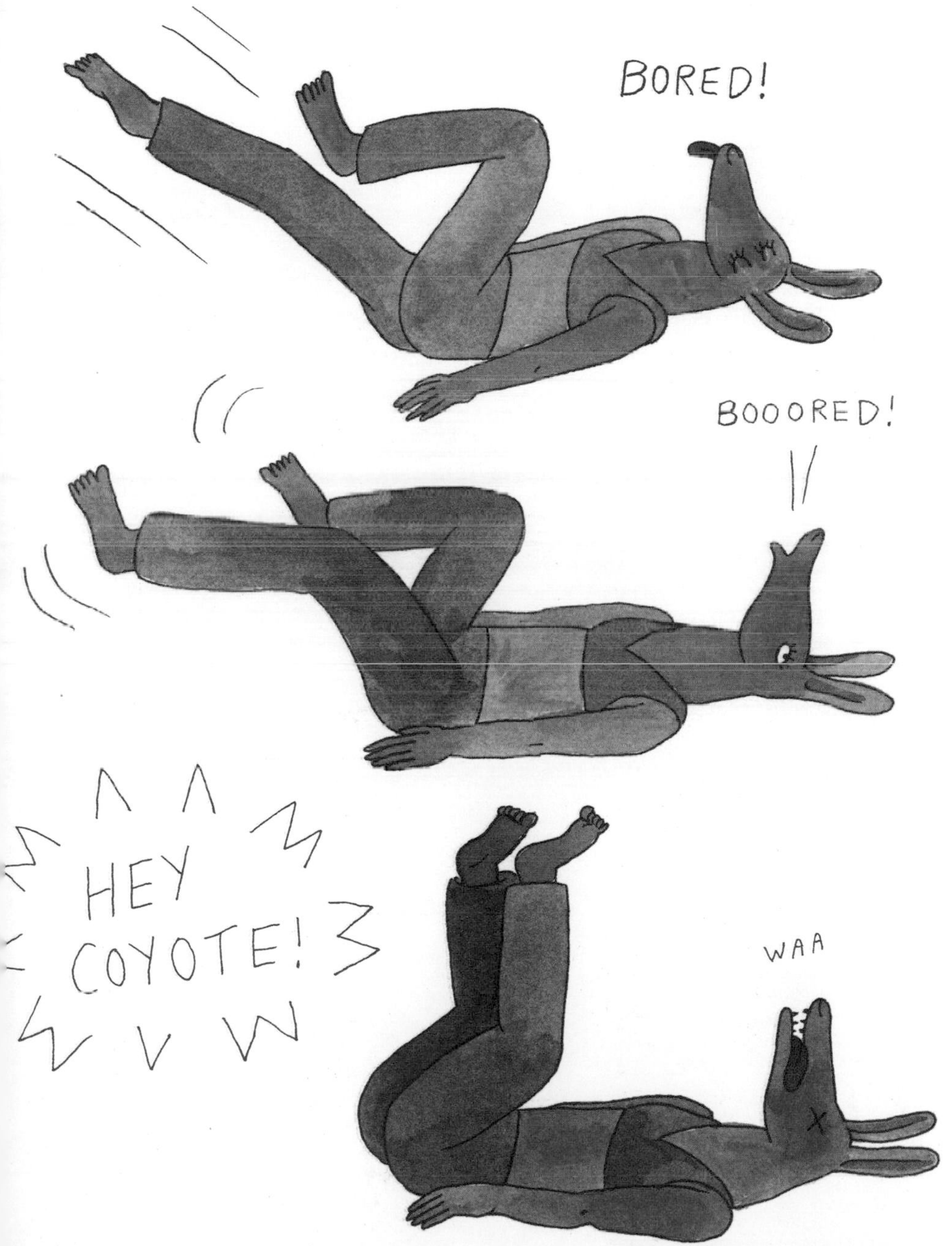
BORED!
BOOORED!
HEY COYOTE!
WAA

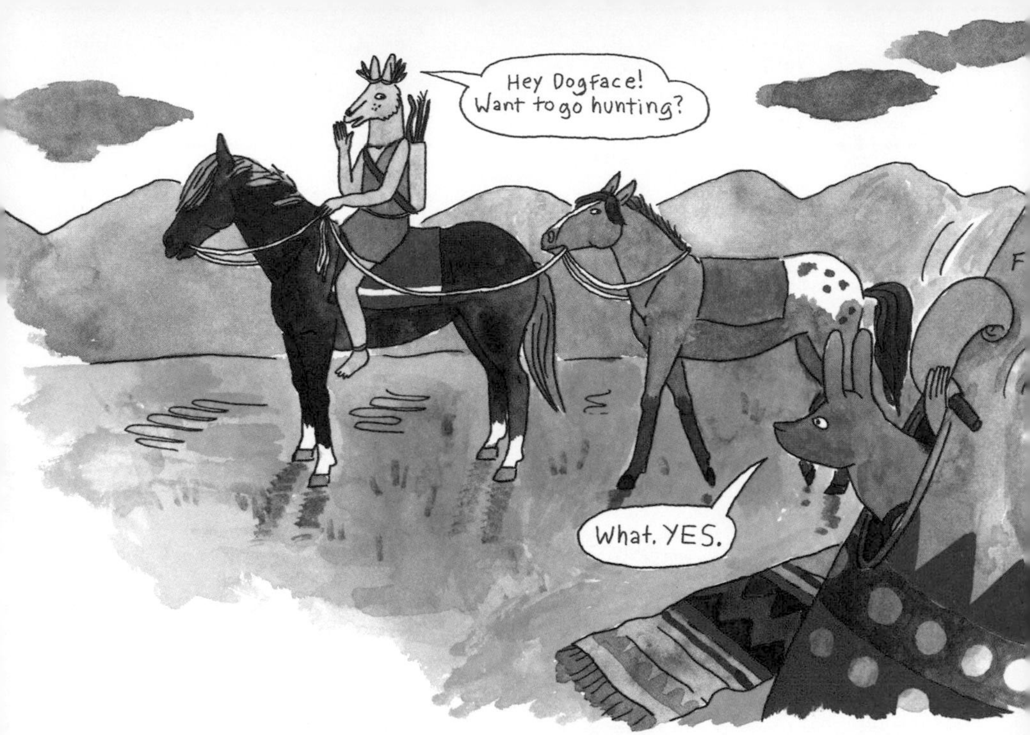
Hey Dogface!
Want to go hunting?
What. YES.

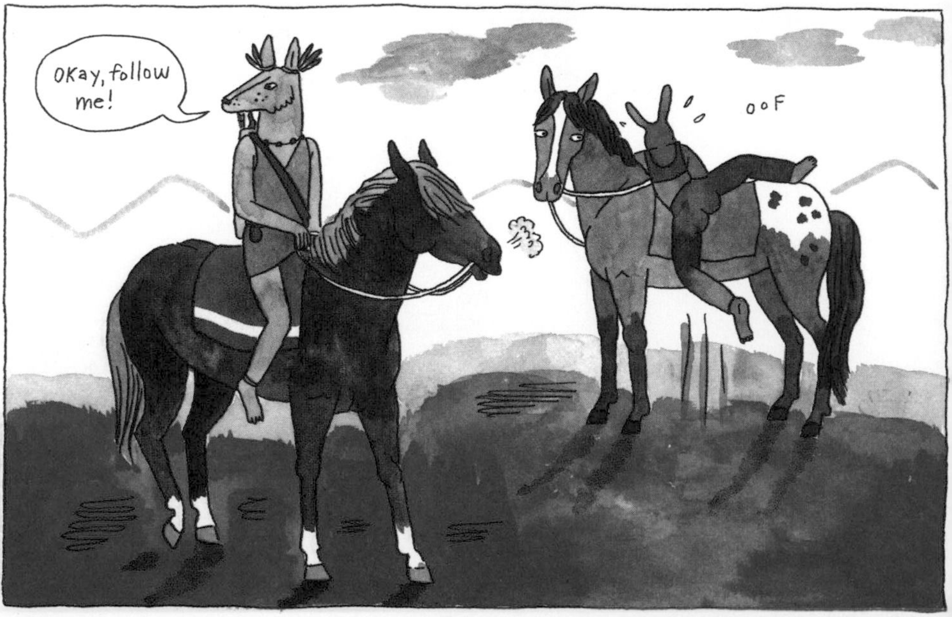
OKay, follow me!
OOF

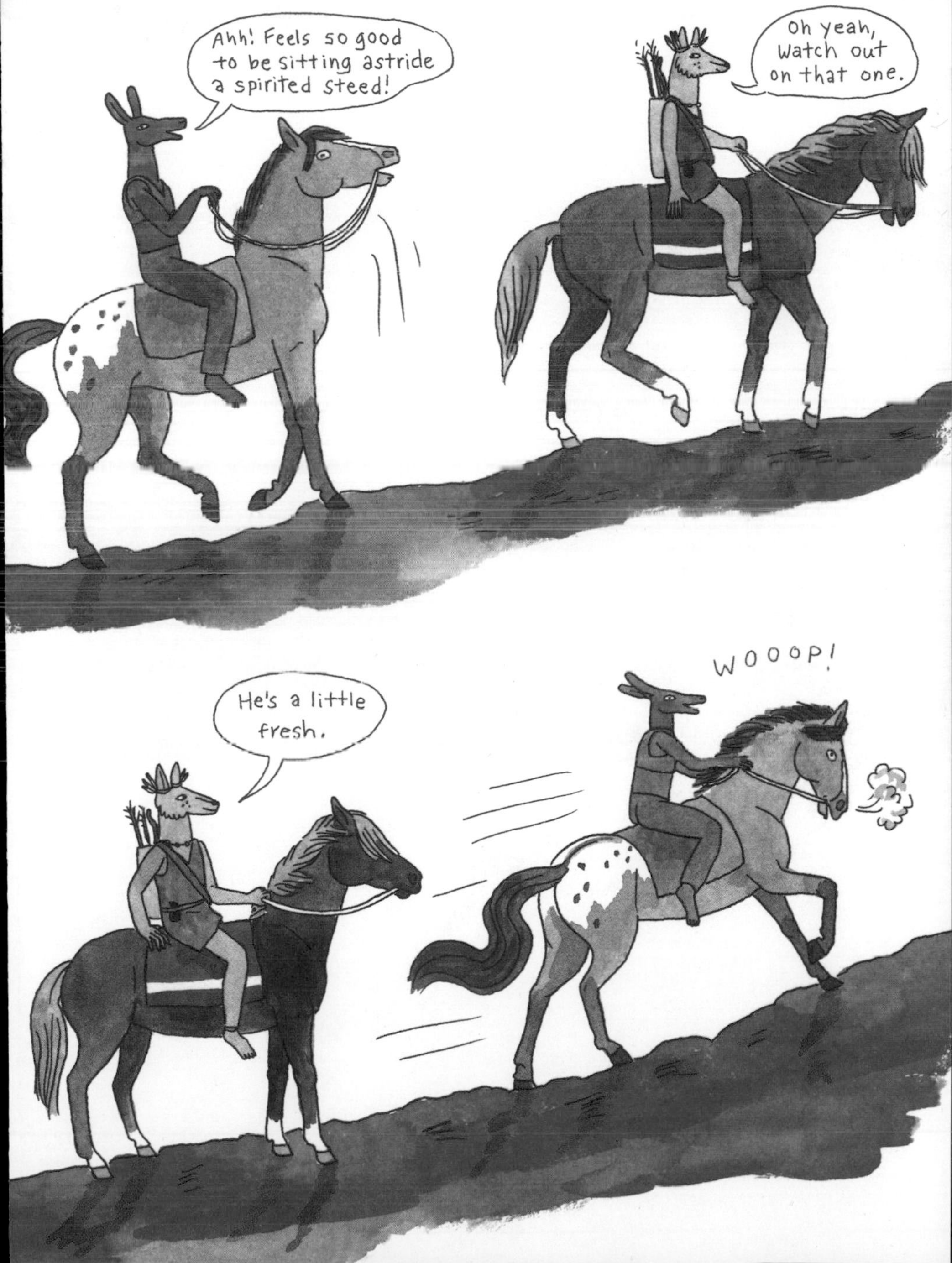
Ahh! Feels so good to be sitting astride a spirited steed!
Oh yeah, Watch out on that one.
He's a little fresh.
WOOOP!

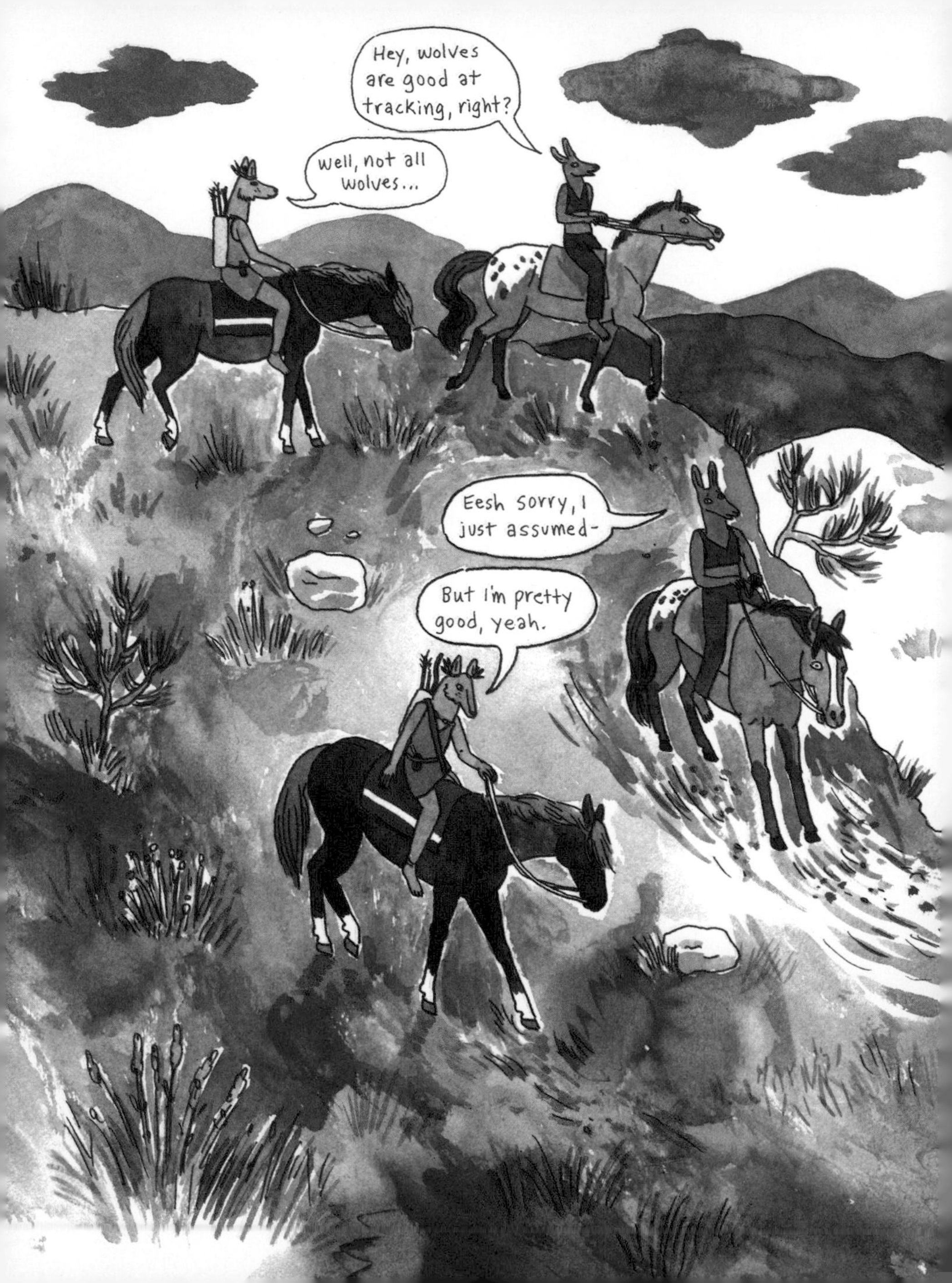
Hey, wolves are good at tracking, right?
well, not all wolves...
Eesh sorry, I just assumed-
But I'm pretty good, yeah.

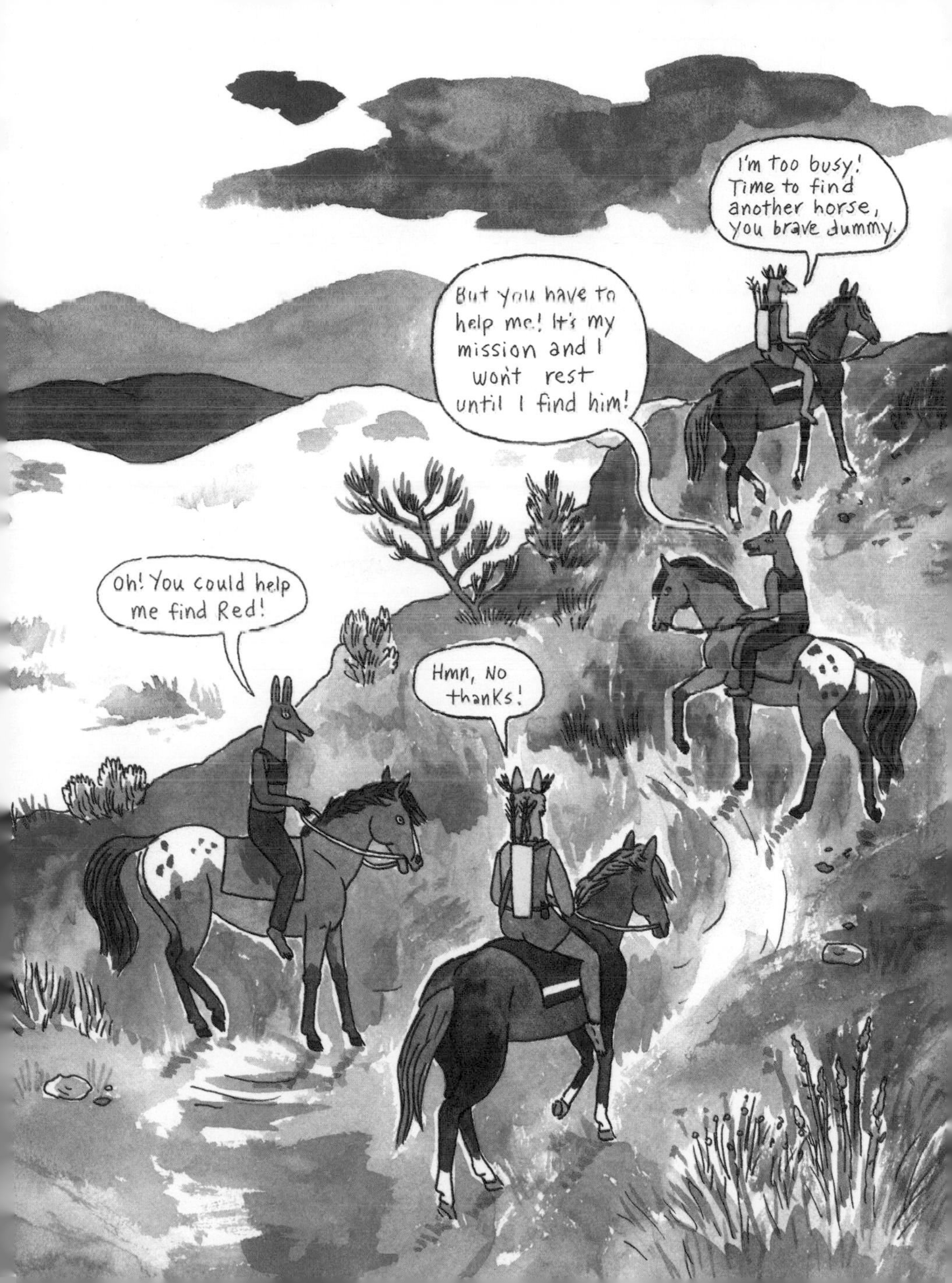
I'm too busy! Time to find another horse, you brave dummy.
But you have to help me! It's my mission and I won't rest until I find him!
Oh! You could help me find Red!
Hmn, No thanks!

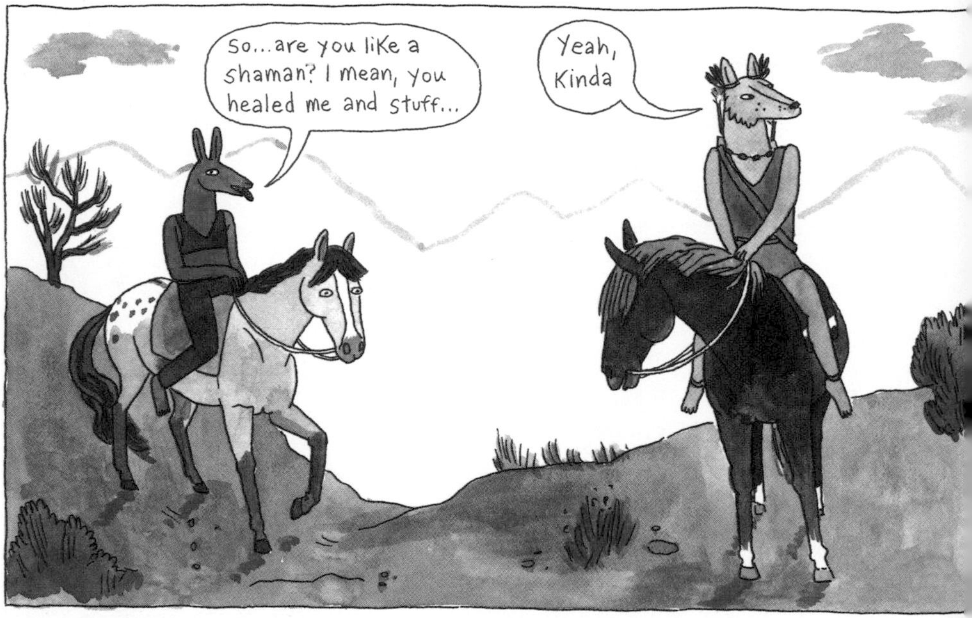
So... are you like a shaman? I mean, you healed me and stuff...
Yeah, Kinda

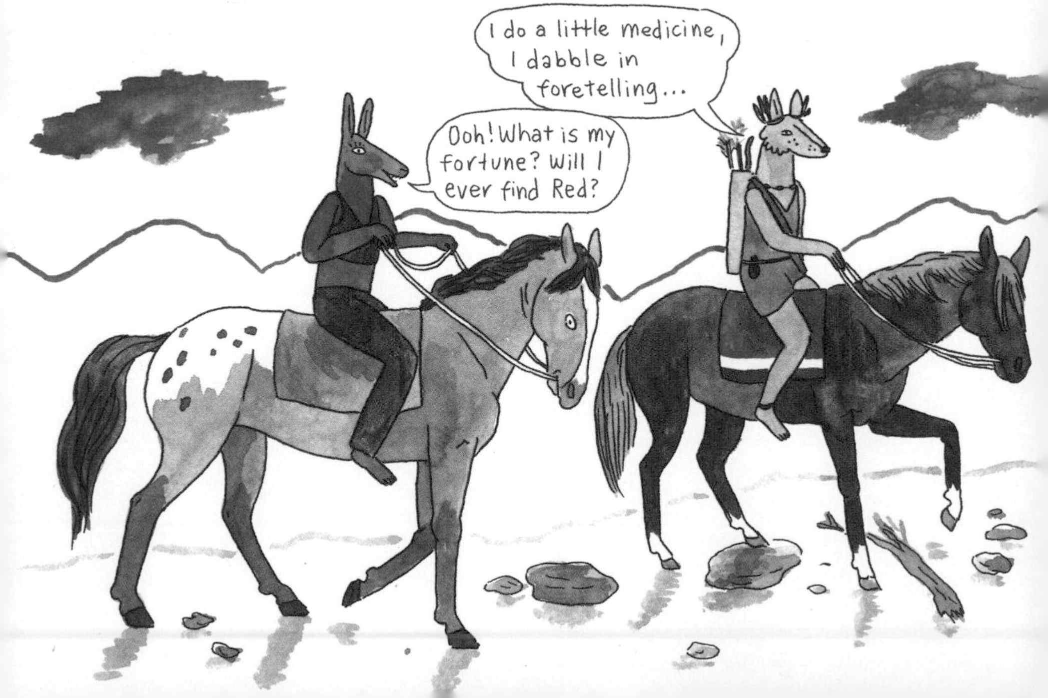
I do a little medicine, I dabble in foretelling...
Ooh! What is my fortune? Will I ever find Red?

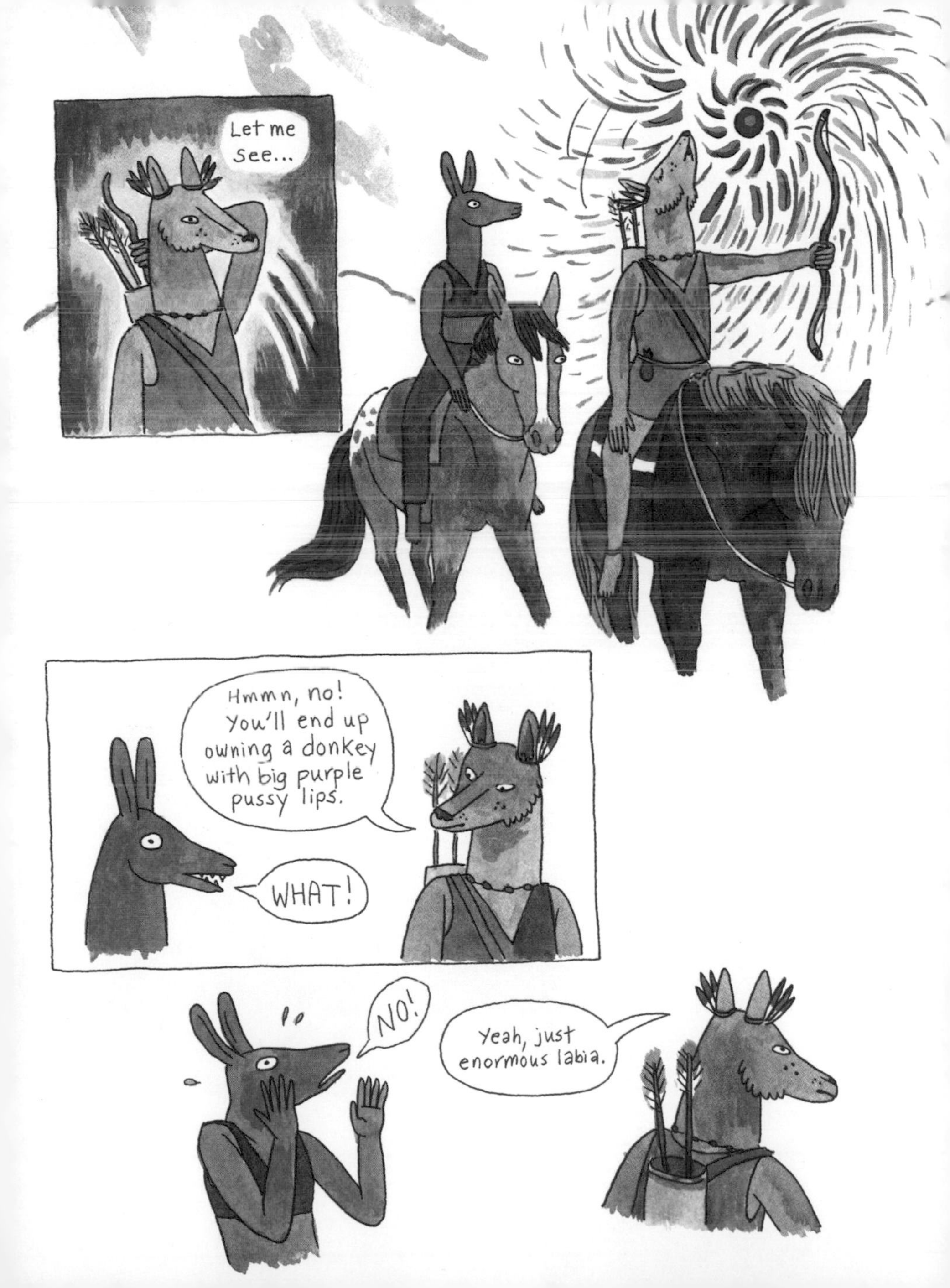

Let me see...
Hmmn, no! You'll end up owning a donkey with big purple pussy lips.
WHAT!
NO!
Yeah, just enormous labia.

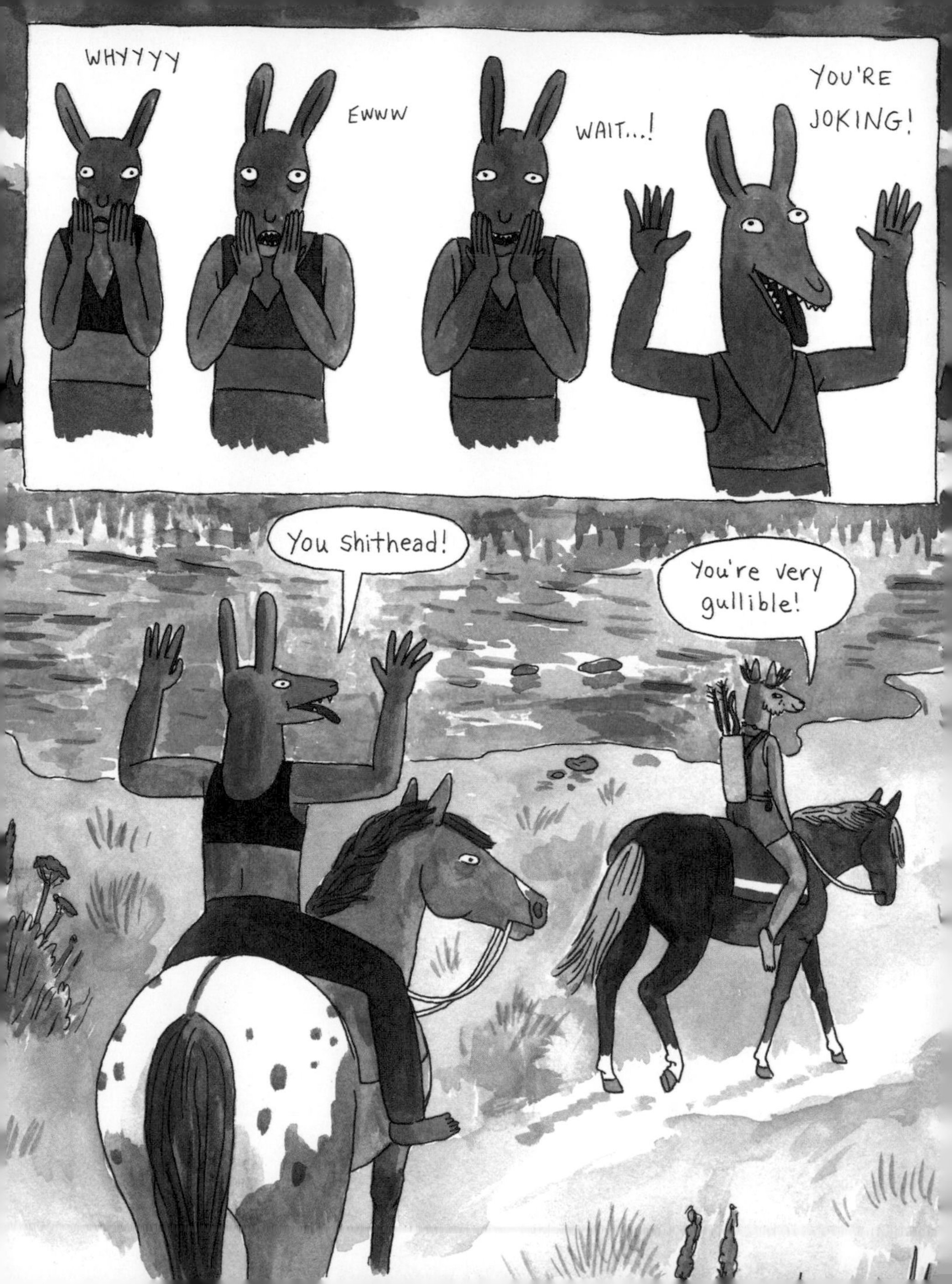
WHYYYY
EWWW
WAIT...!
YOU'RE JOKING!
You shithead!
You're very gullible!

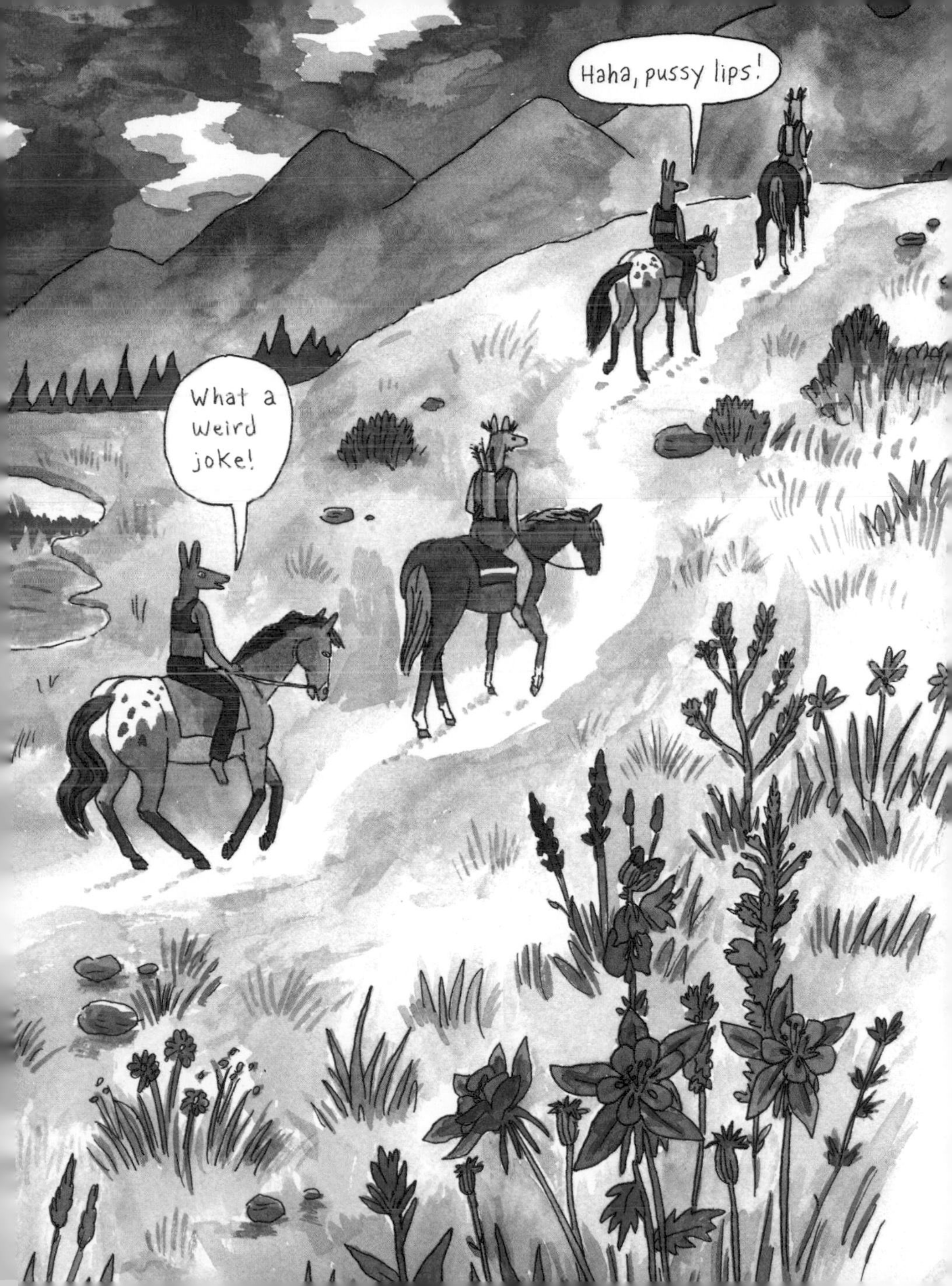
Haha, pussy lips!
What a weird joke!

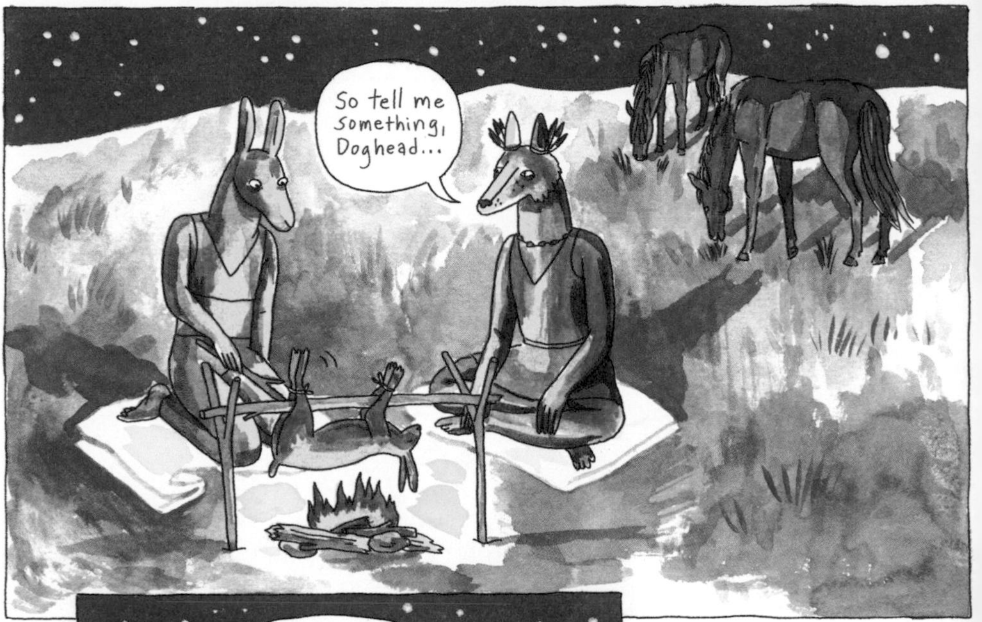
So tell me something, Doghead...

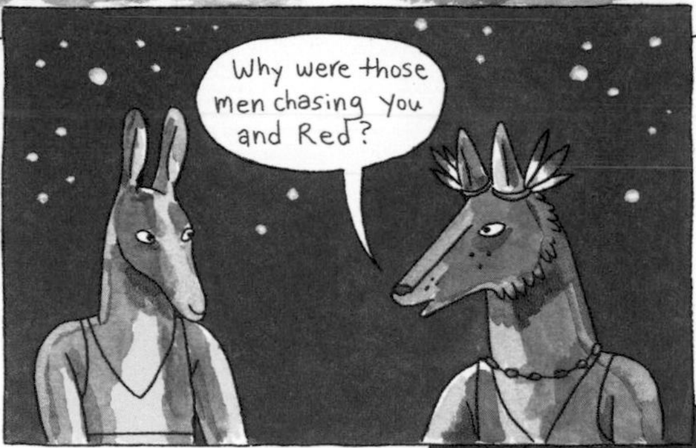
Why were those men chasing you and Red?

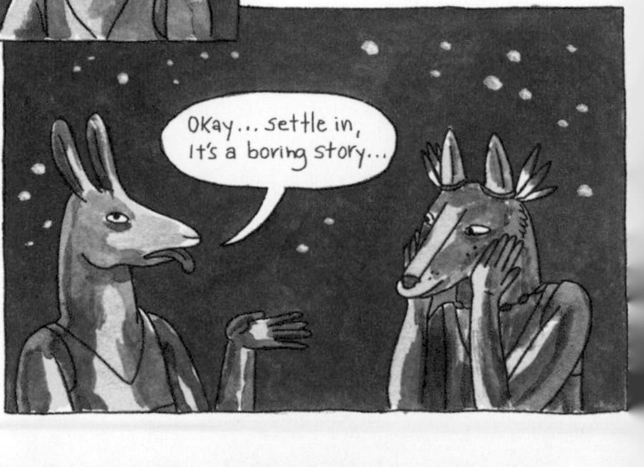
Okay... settle in, It's a boring story...

I had a little home on the outskirts of a town up north.

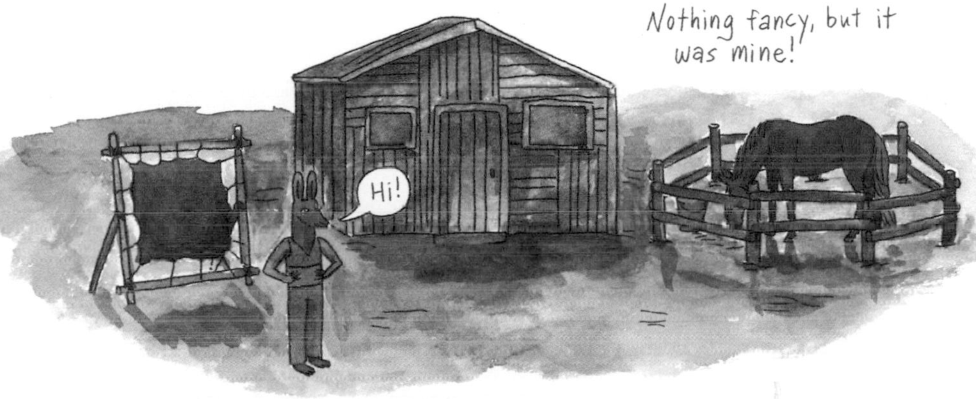
Nothing fancy, but it was mine!
Hi!

I kept to myself mostly. I didn't socialize.

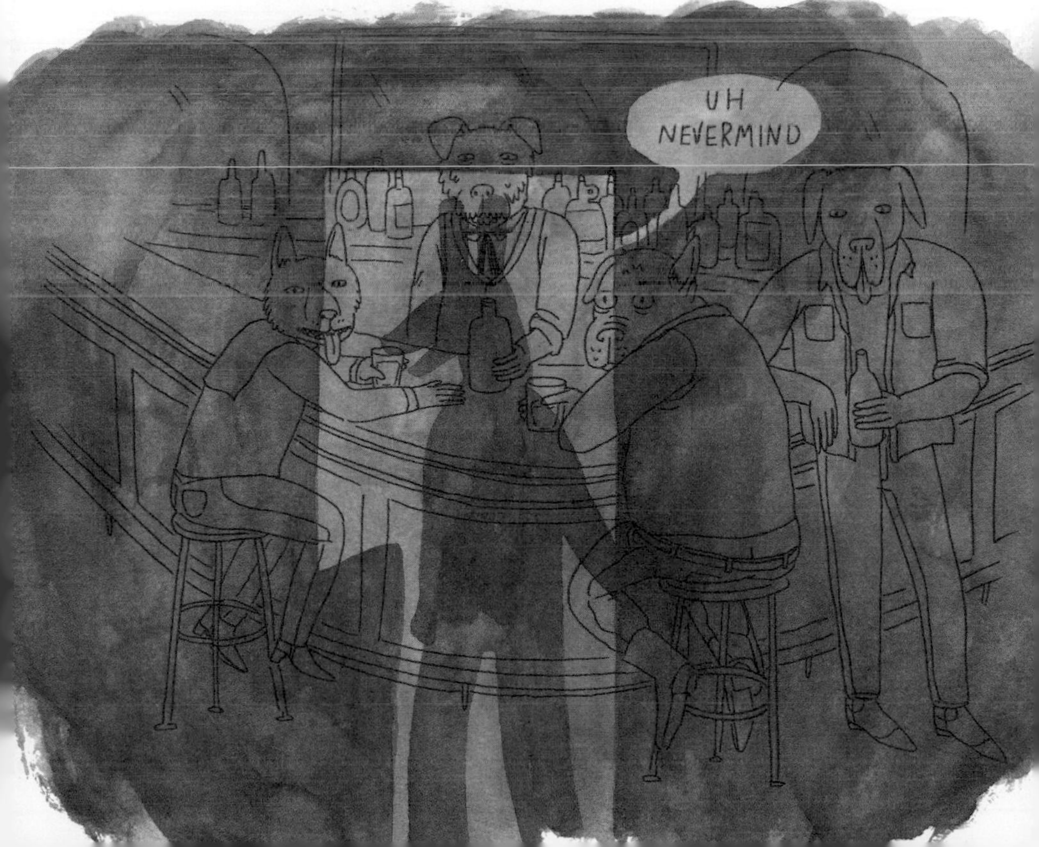
UH NEVERMIND

There was one man I dealt with regularly.
I found his prices and practices to be fair.

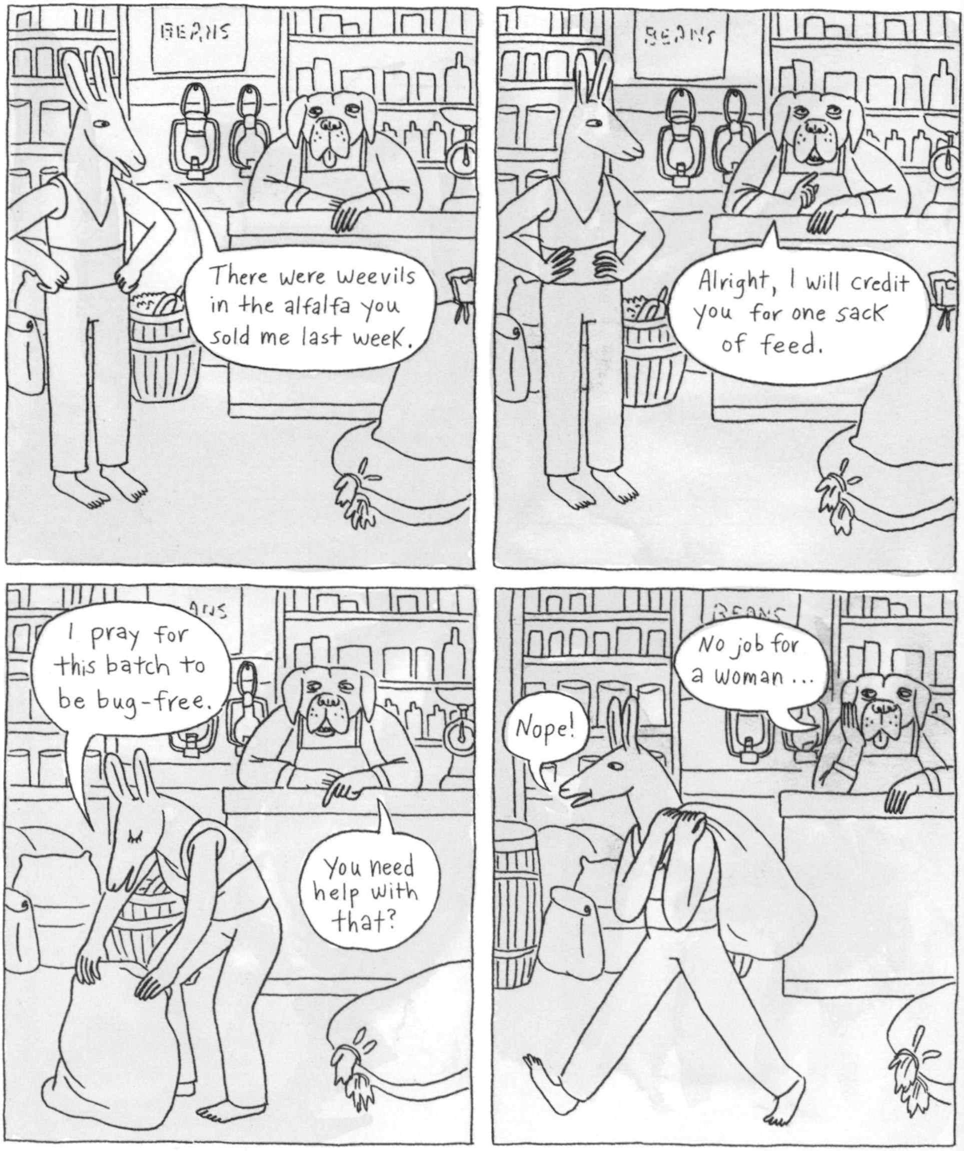
There were weevils in the alfalfa you sold me last week.
Alright, I will credit you for one sack of feed.
I pray for this batch to be bug-free.
You need help with that?
No job for a woman ...
Nope!

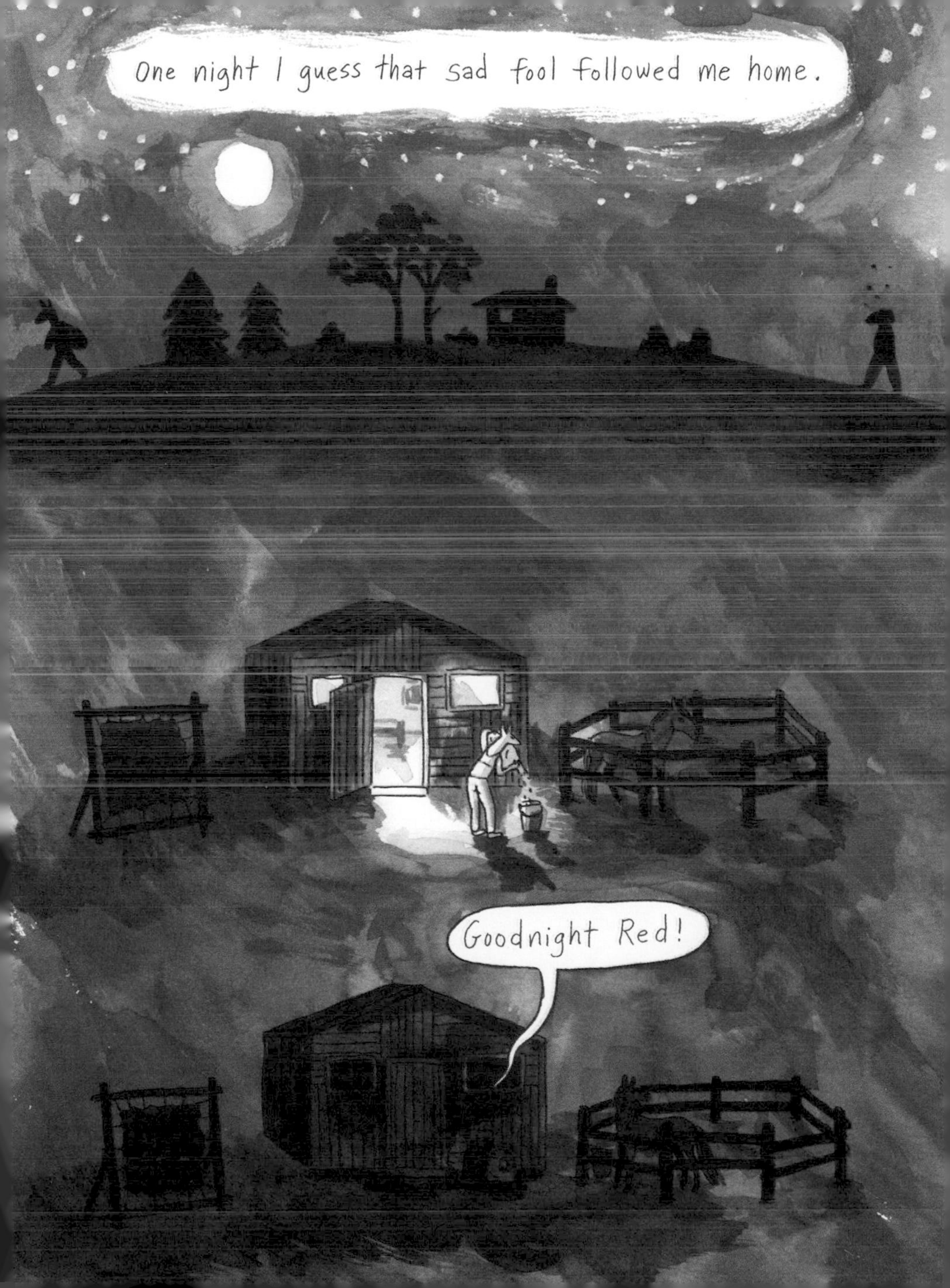
One night I guess that sad fool followed me home.
Goodnight Red!

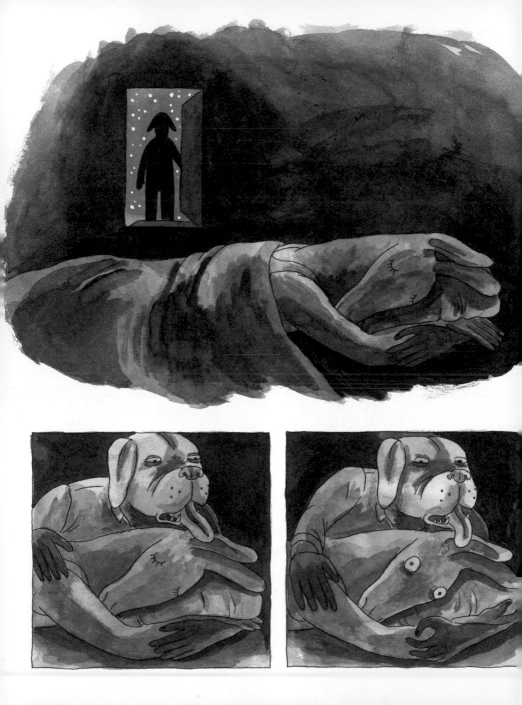

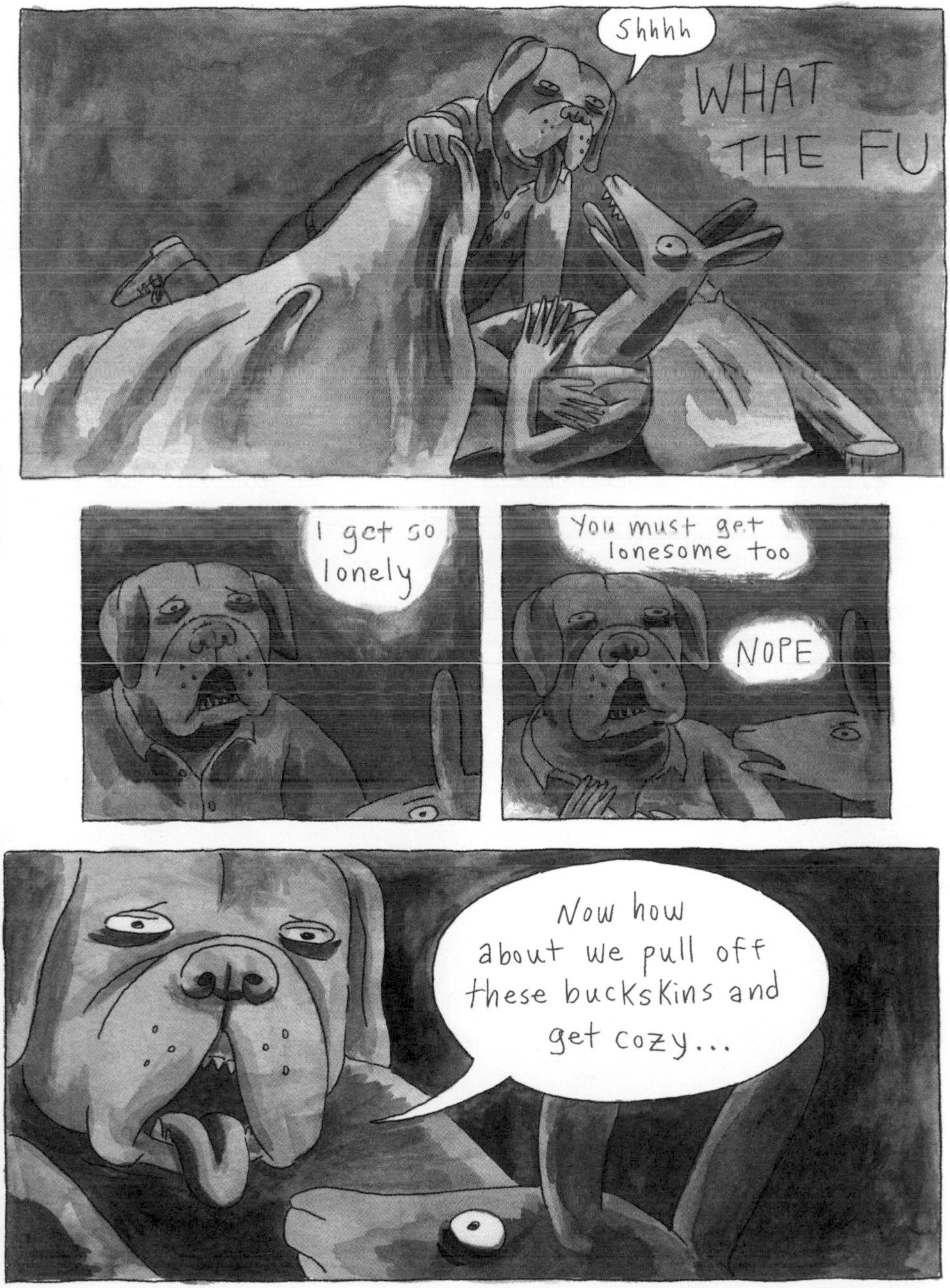

Shhhh
WHAT THE FU
I get so lonely
You must get lonesome too
NOPE
Now how about we pull off these buckskins and get cozy...

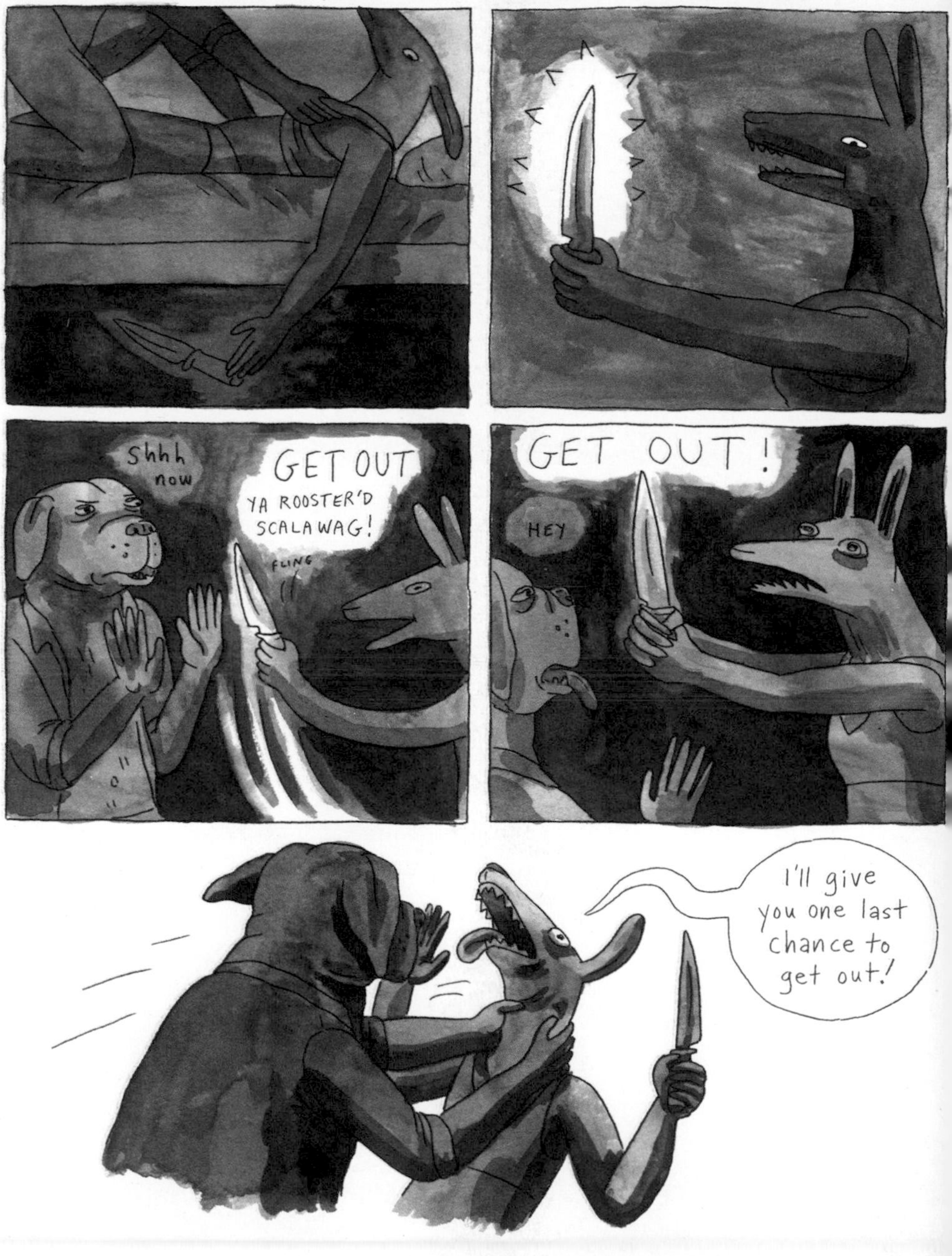
Shhh now
GET OUT
YA ROOSTER'D SCALAWAG!
FLING
GET OUT!
HEY
I'll give you one last chance to get out!

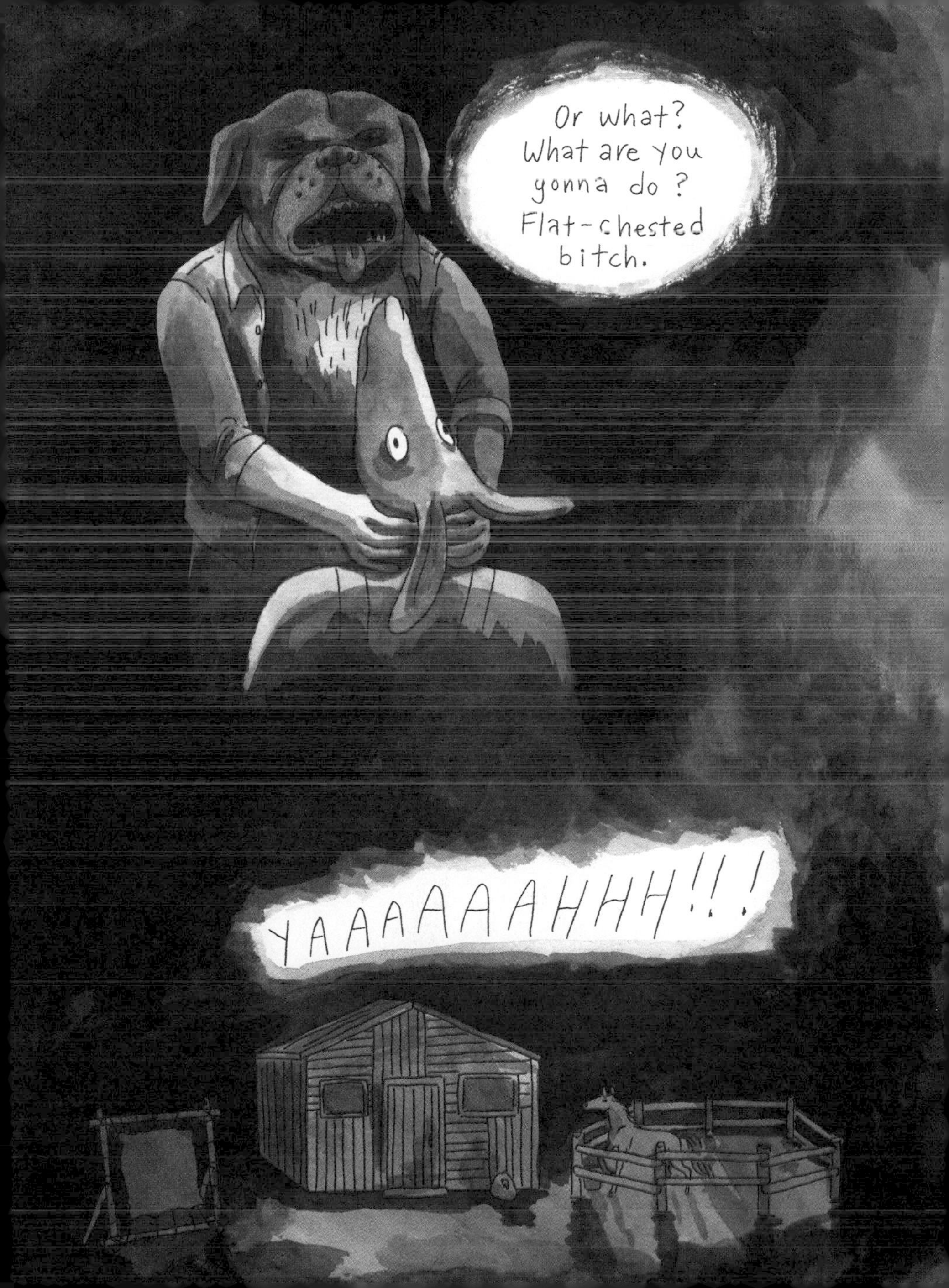
Or what? What are you yonna do? Flat-chested bitch.
YAAAAAAHHH!!!

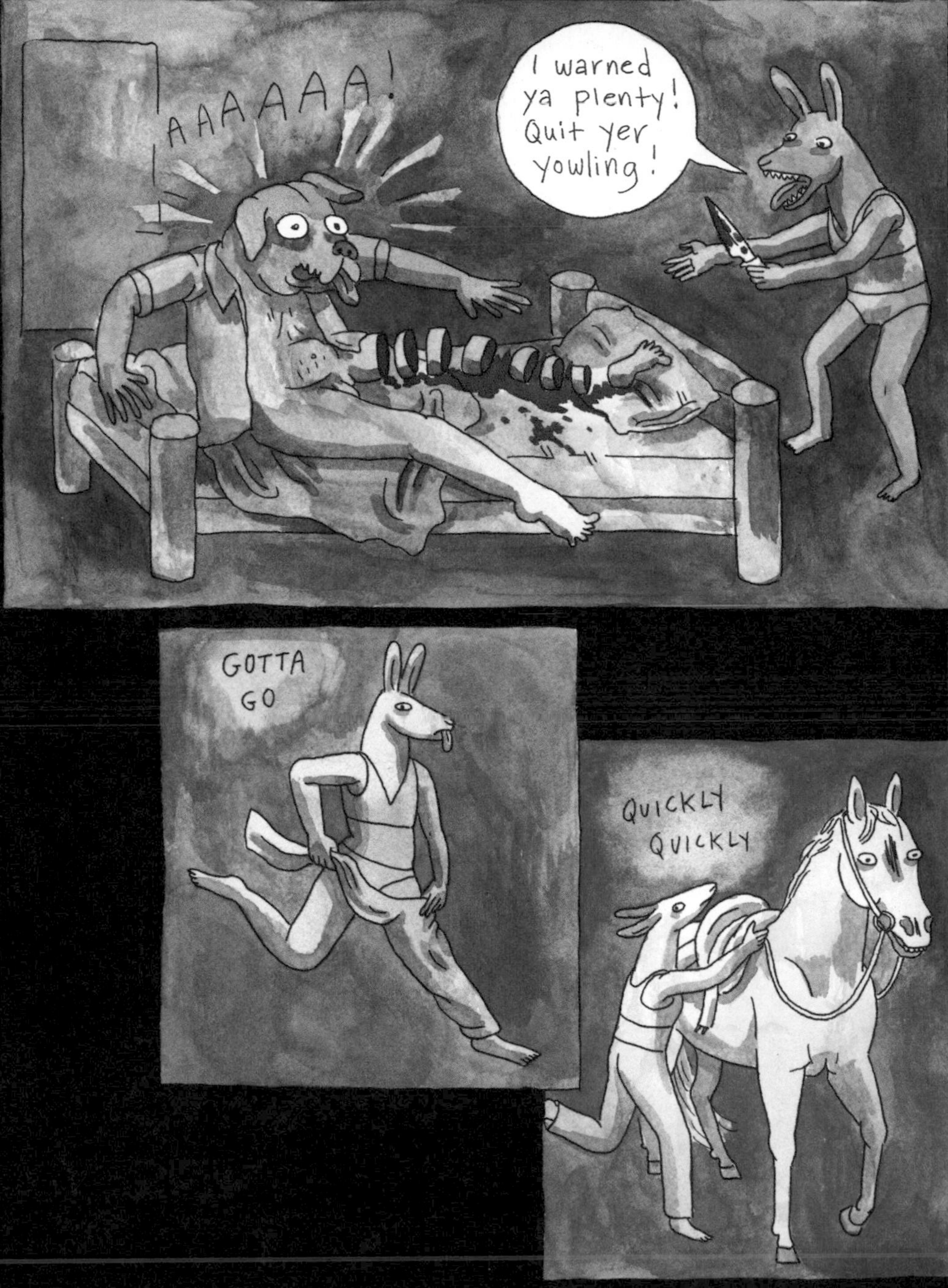
AAAAAAA!
I warned ya plenty! Quit yer yowling!
GOTTA GO
QUICKLY QUICKLY

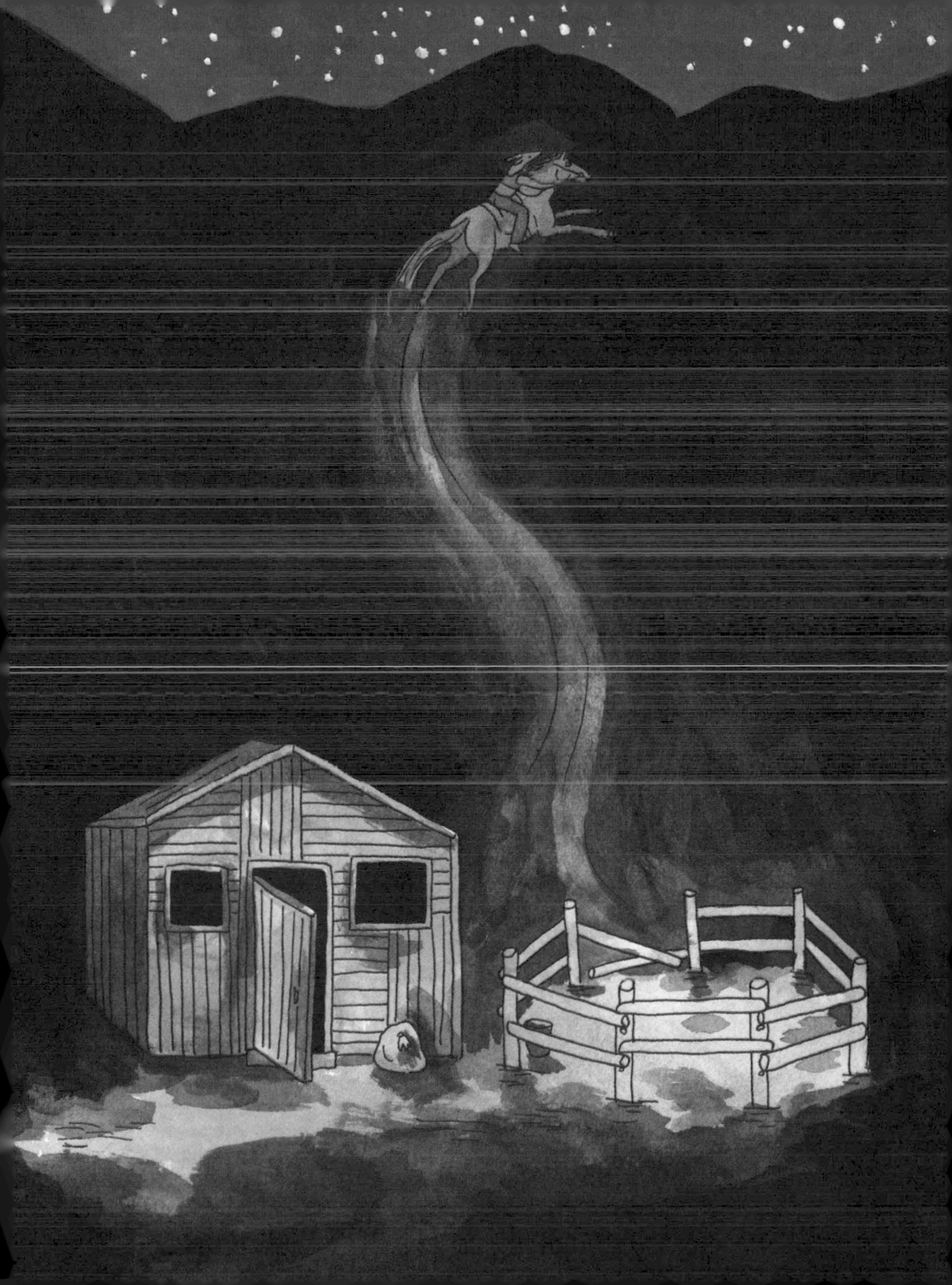

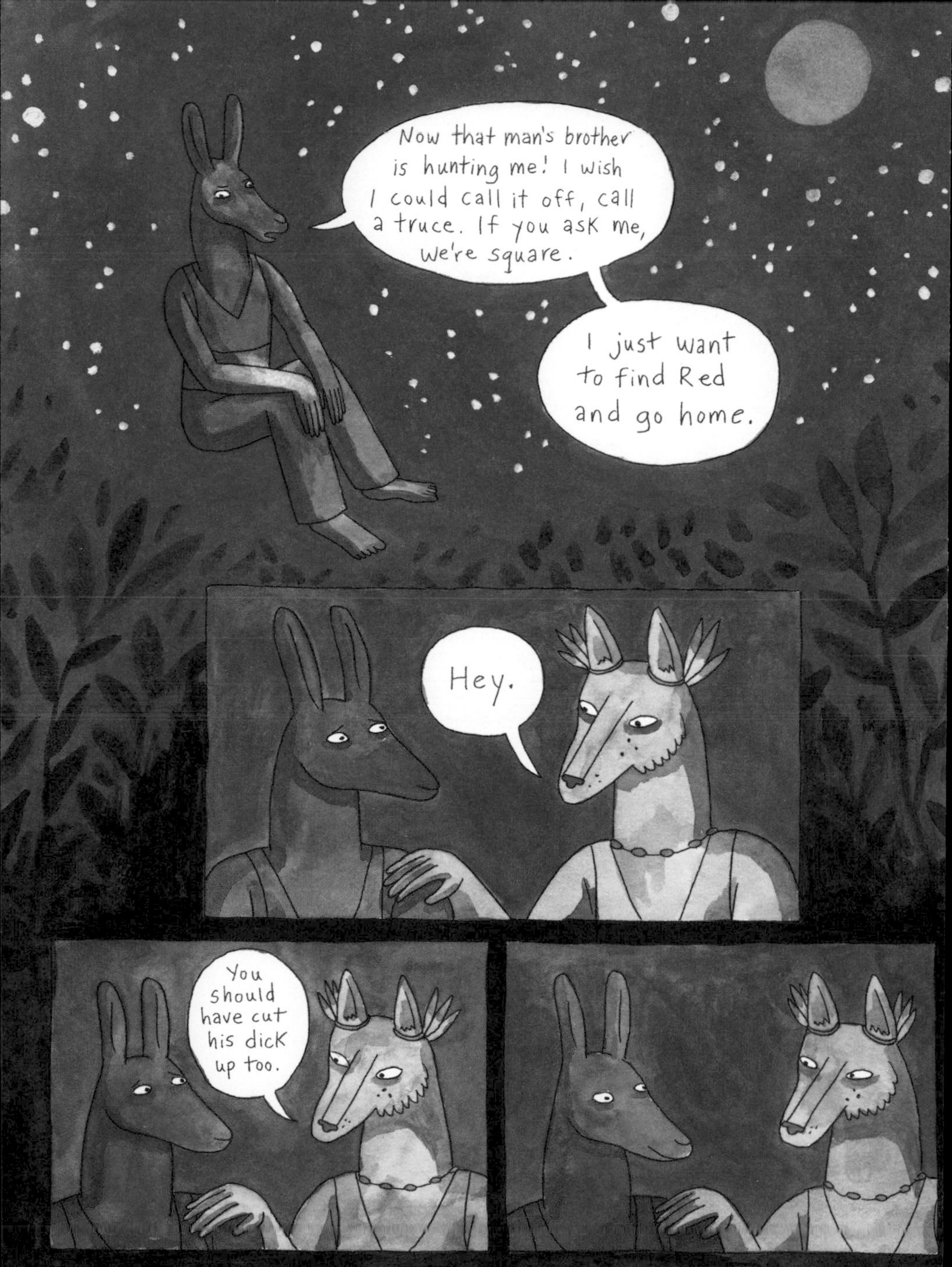
Now that man's brother is hunting me! I wish I could call it off, call a truce. If you ask me, we're square.
I just want to find Red and go home.
Hey.
You should have cut his dick up too.

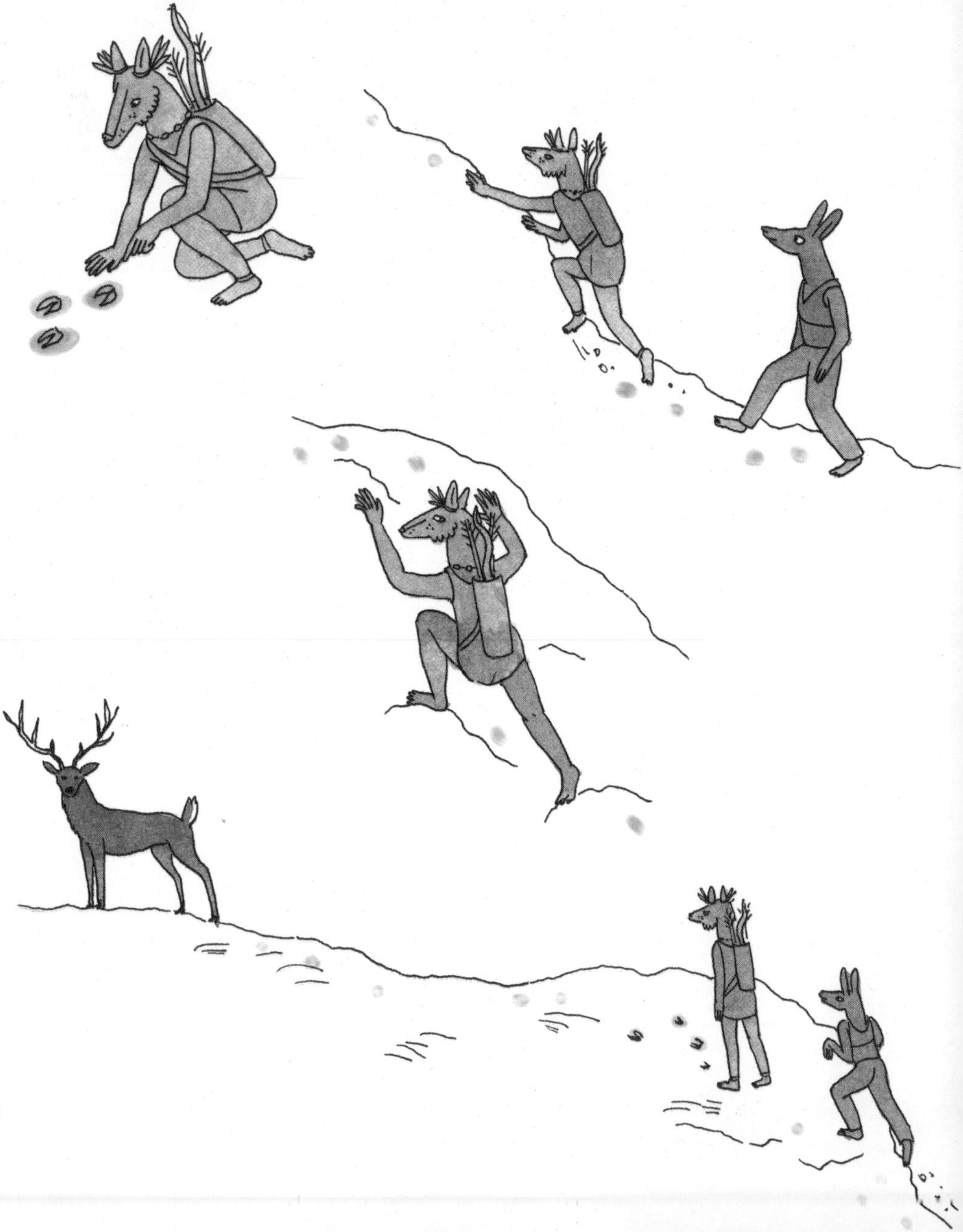

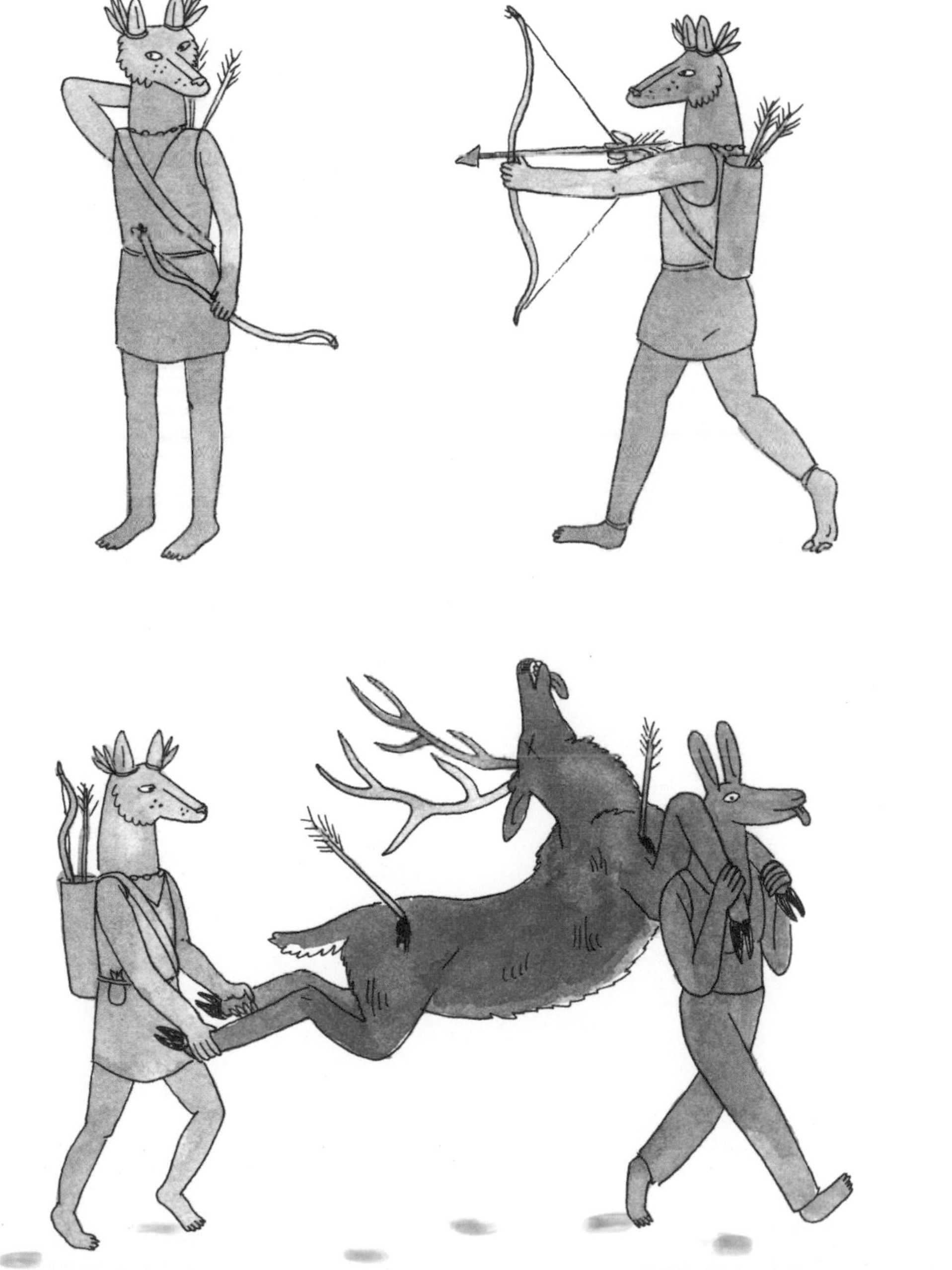

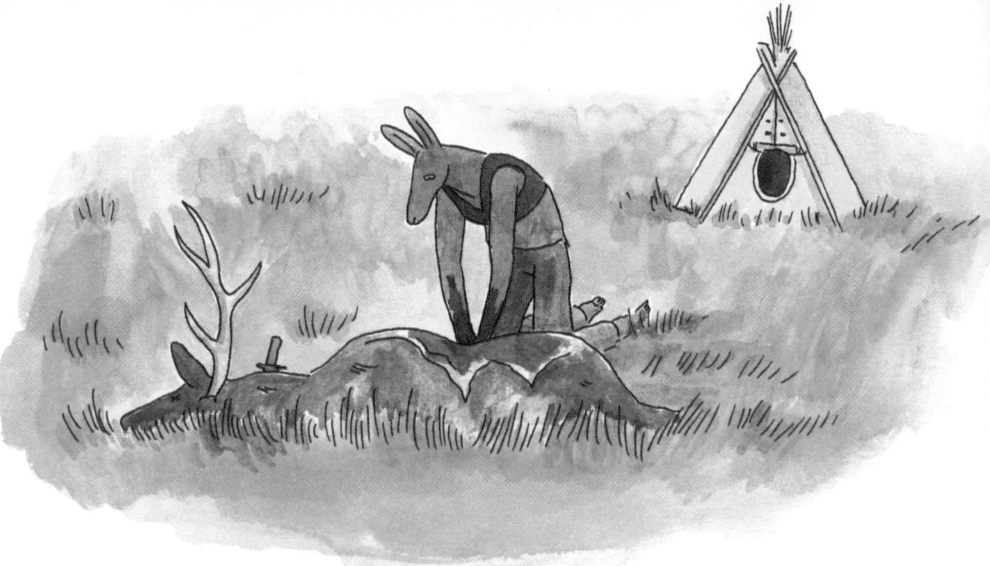

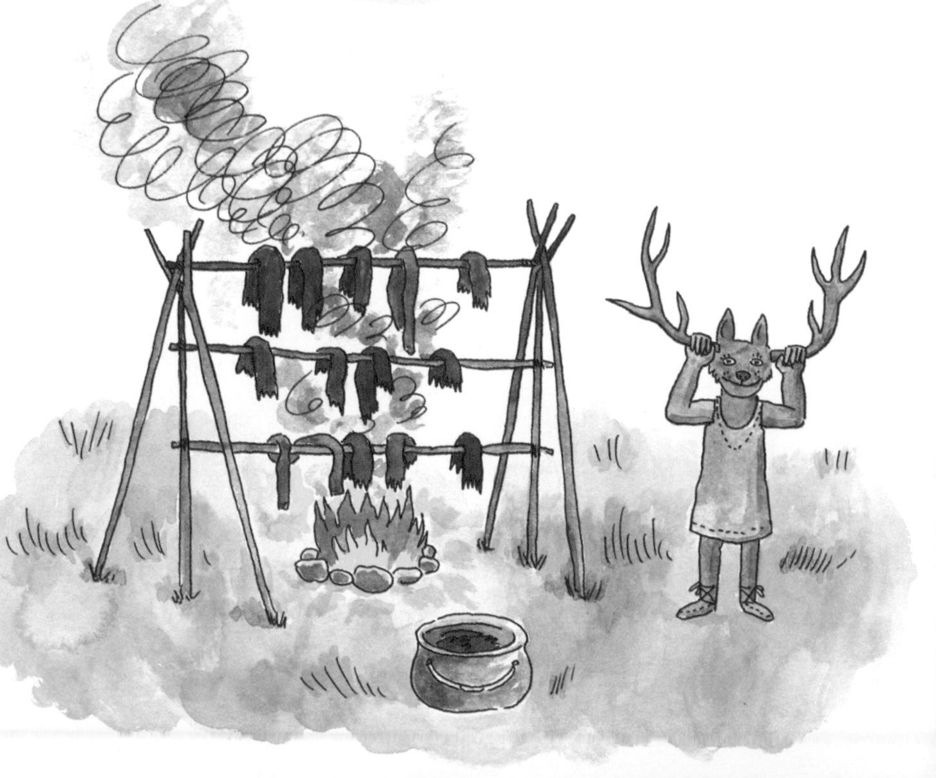

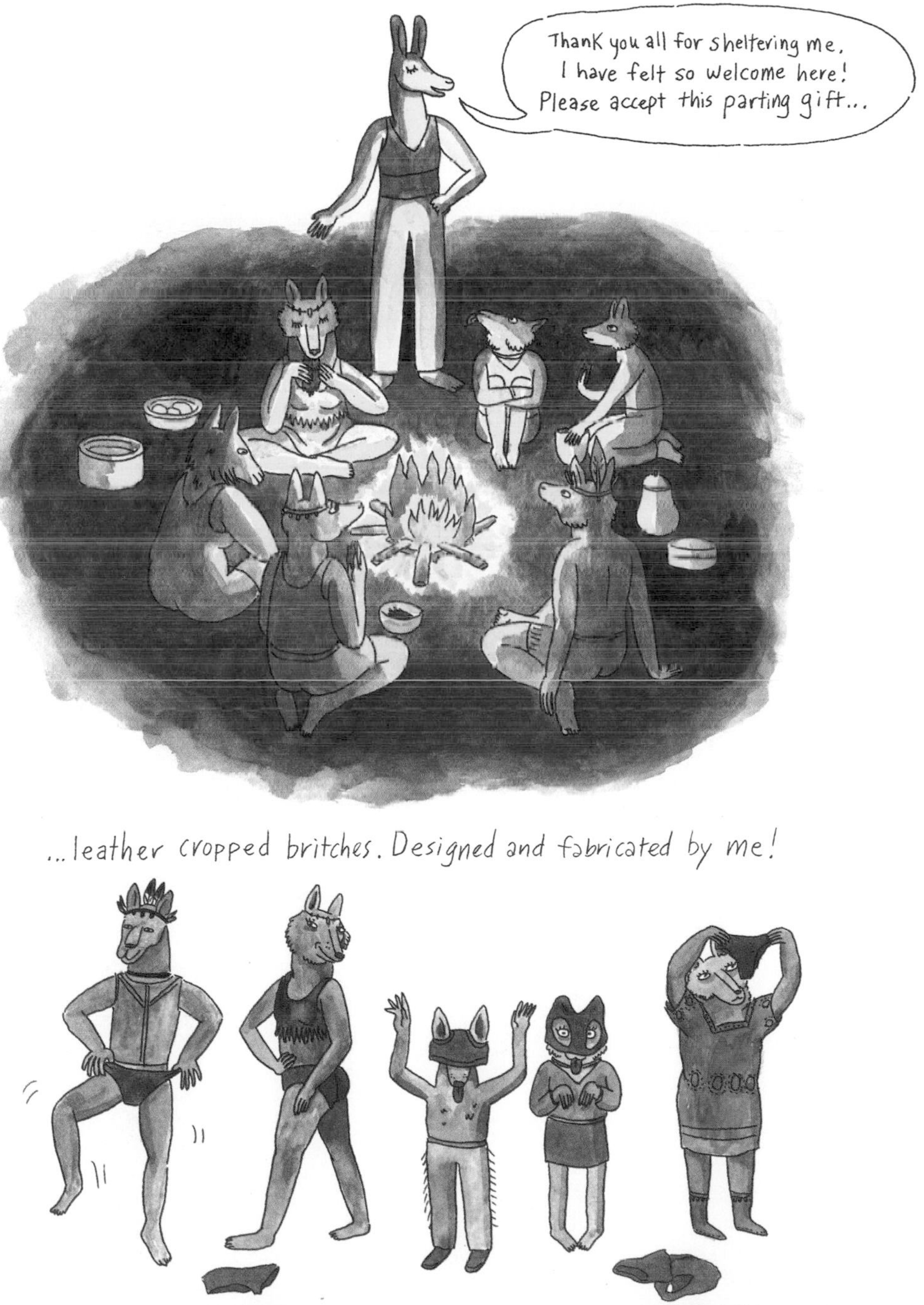
Thank you all for sheltering me. I have felt so welcome here! Please accept this parting gift...
...leather cropped britches. Designed and fabricated by me!

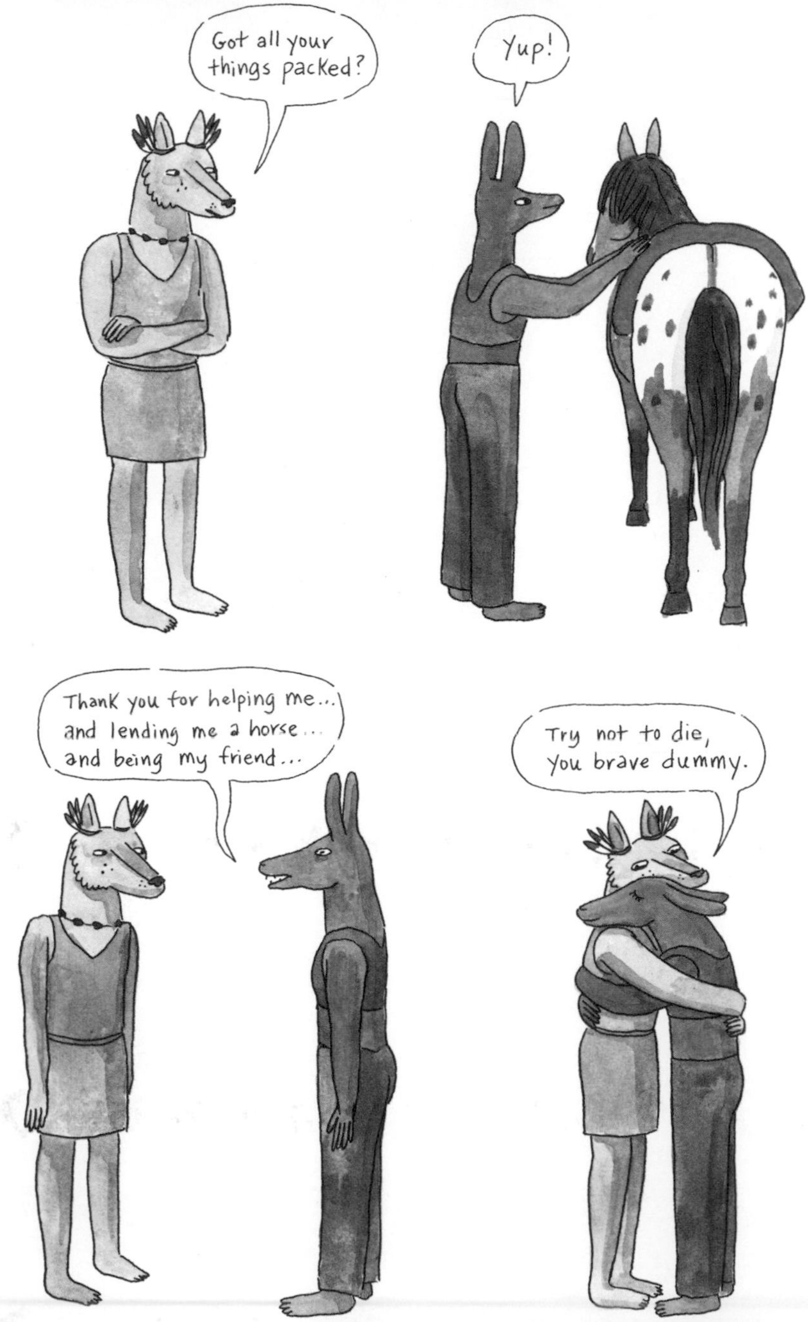

Got all your things packed?
Yup!
Thank you for helping me... and lending me a horse... and being my friend...
Try not to die, you brave dummy.

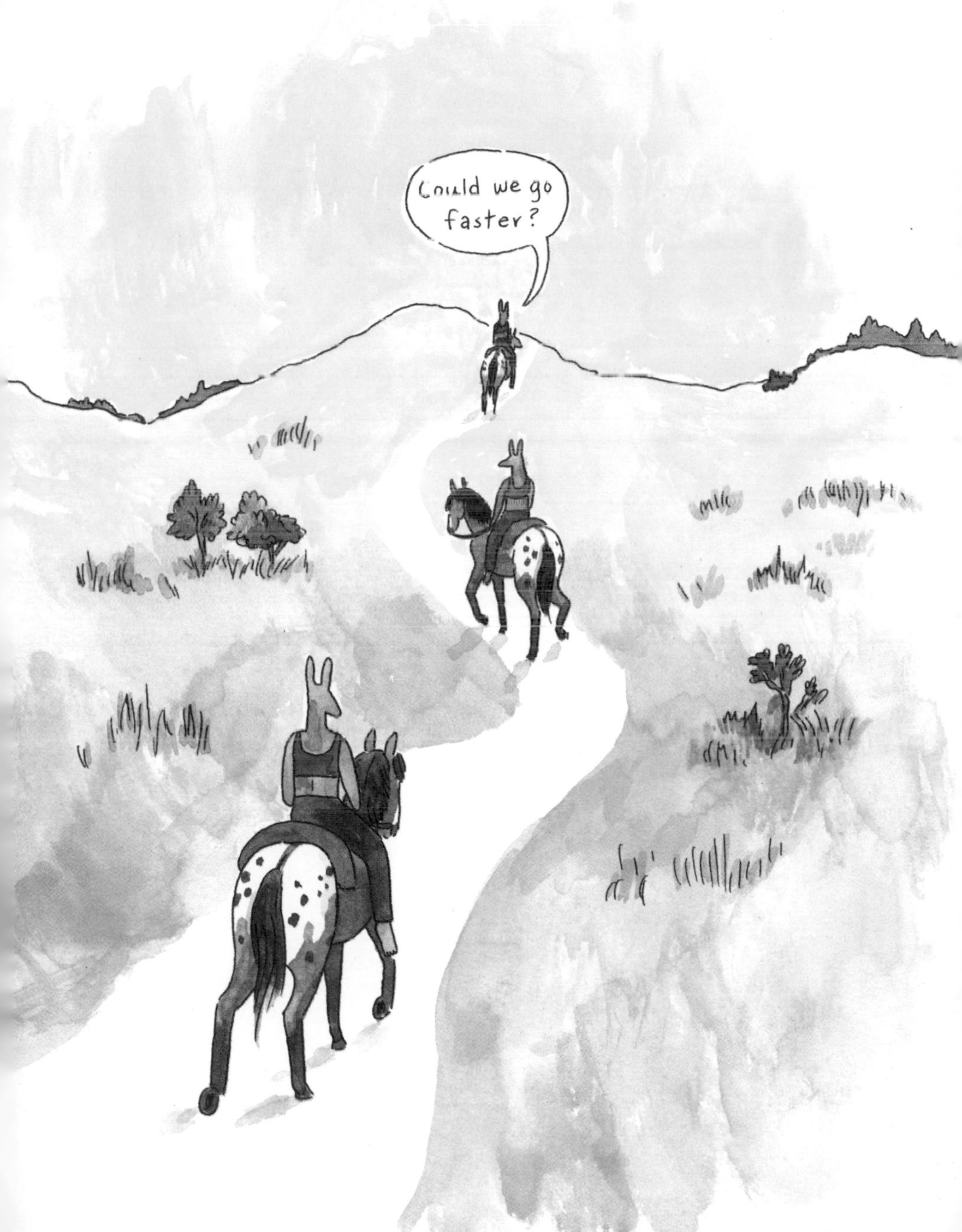
Could we go faster?

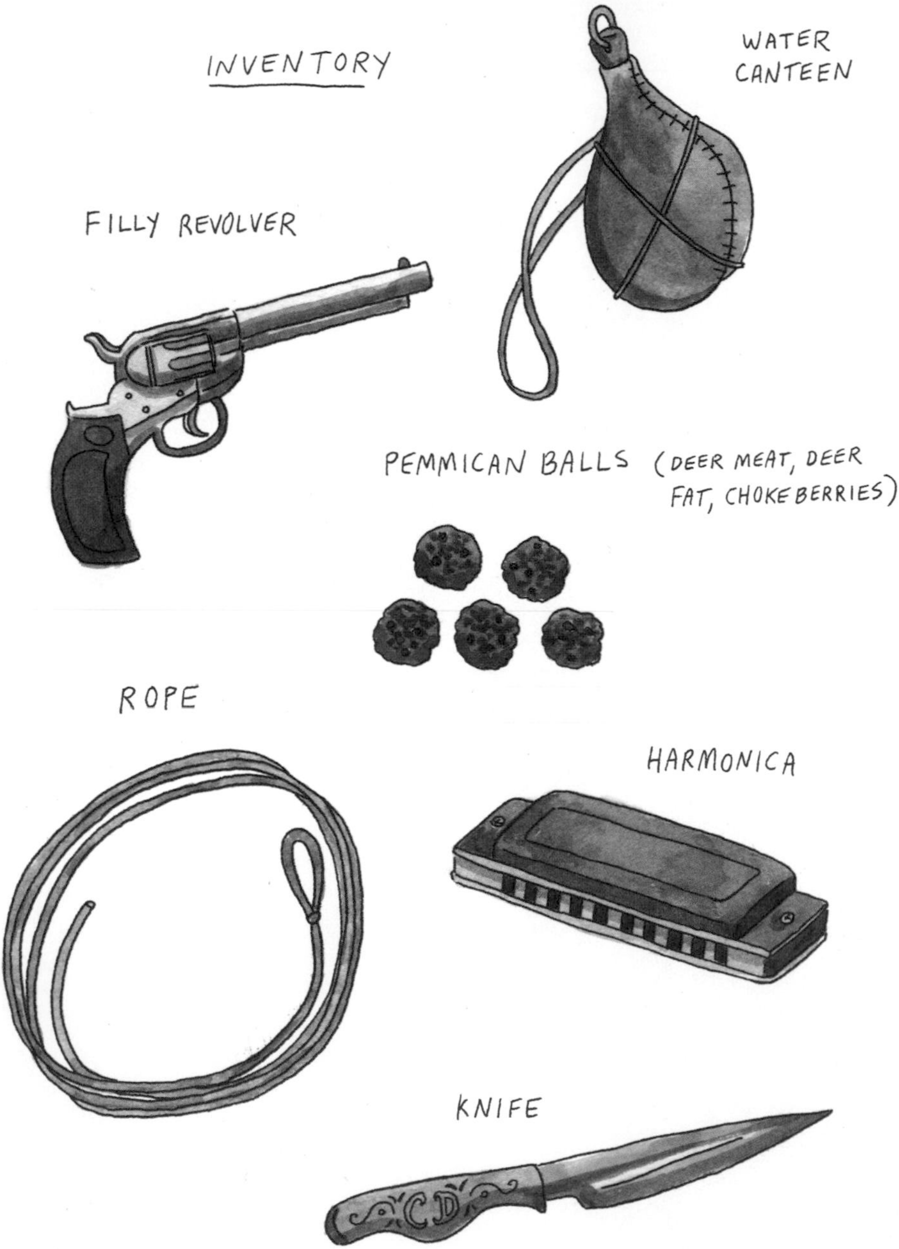
INVENTORY
WATER CANTEEN
FILLY REVOLVER
PEMMICAN BALLS (DEER MEAT, DEER FAT, CHOKEBERRIES)
ROPE
HARMONICA
KNIFE
CD

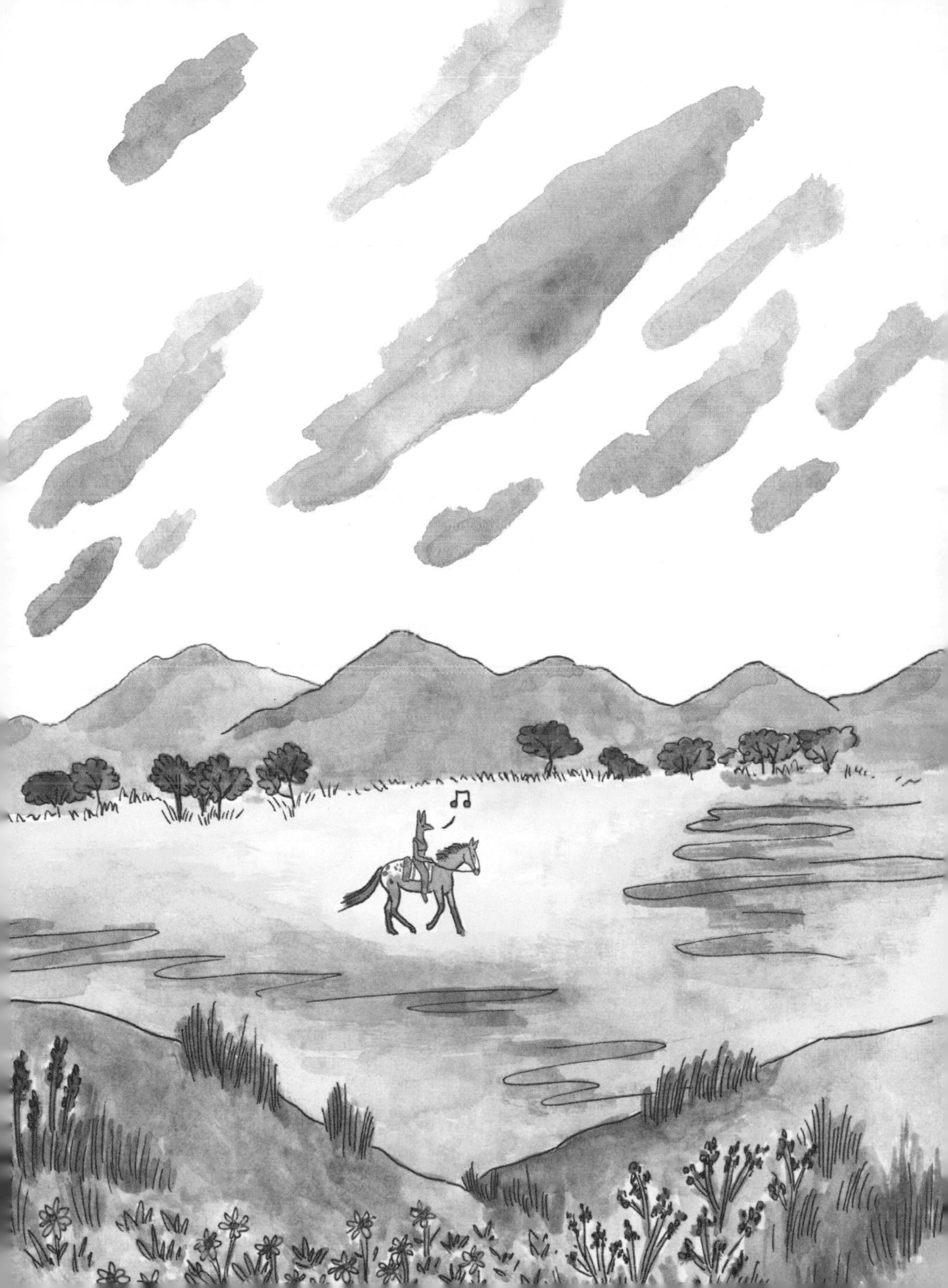

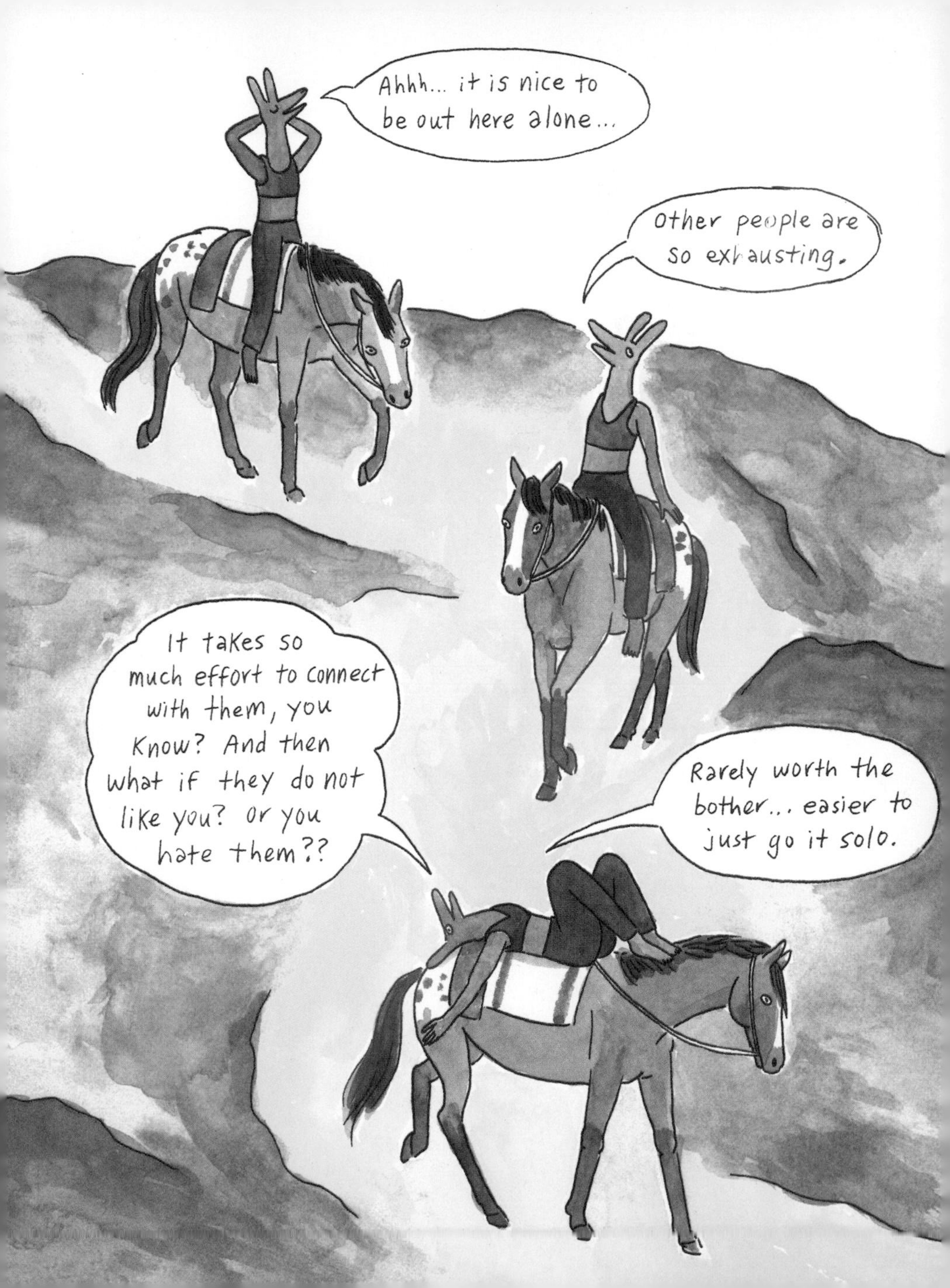
Ahhh... it is nice to be out here alone...
Other people are so exhausting.
It takes so much effort to connect with them, you Know? And then what if they do not like you? or you hate them??
Rarely worth the bother... easier to just go it solo.

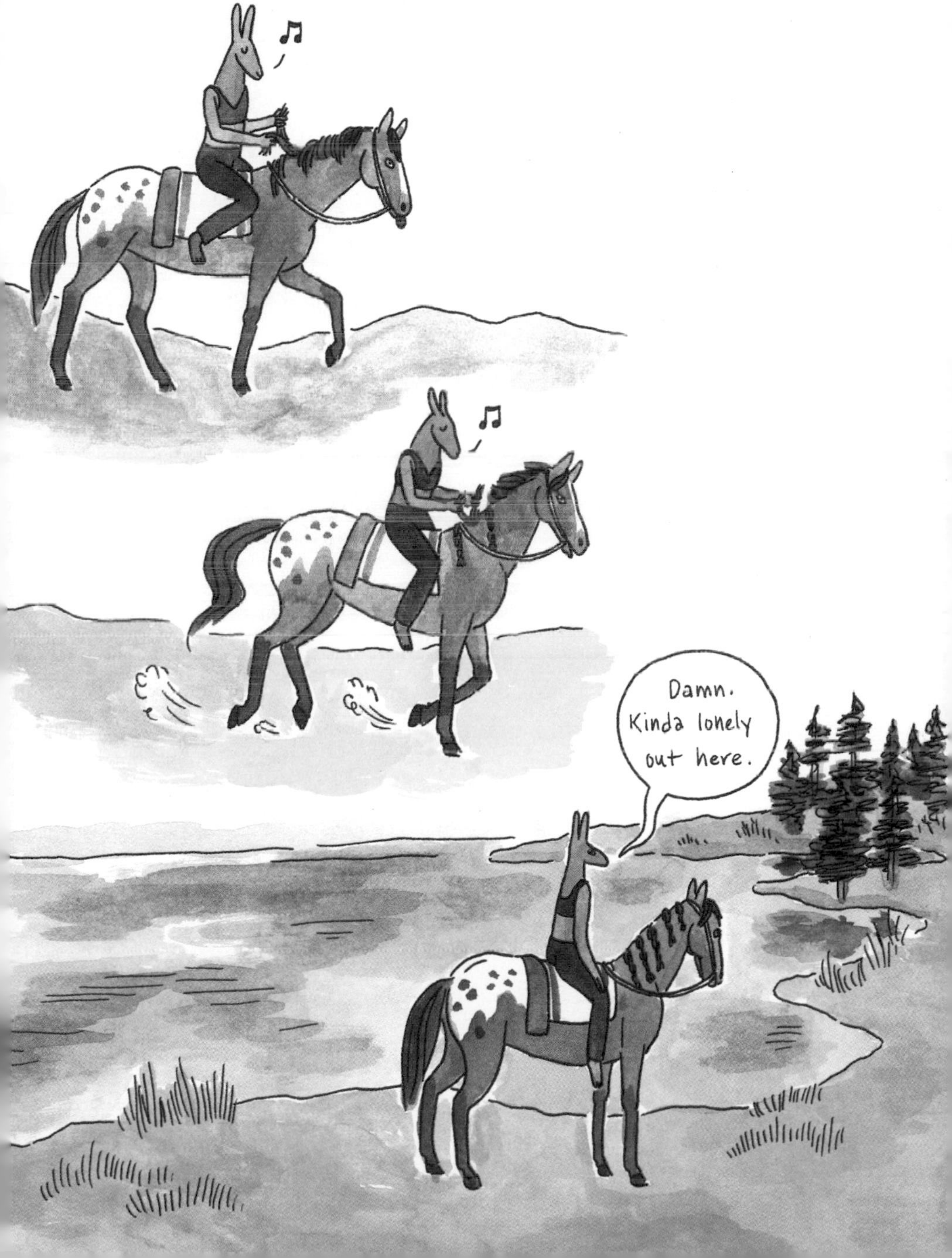
Damn. Kinda lonely out here.

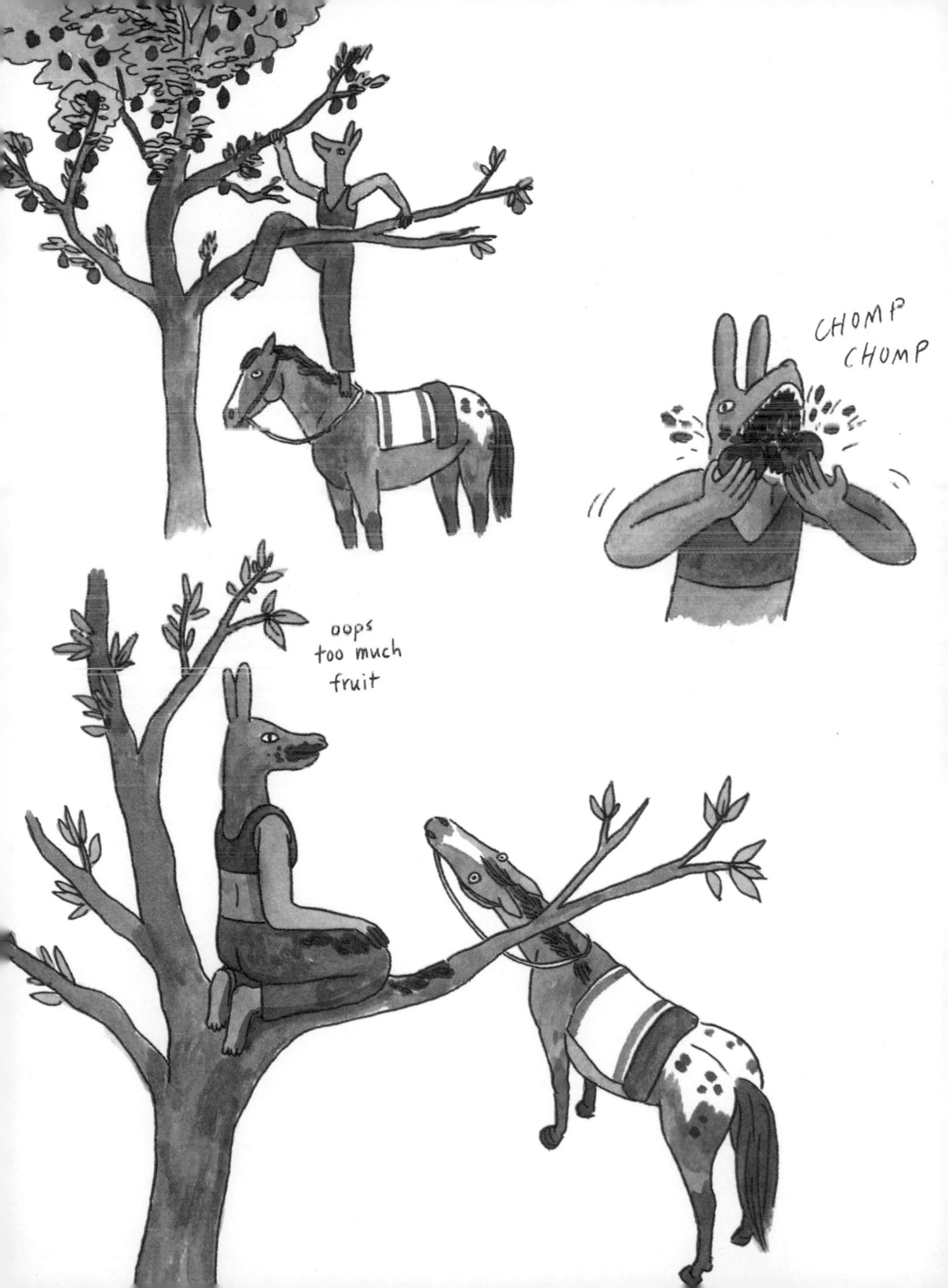
CHOMP
CHOMP
oops
too much
fruit

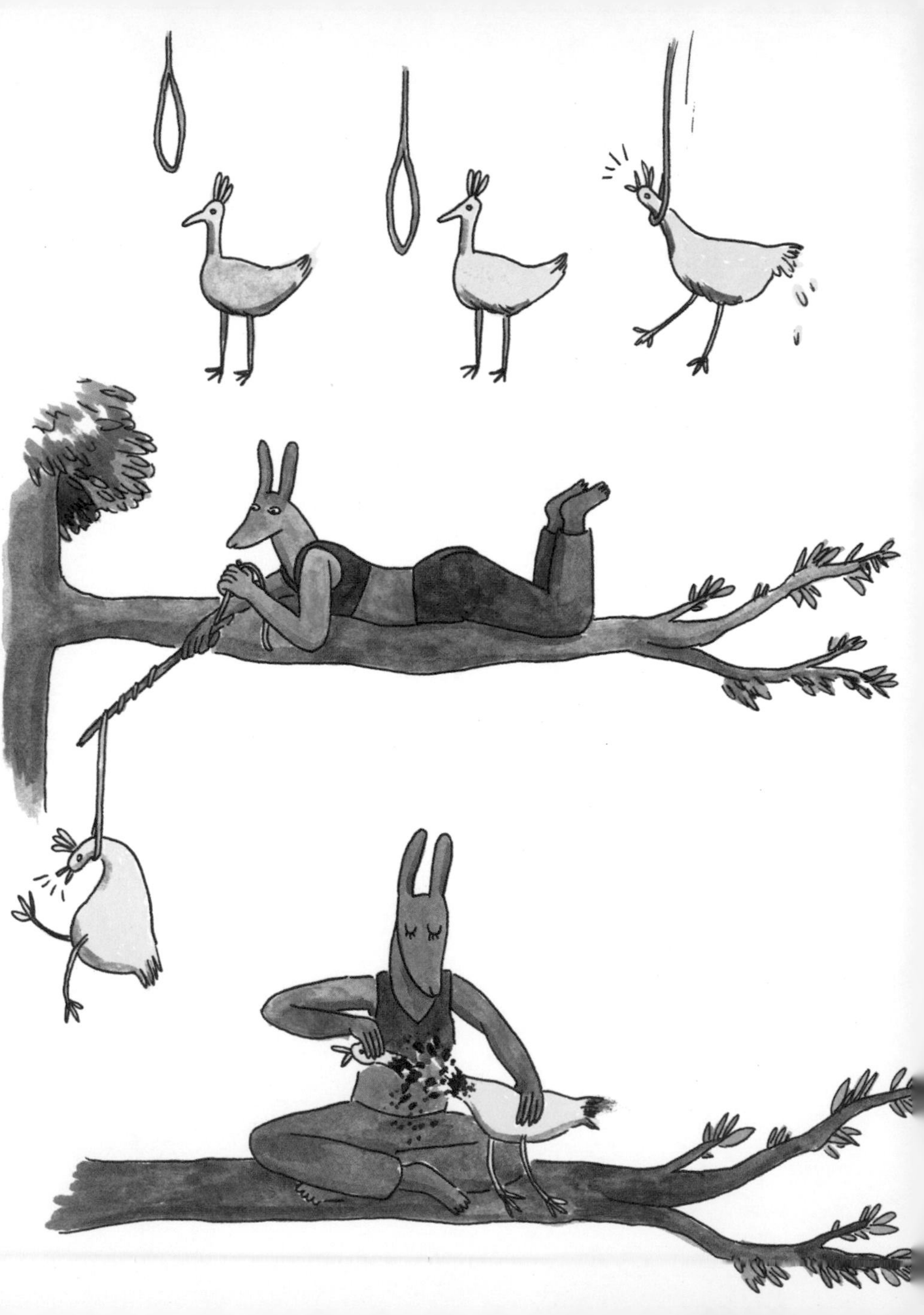

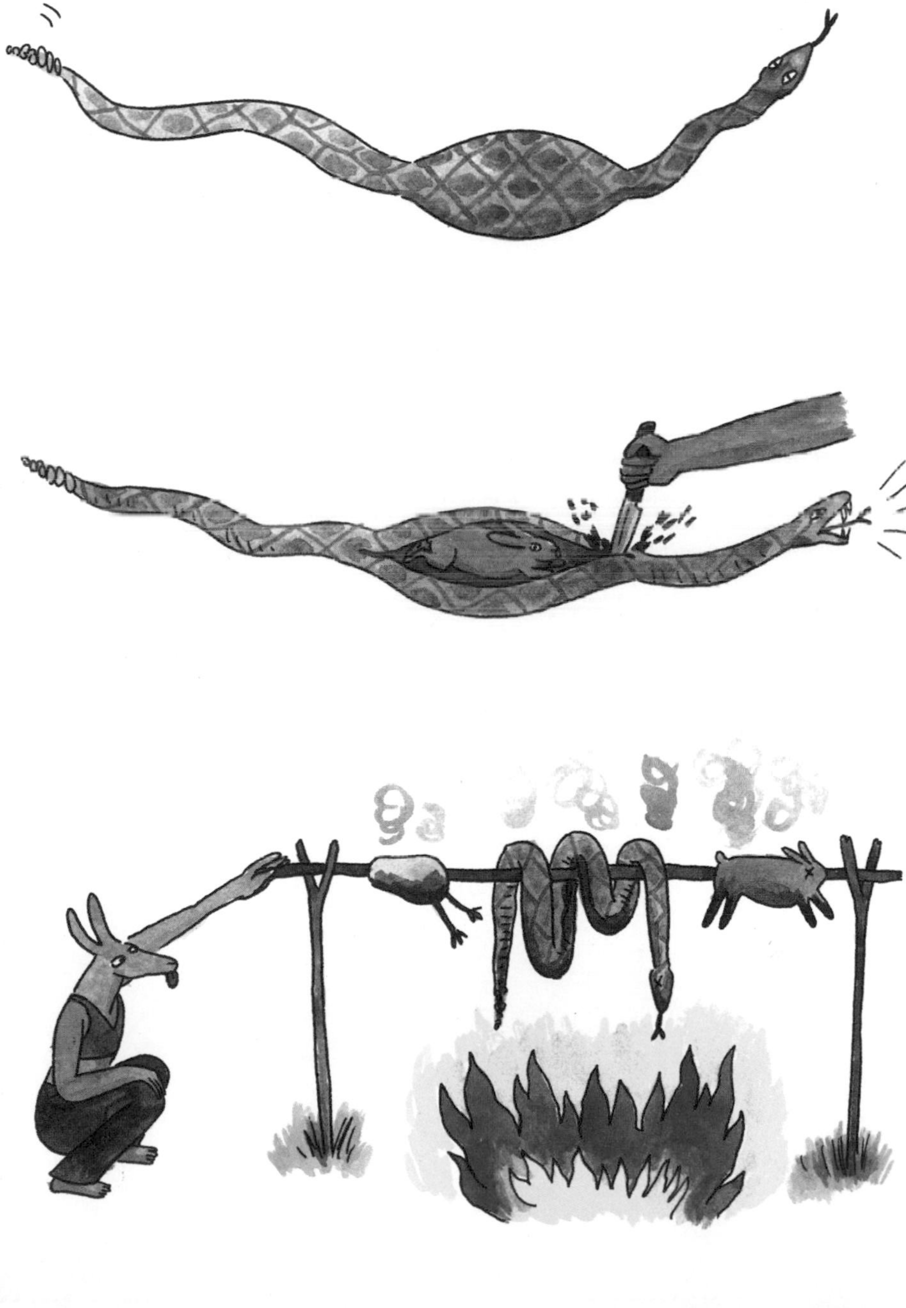

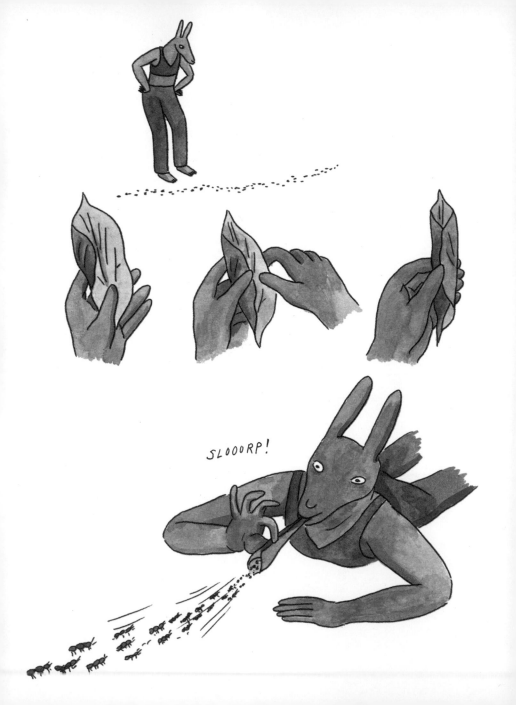

SLOOORP!

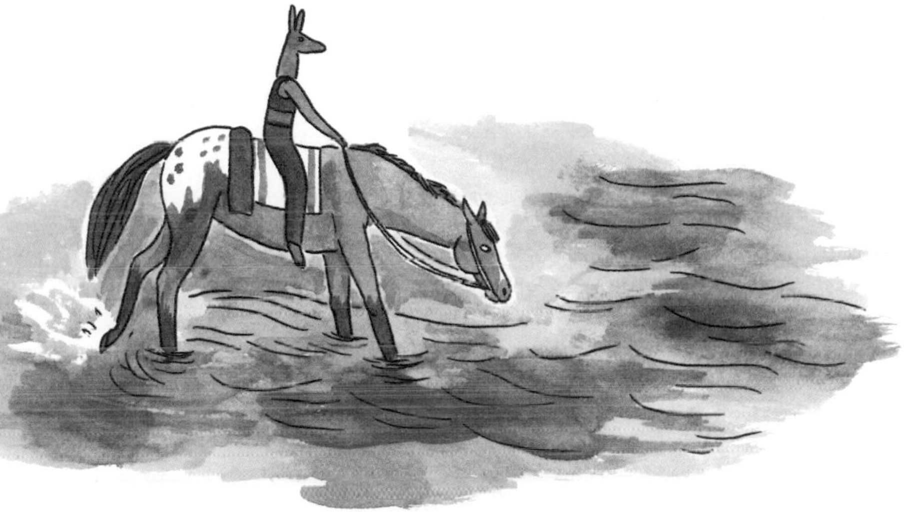

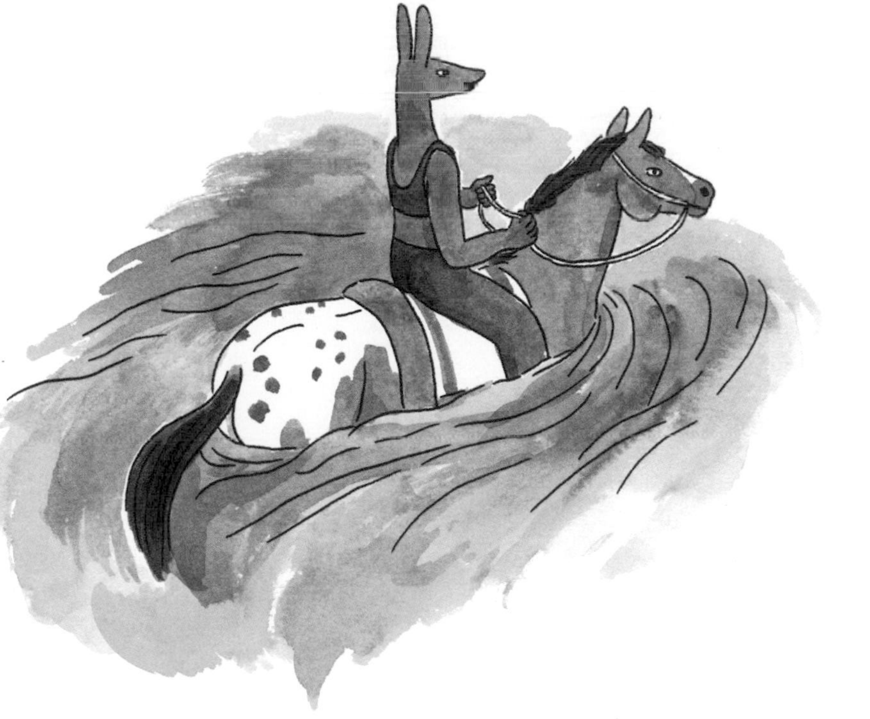

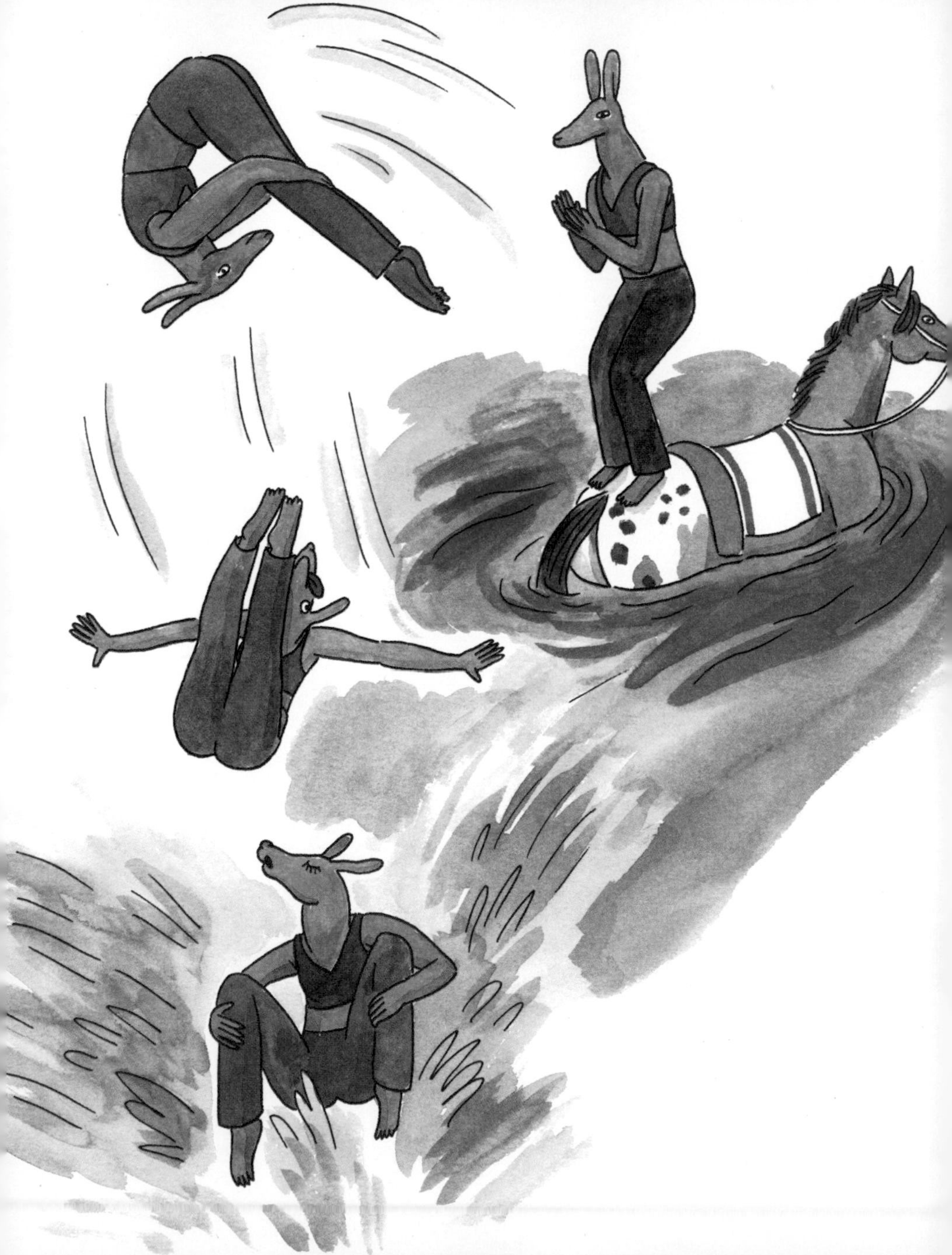

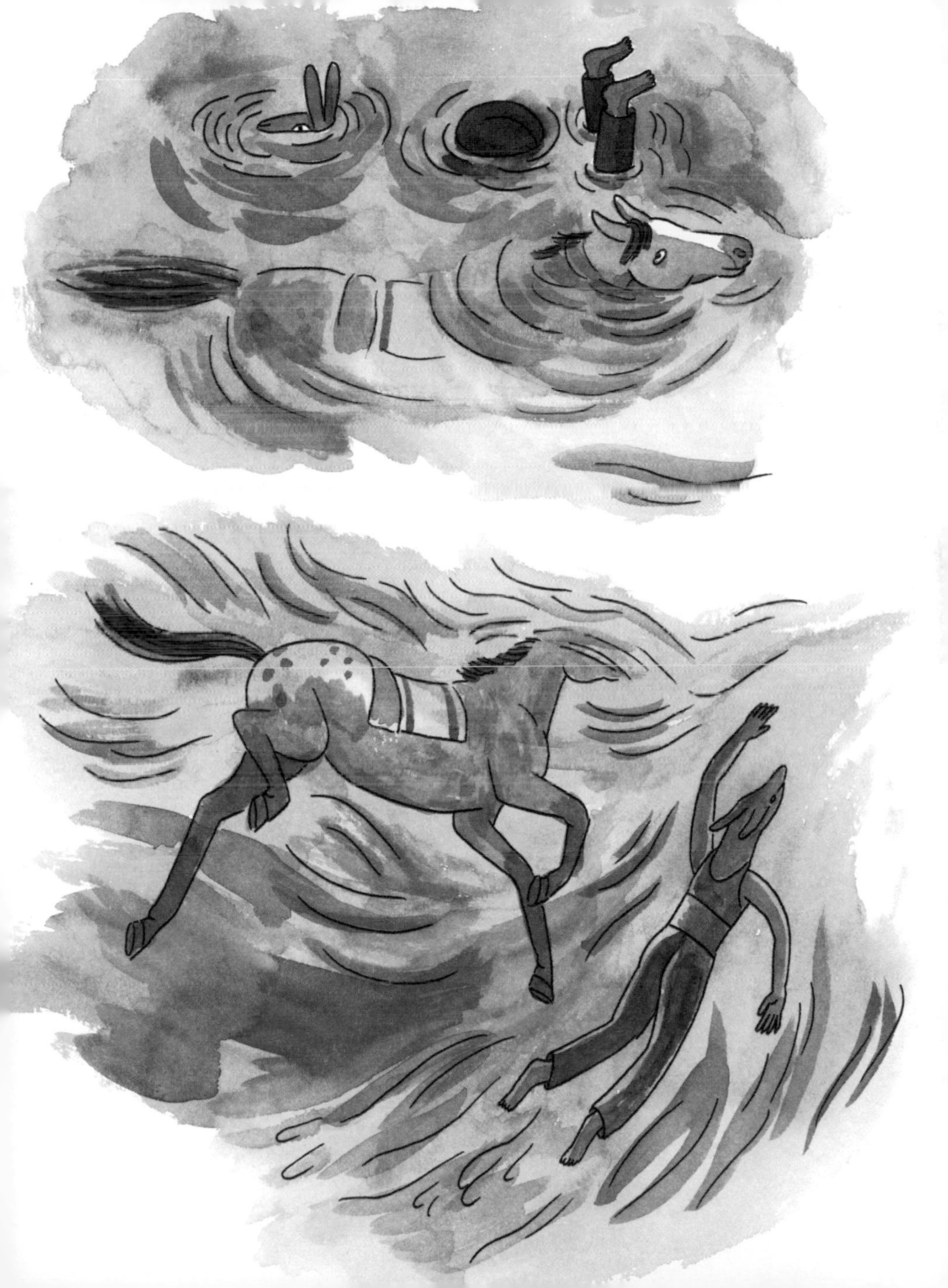

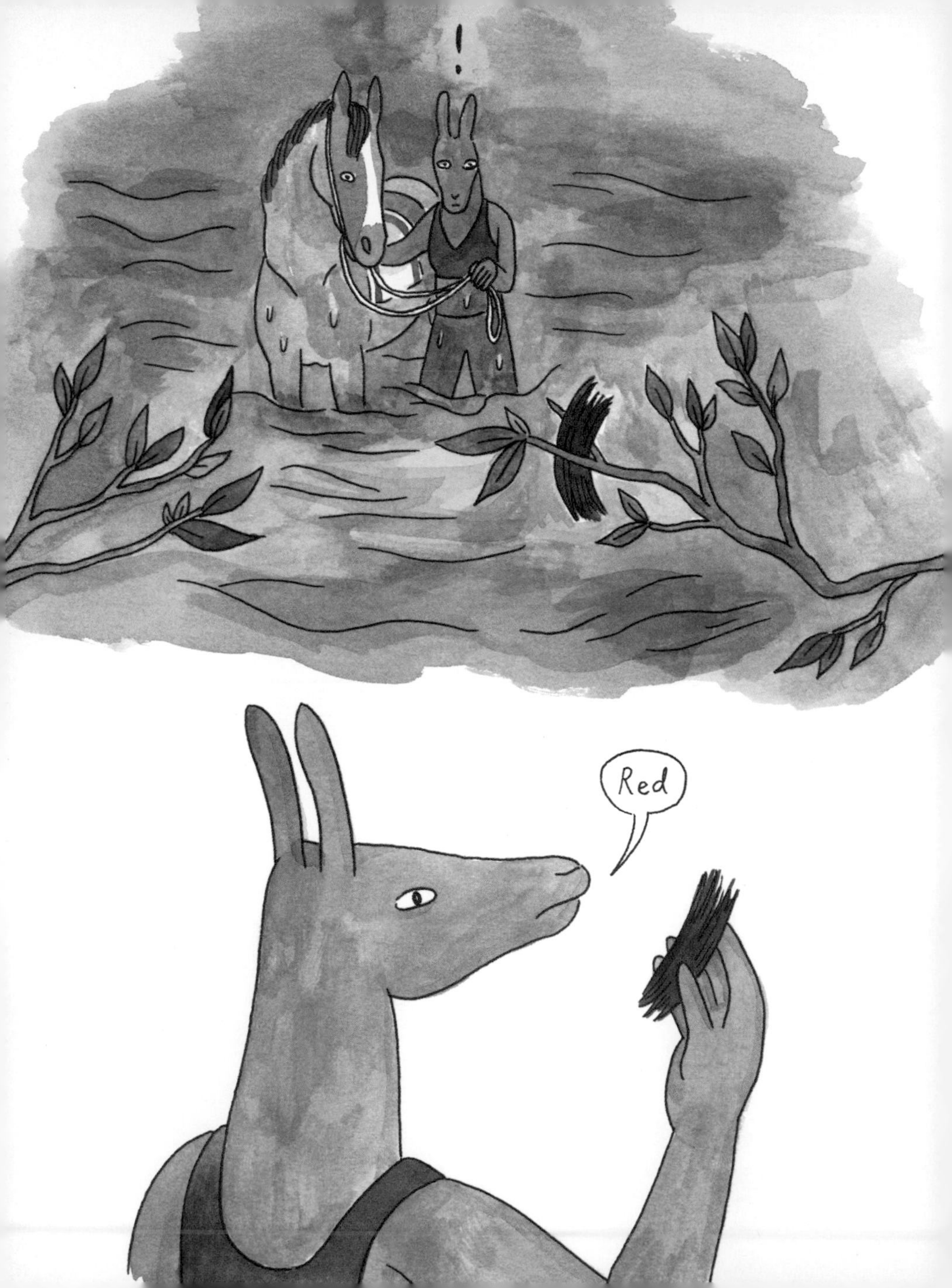
!
Red

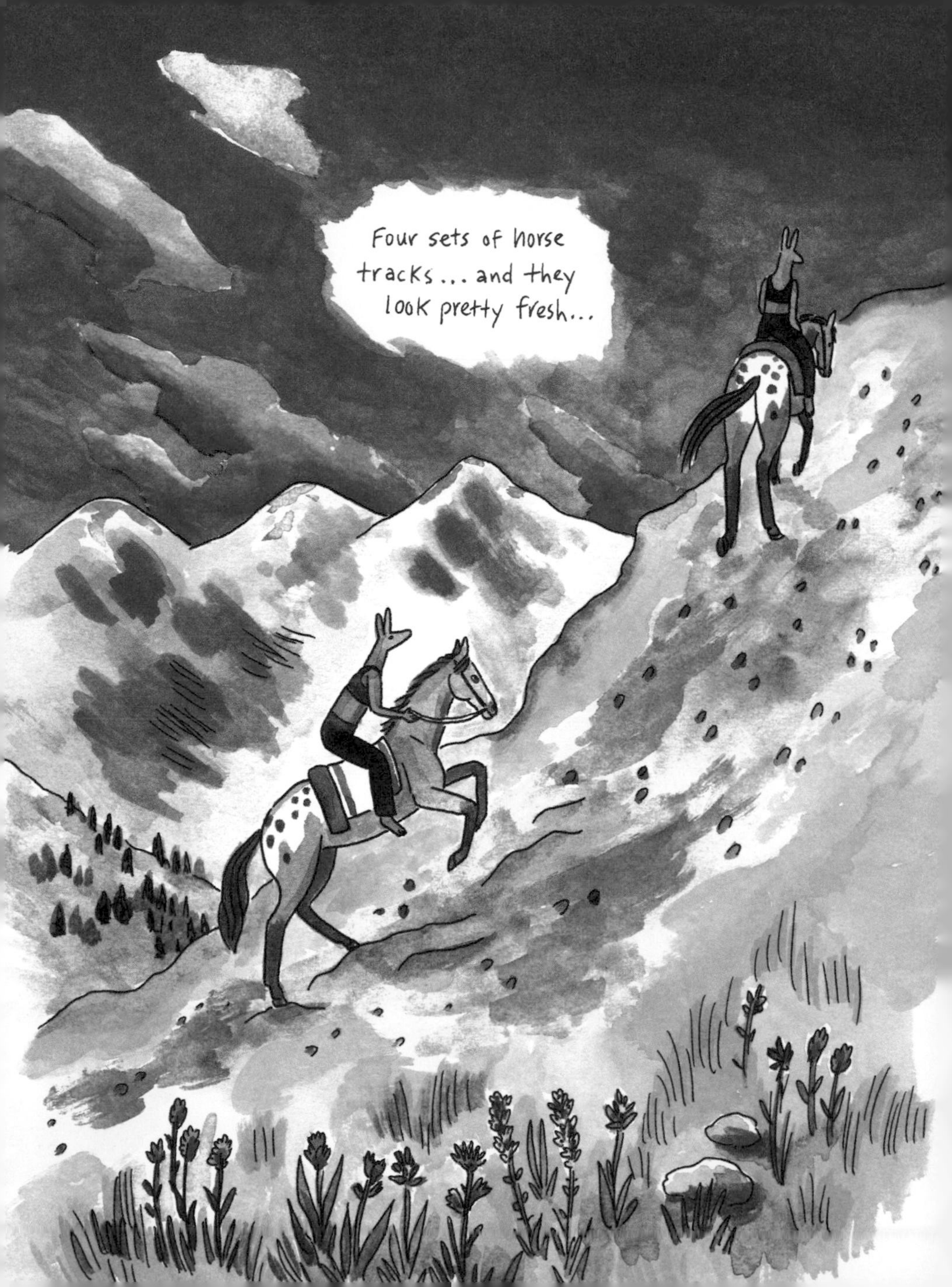
Four sets of horse tracks... and they look pretty fresh...

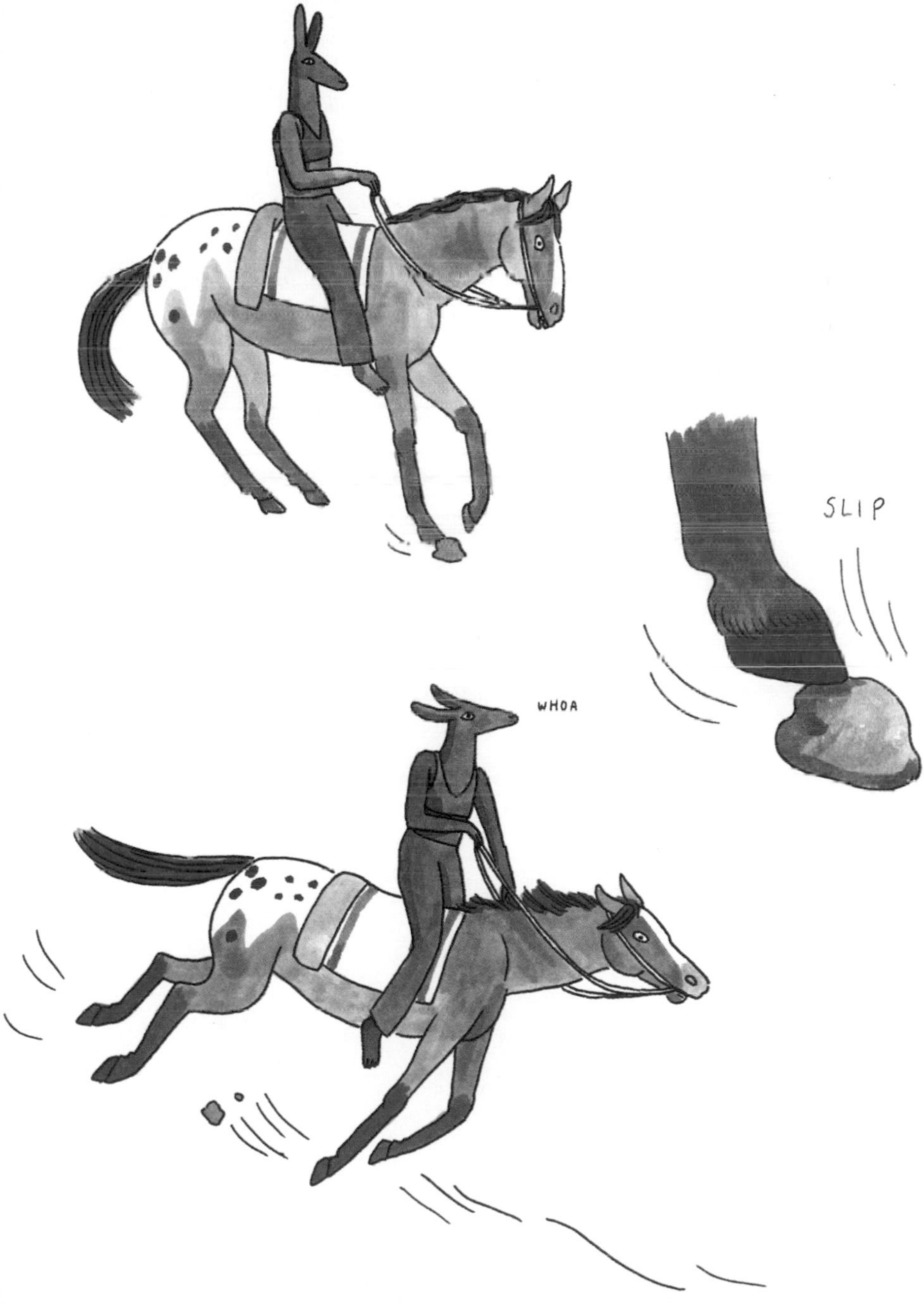
SLIP
WHOA

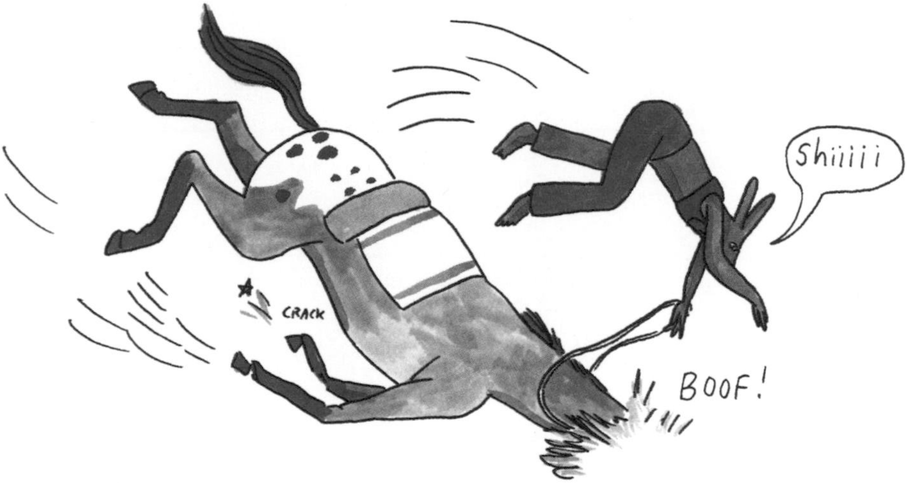
Shiiiii
CRACK
BOOF!
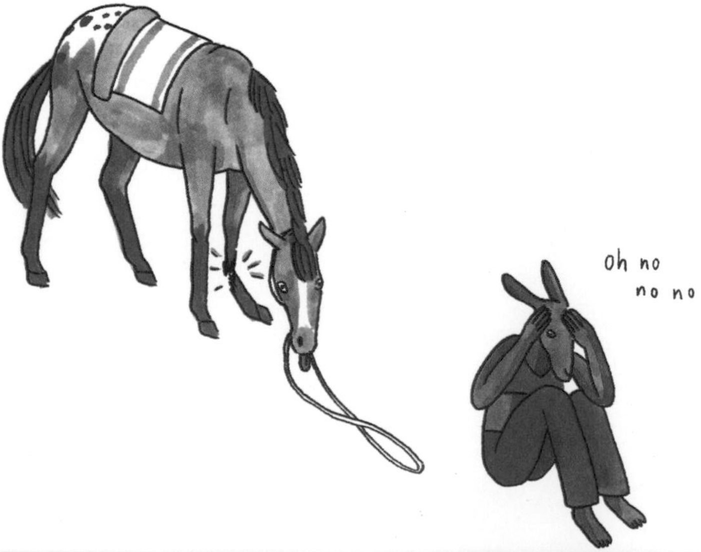
oh no
no no

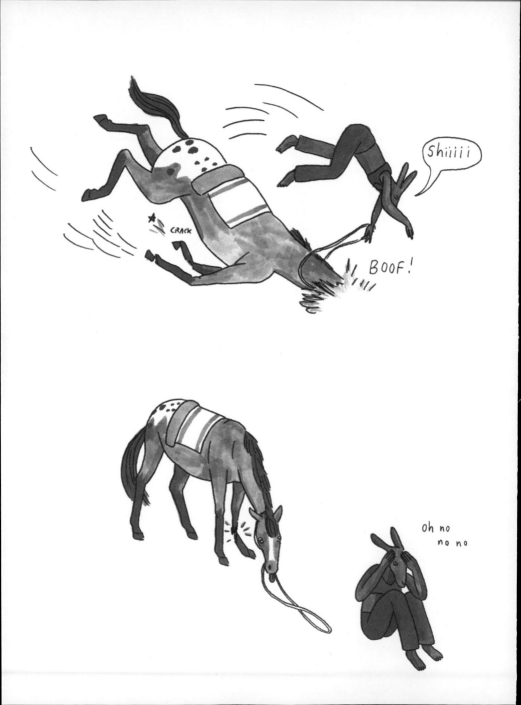

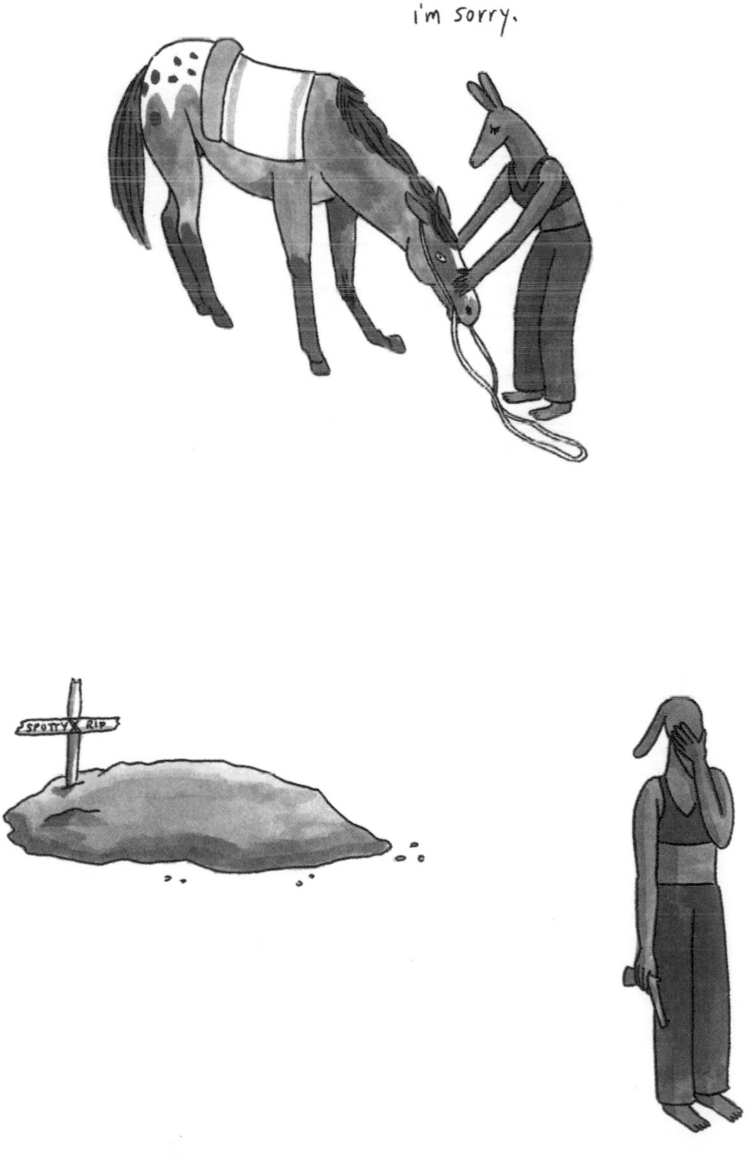
i'm sorry.
SPOTTY RIP

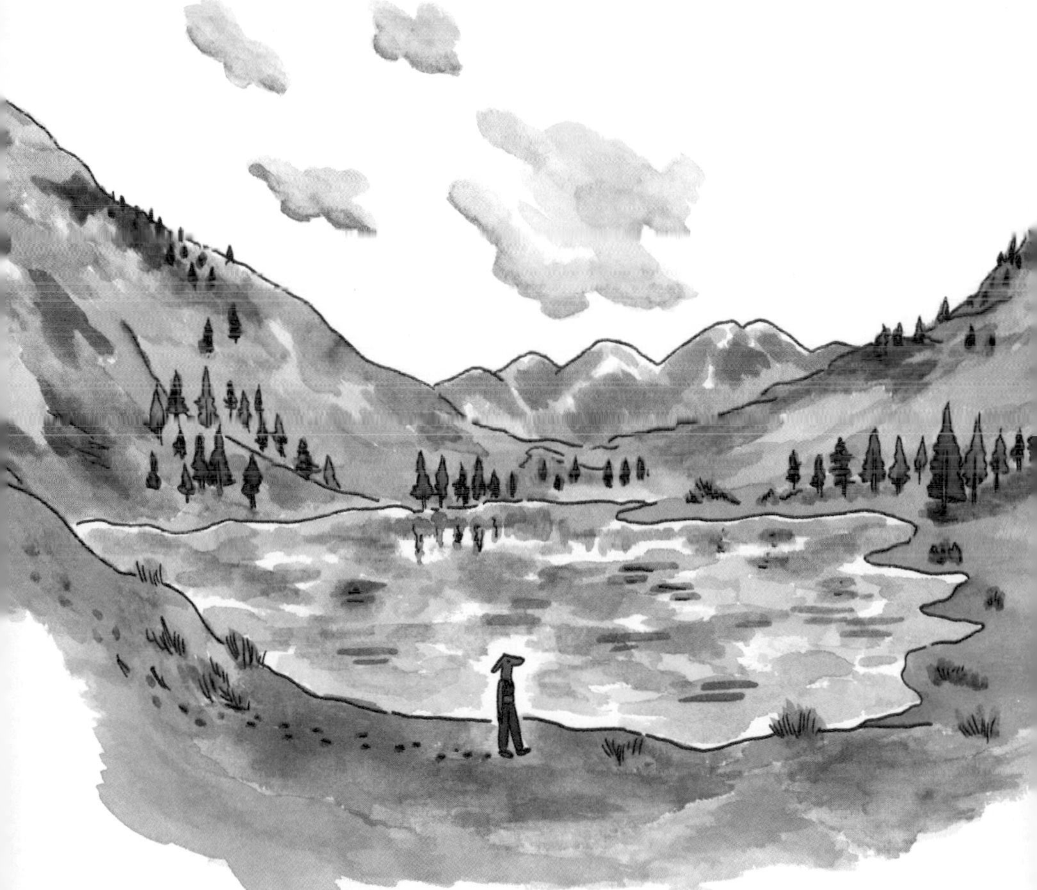

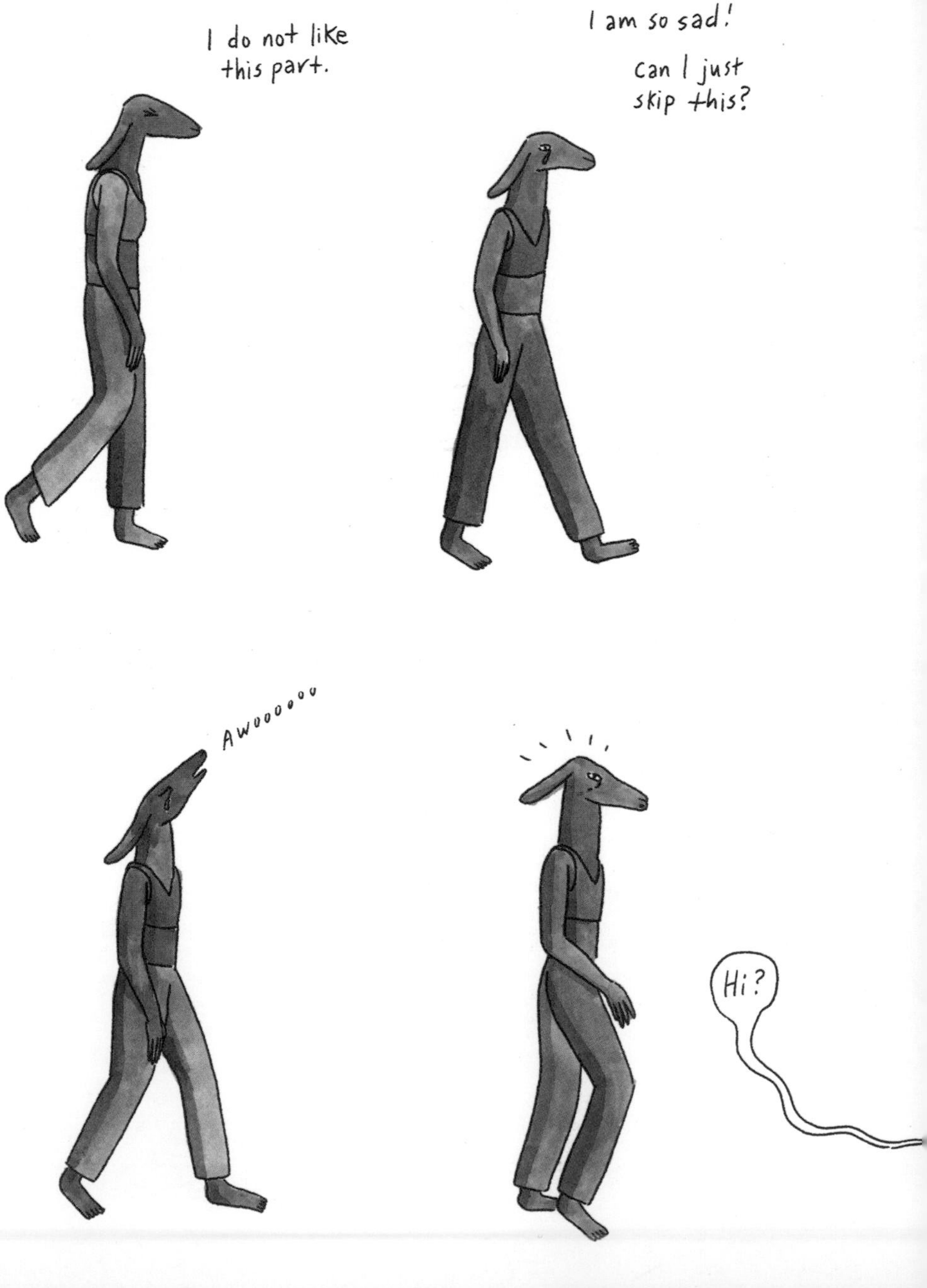
I do not like this part.
I am so sad!
Can I just skip this?
Awoooooo
Hi?

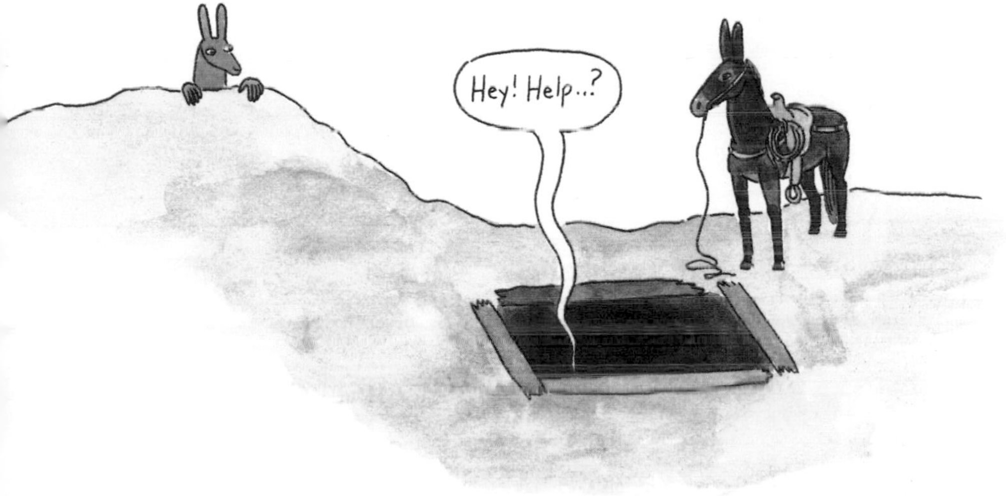
Hey! Help...?

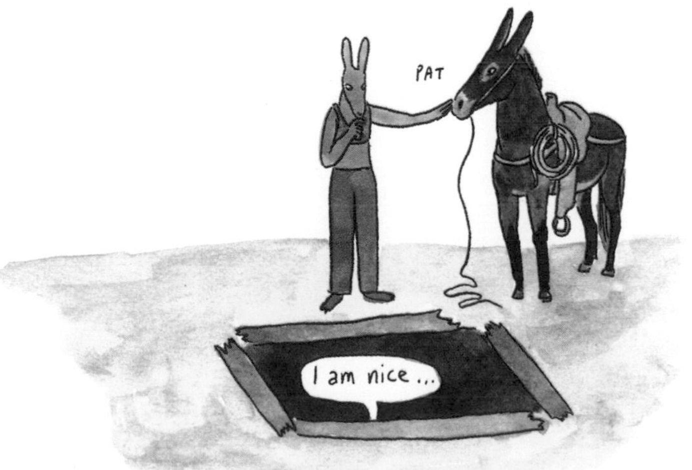
PAT
I am nice...

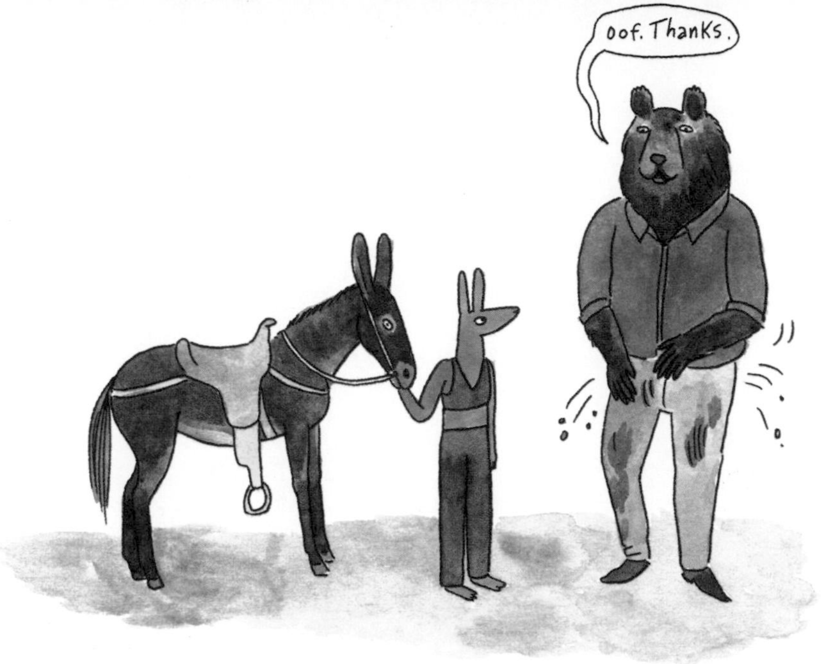
oof. Thanks.

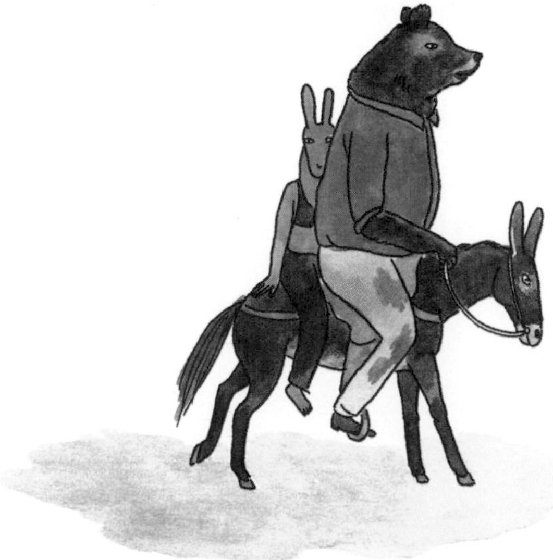

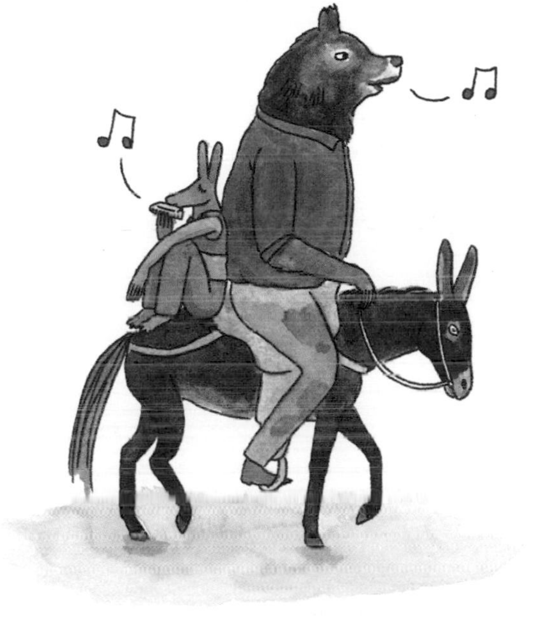

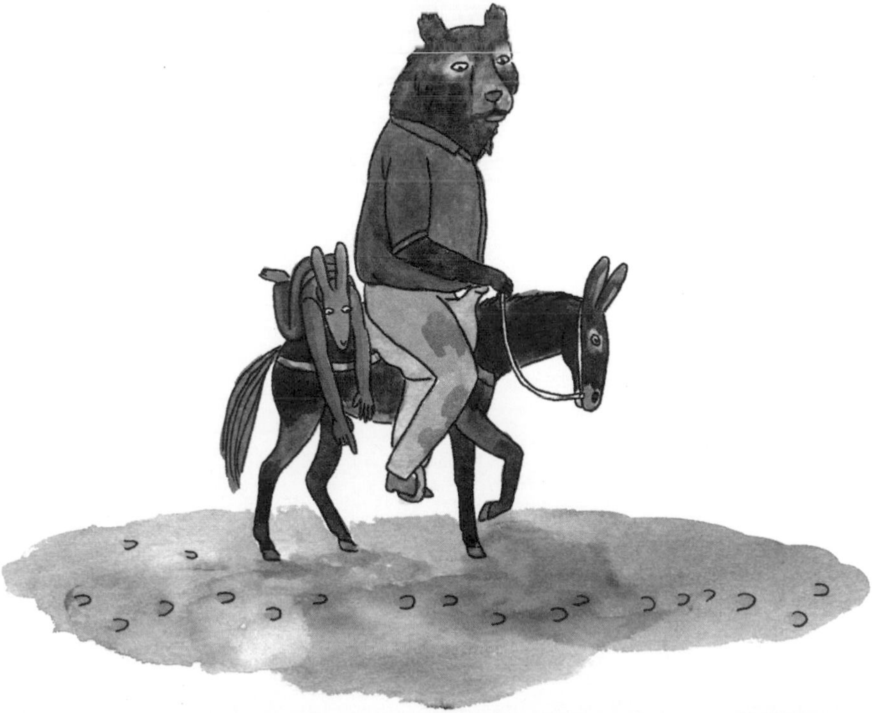

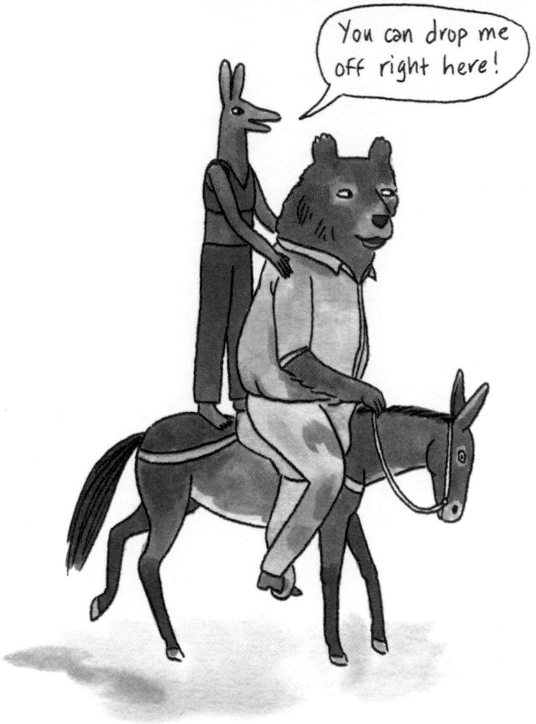
You can drop me off right here!

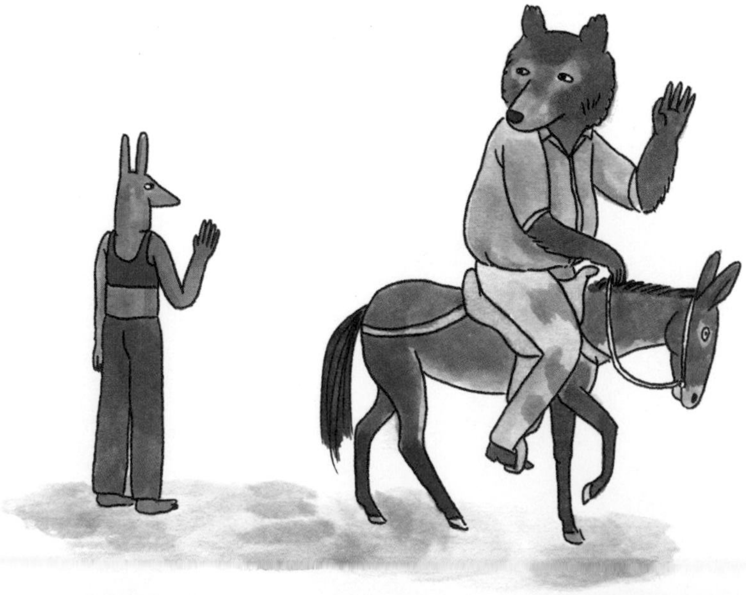

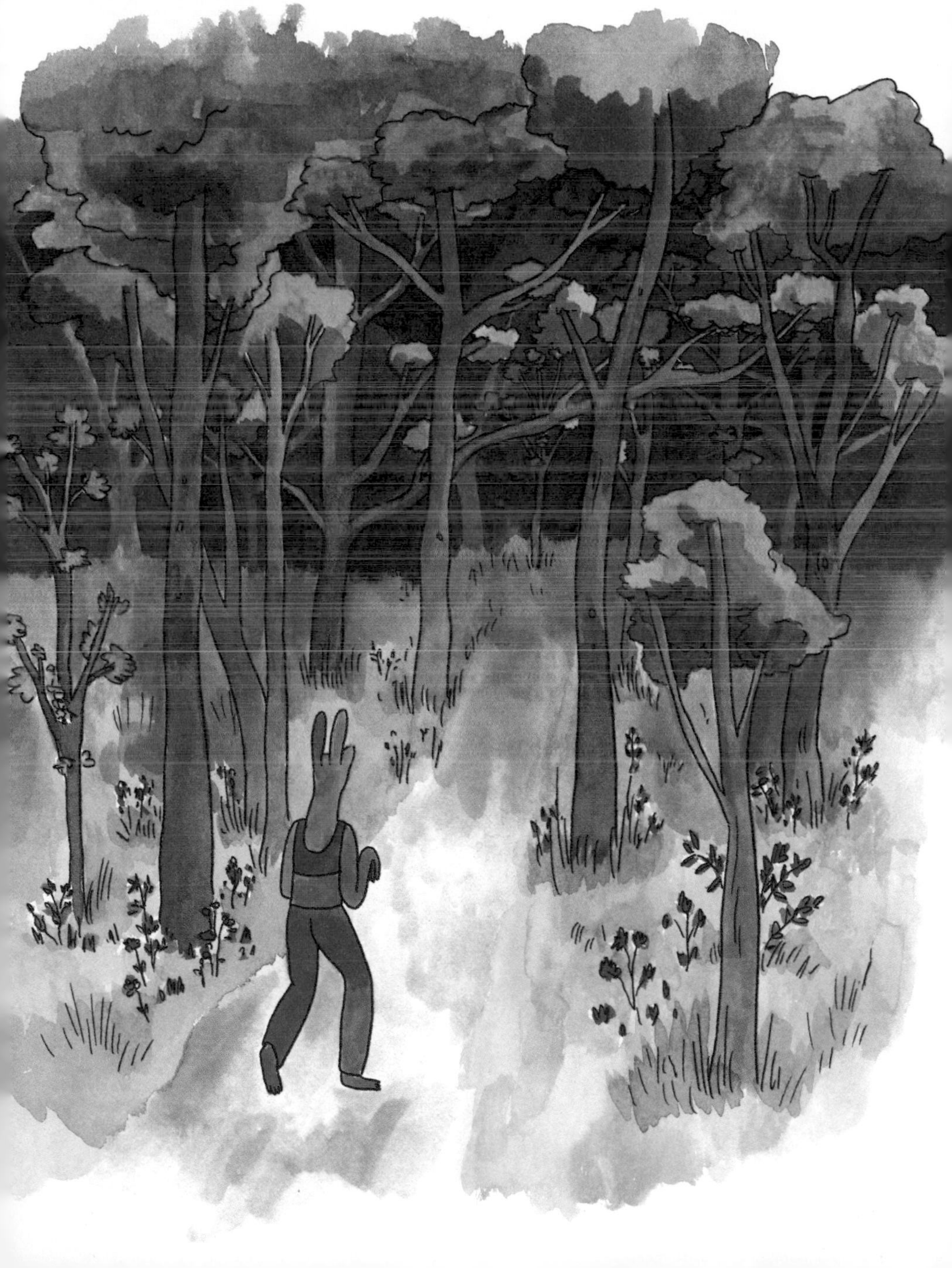

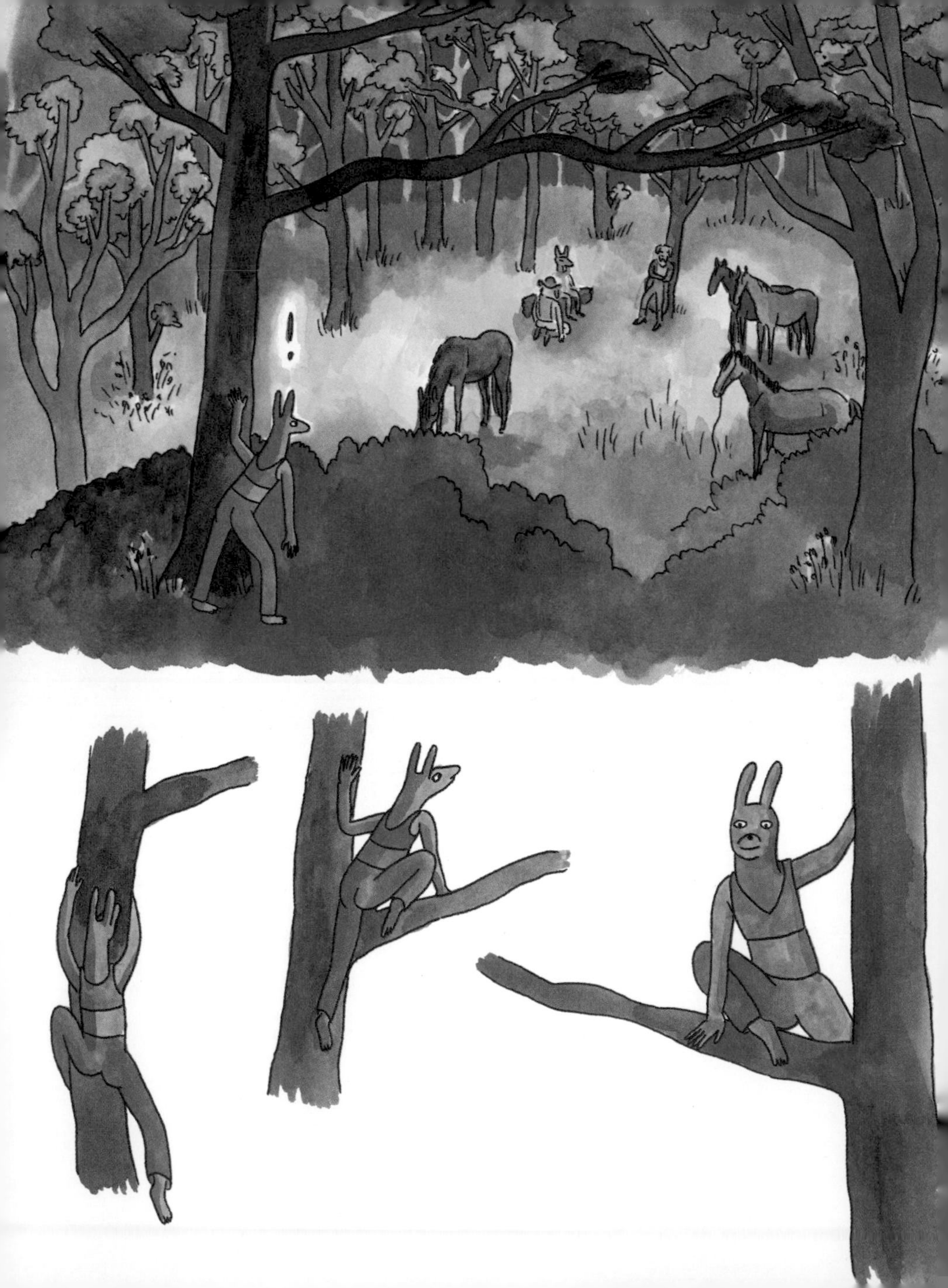
!

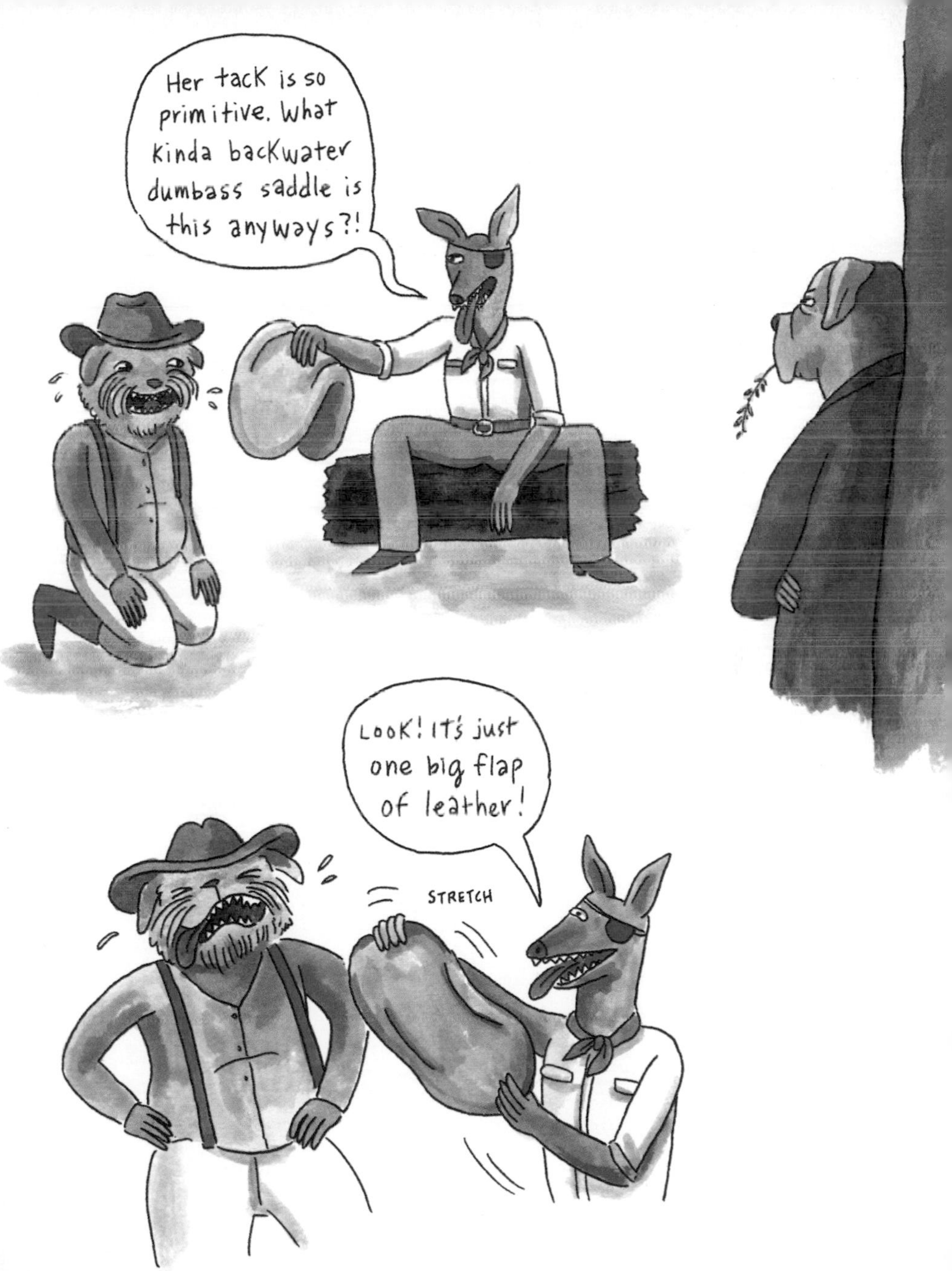
Her tack is so primitive. What kinda backwater dumbass saddle is this anyways?!
LOOK! IT's just one big flap of leather!
STRETCH

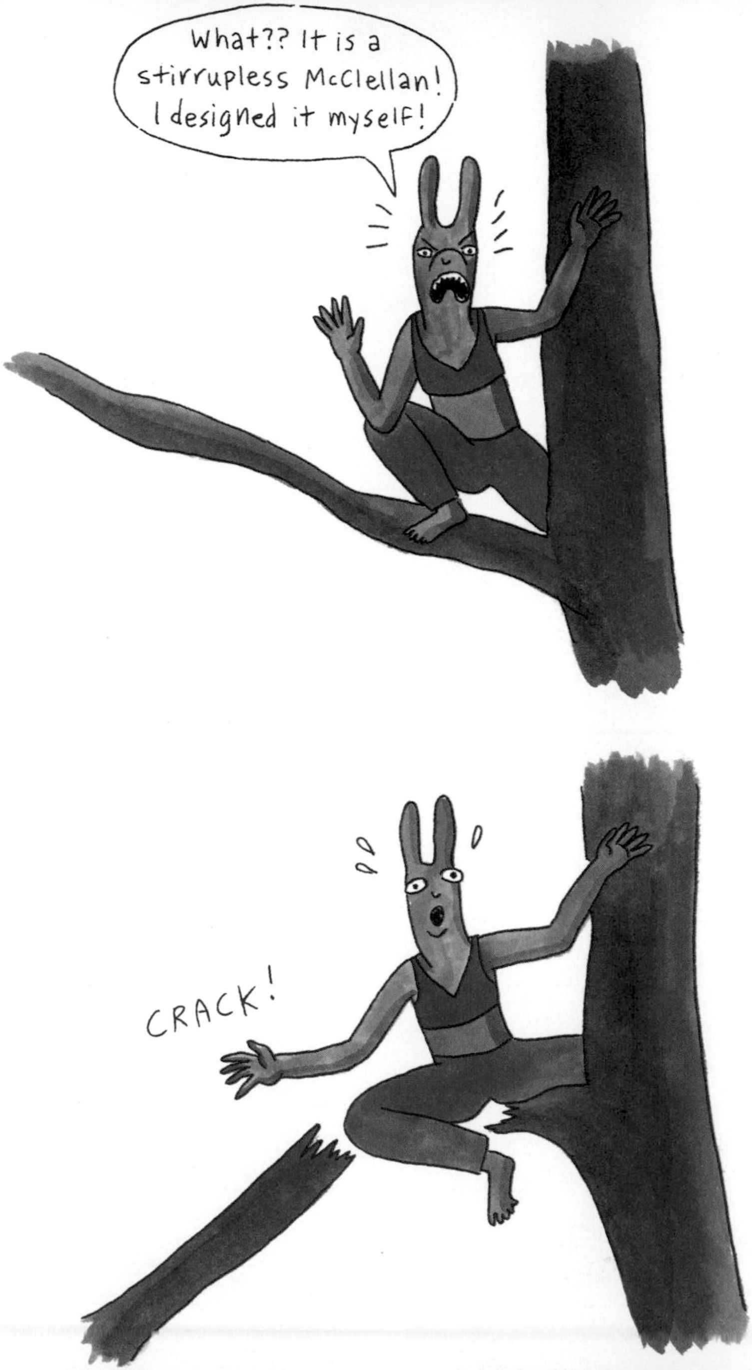
What?? It is a stirrupless McClellan! I designed it myself!
CRACK!

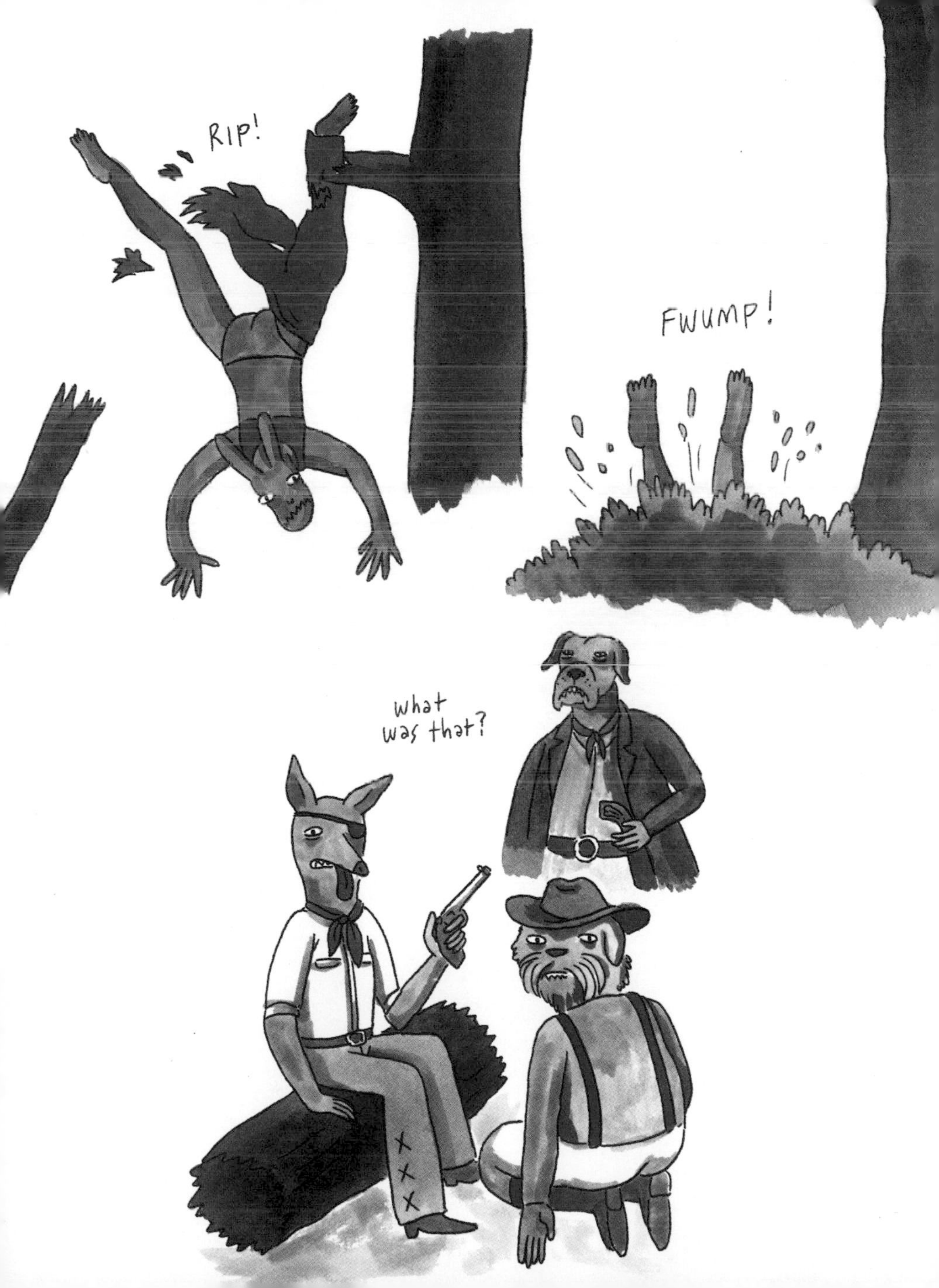
RIP!
FWUMP!
what was that?

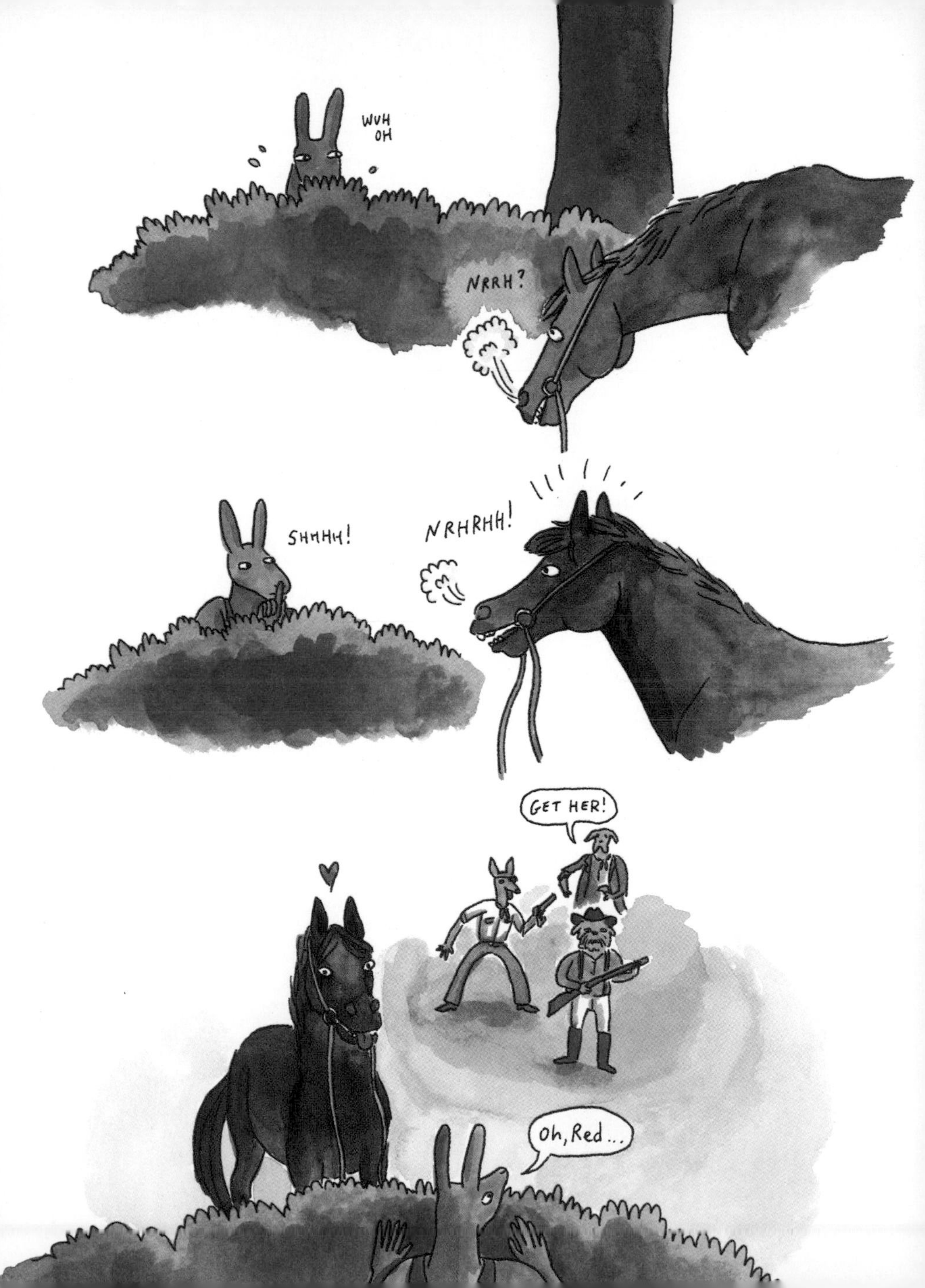
WUH OH
NRRH?
SHHHH!
NRHRHH!
GET HER!
Oh, Red...

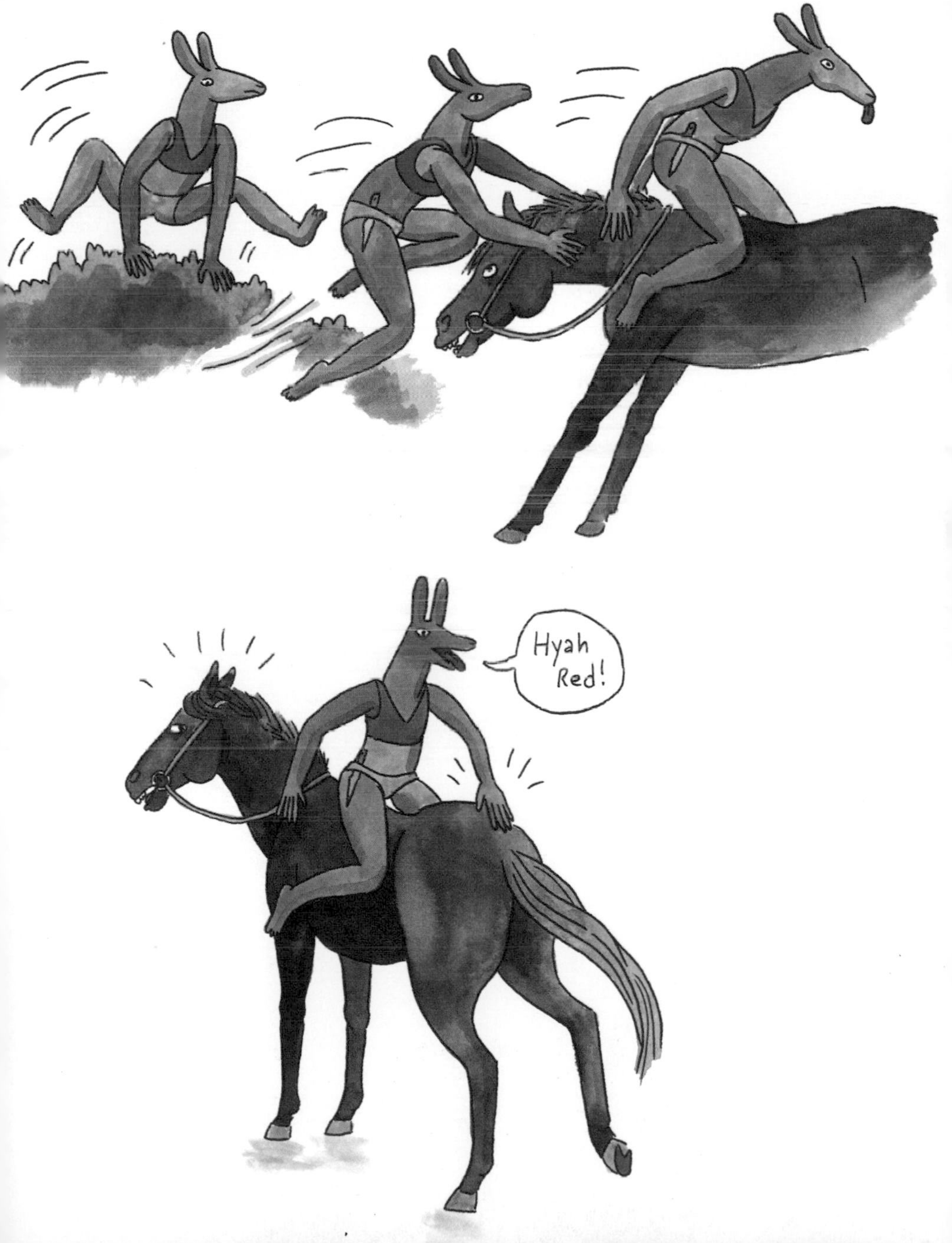
Hyah Red!

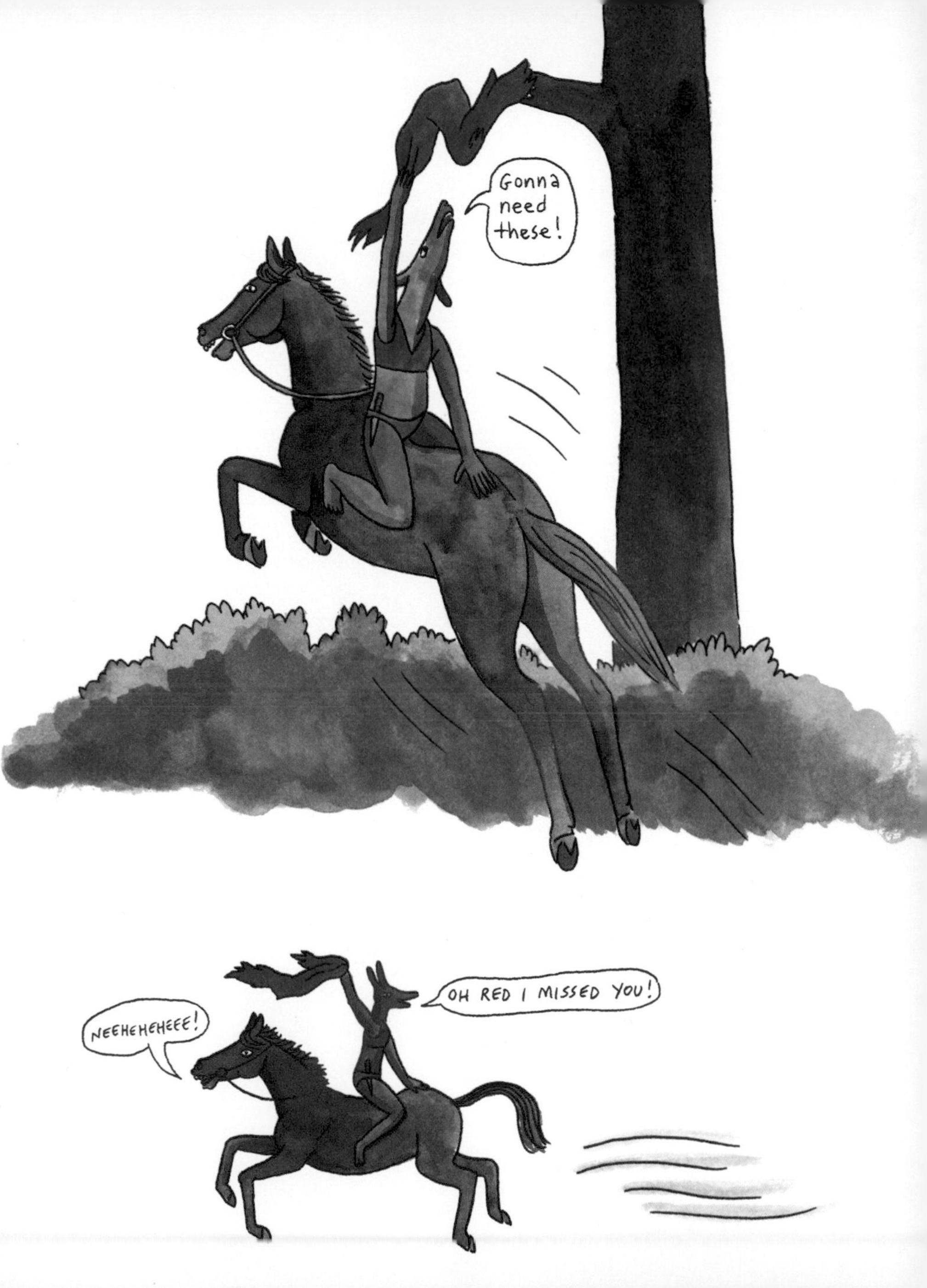
Gonna need these!
NEEHEHEHEEE!
OH RED I MISSED YOU!

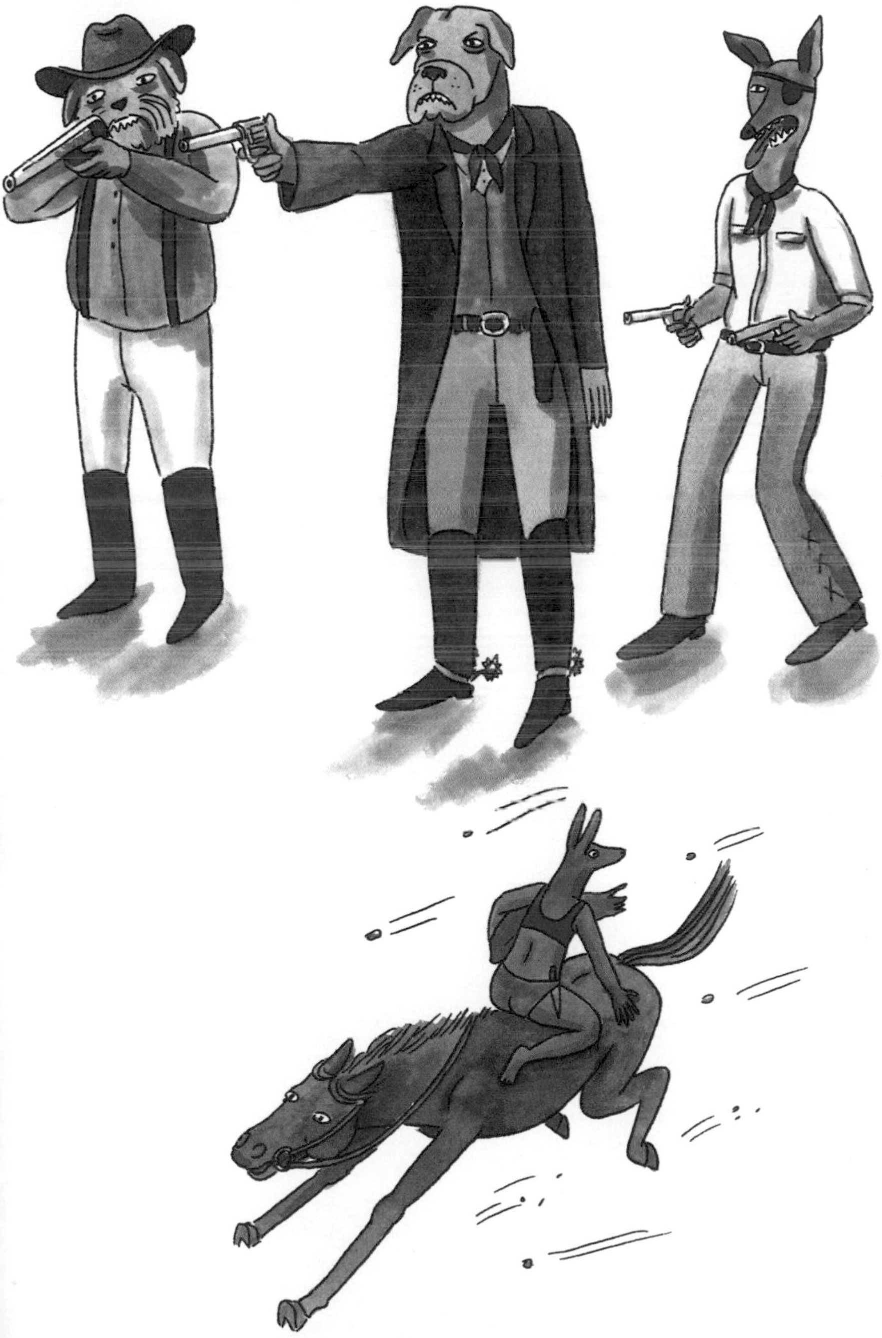

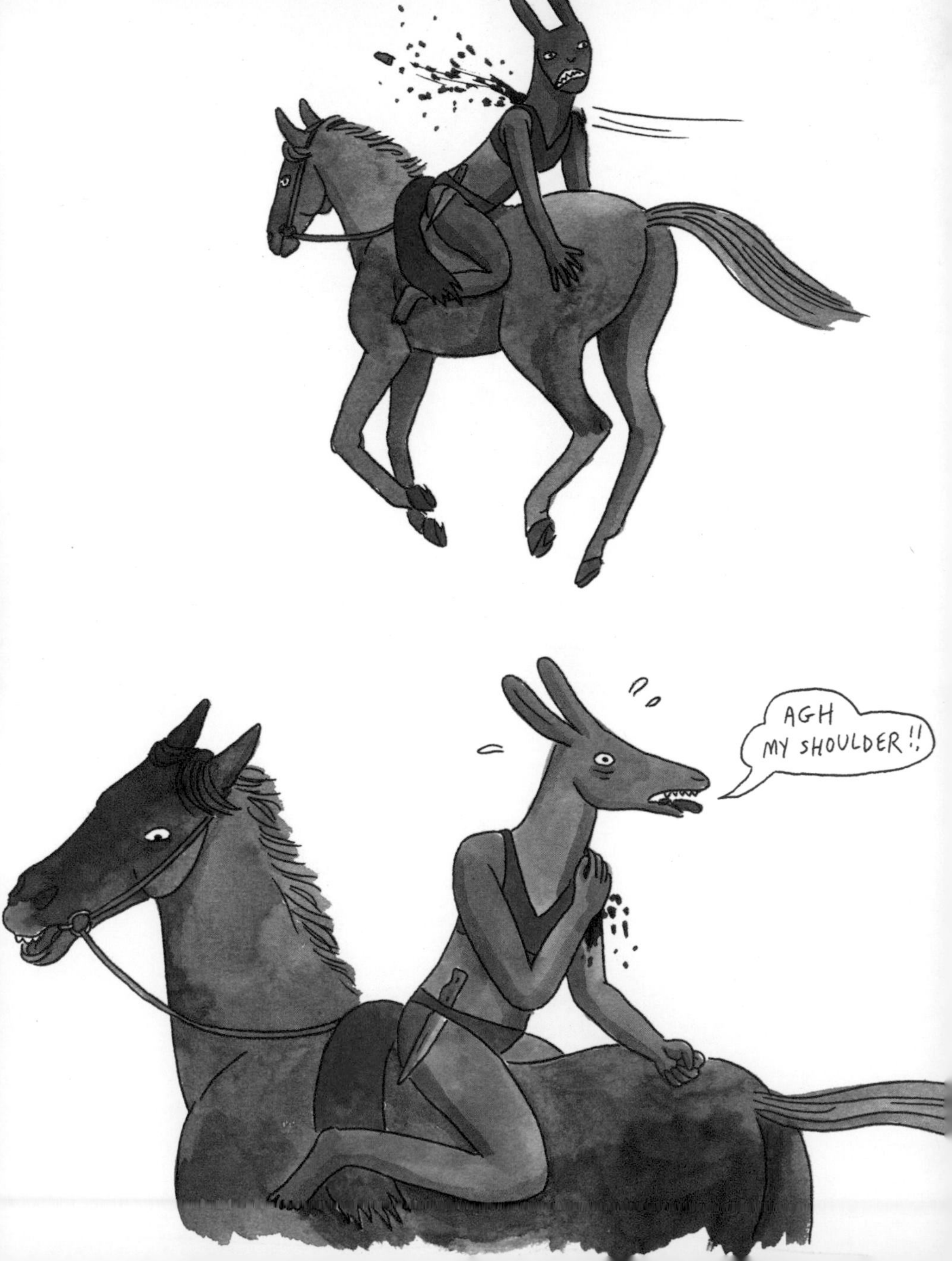
AGH
MY SHOULDER !!

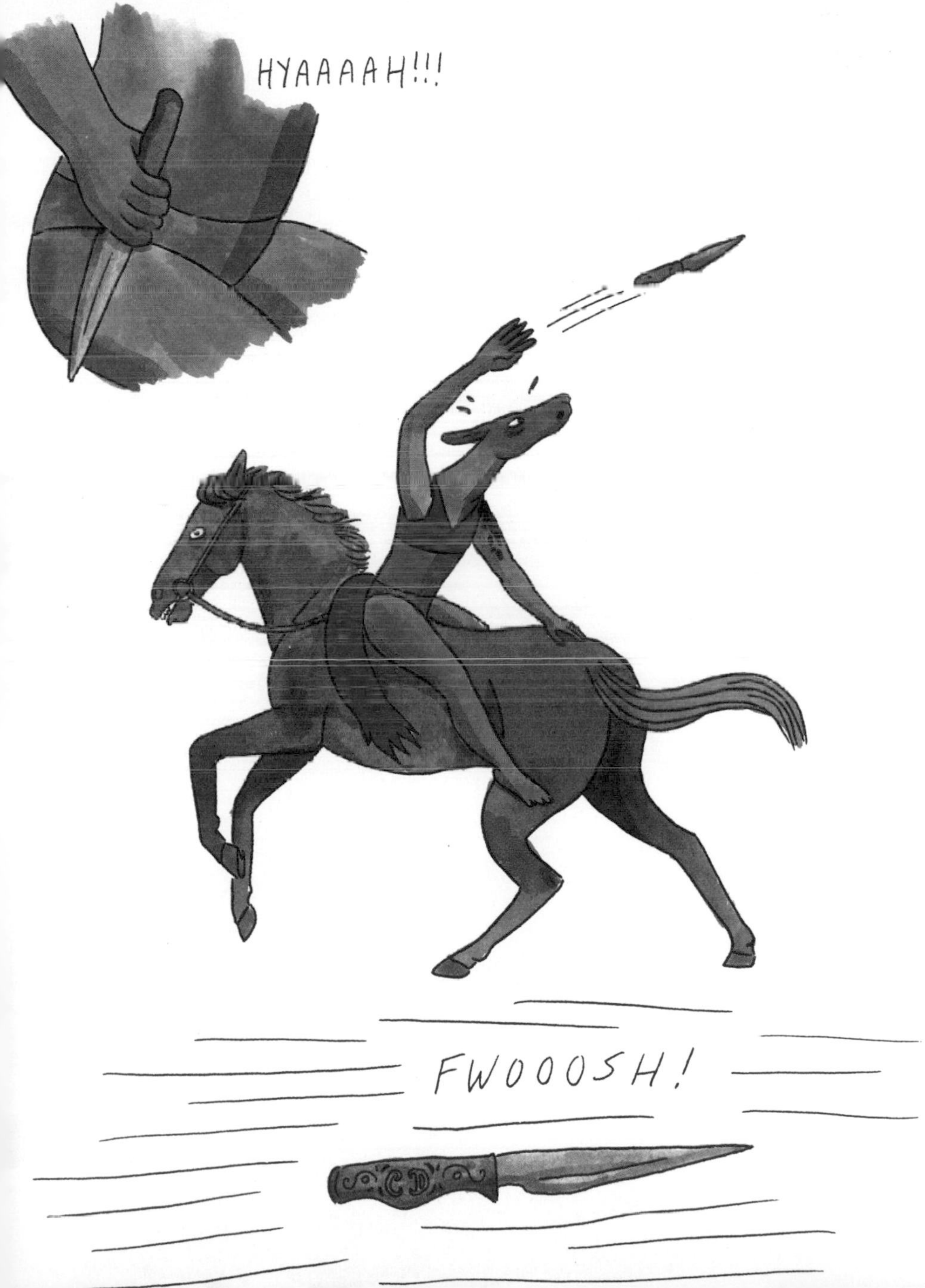
HYAAAAH!!!
FWOOOSH!
CD

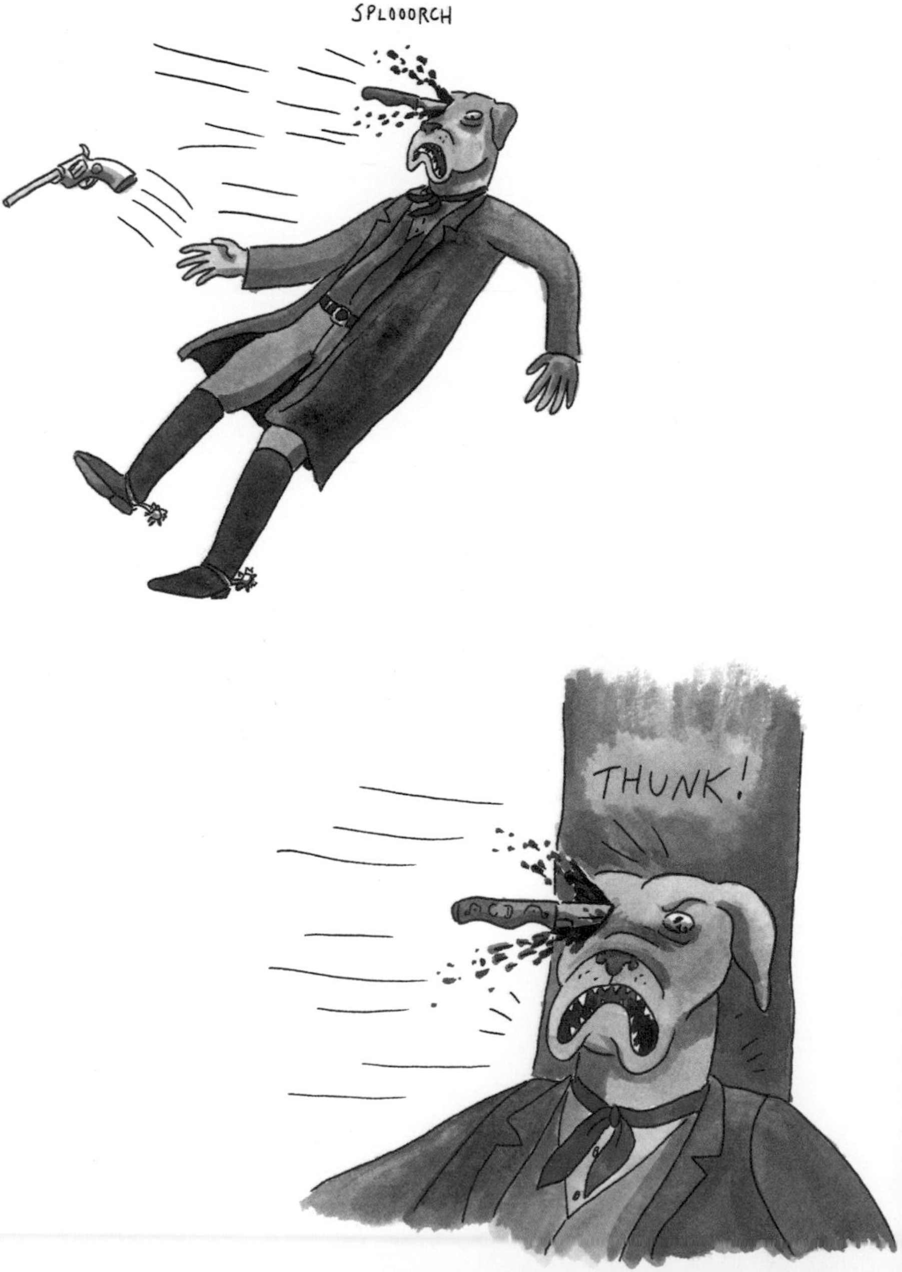
SPLOOORCH
THUNK!

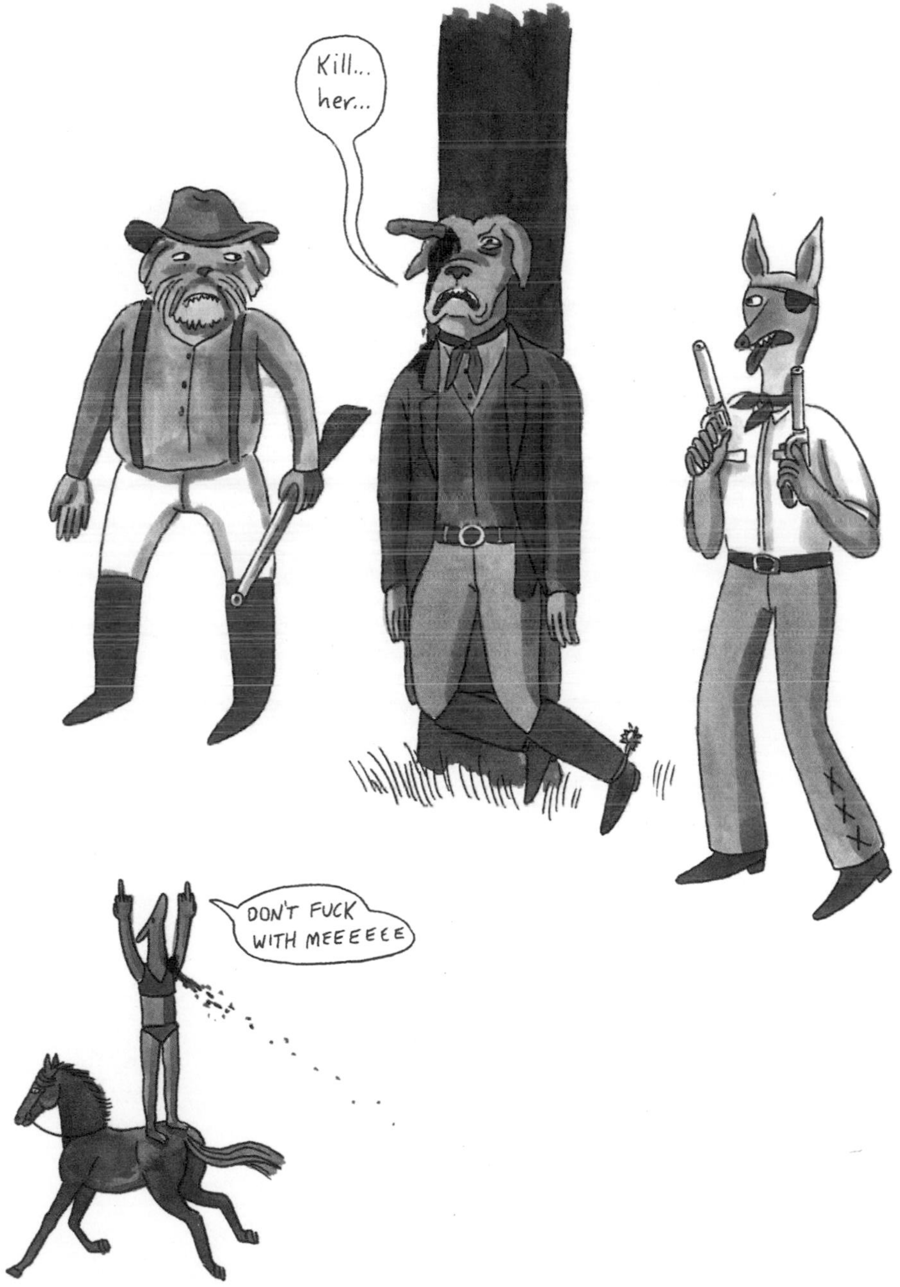
Kill... her...
DON'T FUCK WITH MEEEEEE

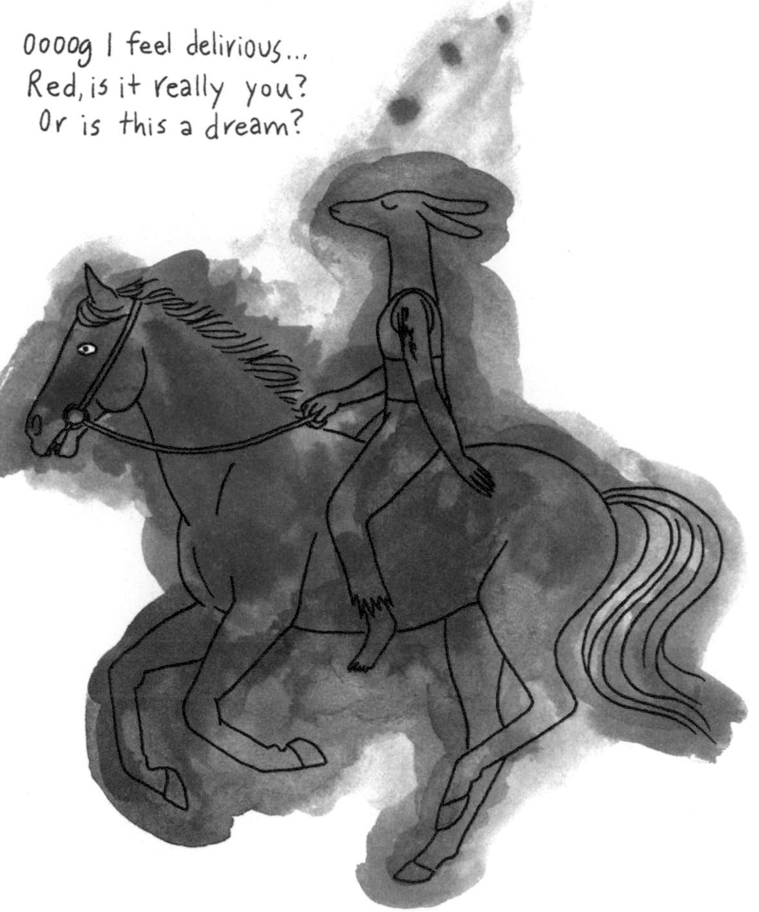
Oooog I feel delirious...
Red, is it really you?
Or is this a dream?

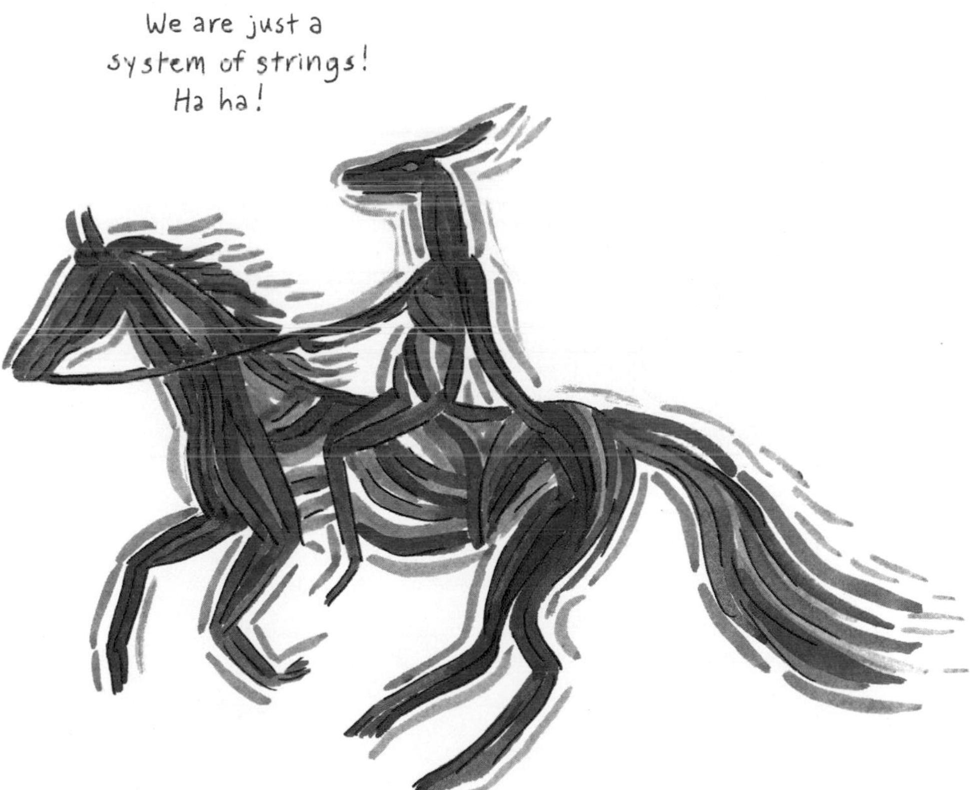
We are just a
system of strings!
Ha ha!

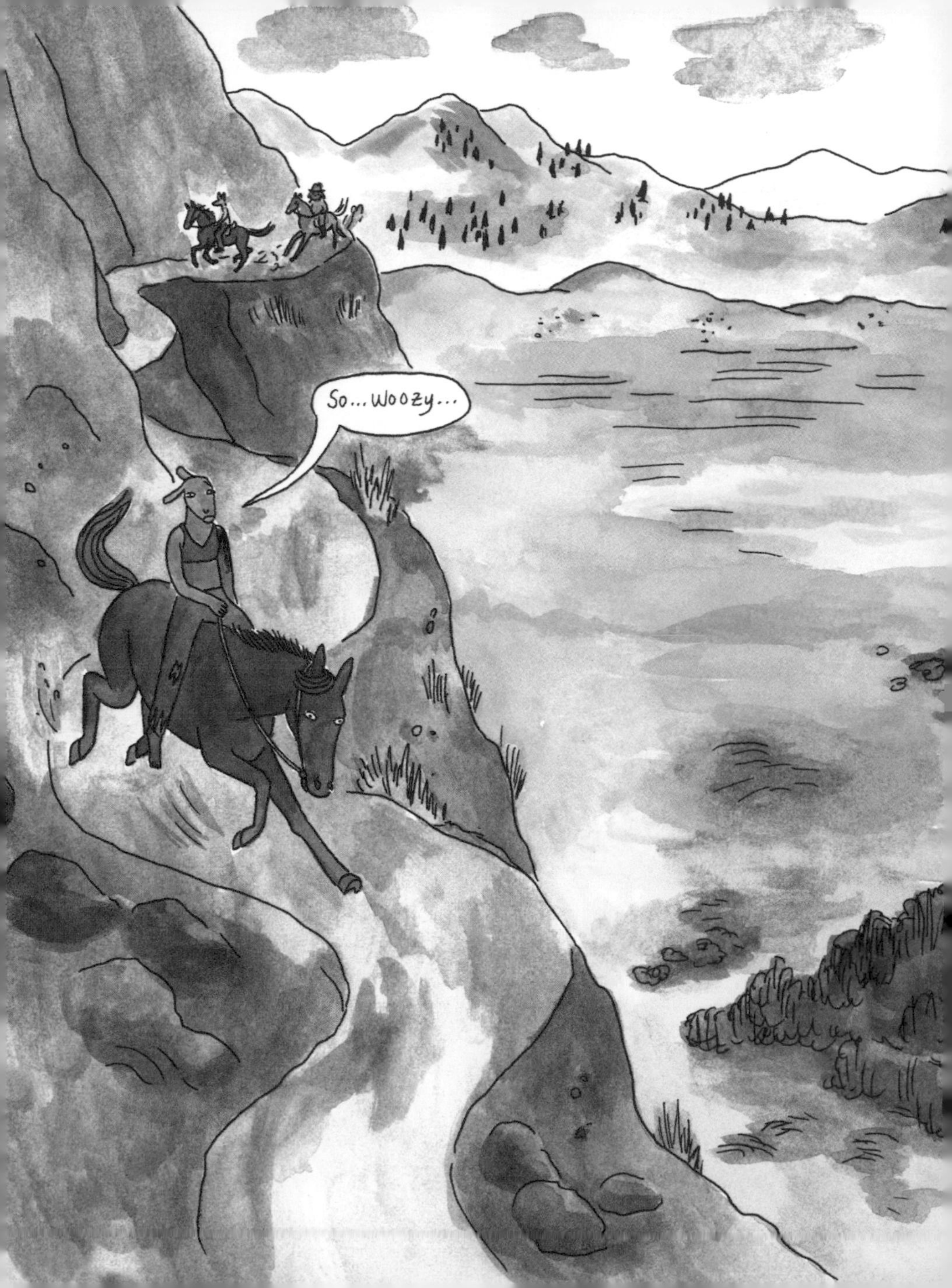
So... woozy...

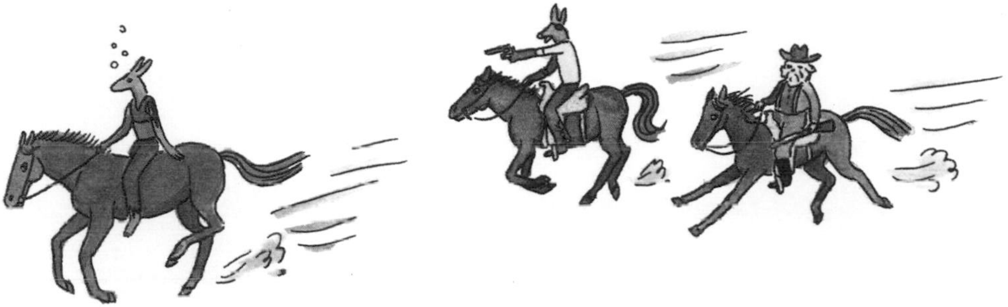

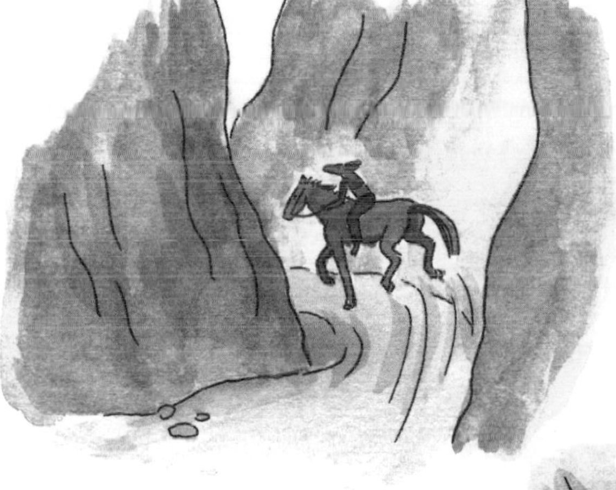

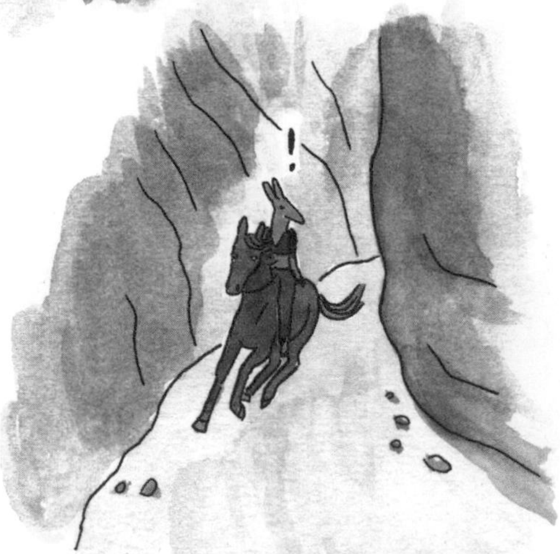
!

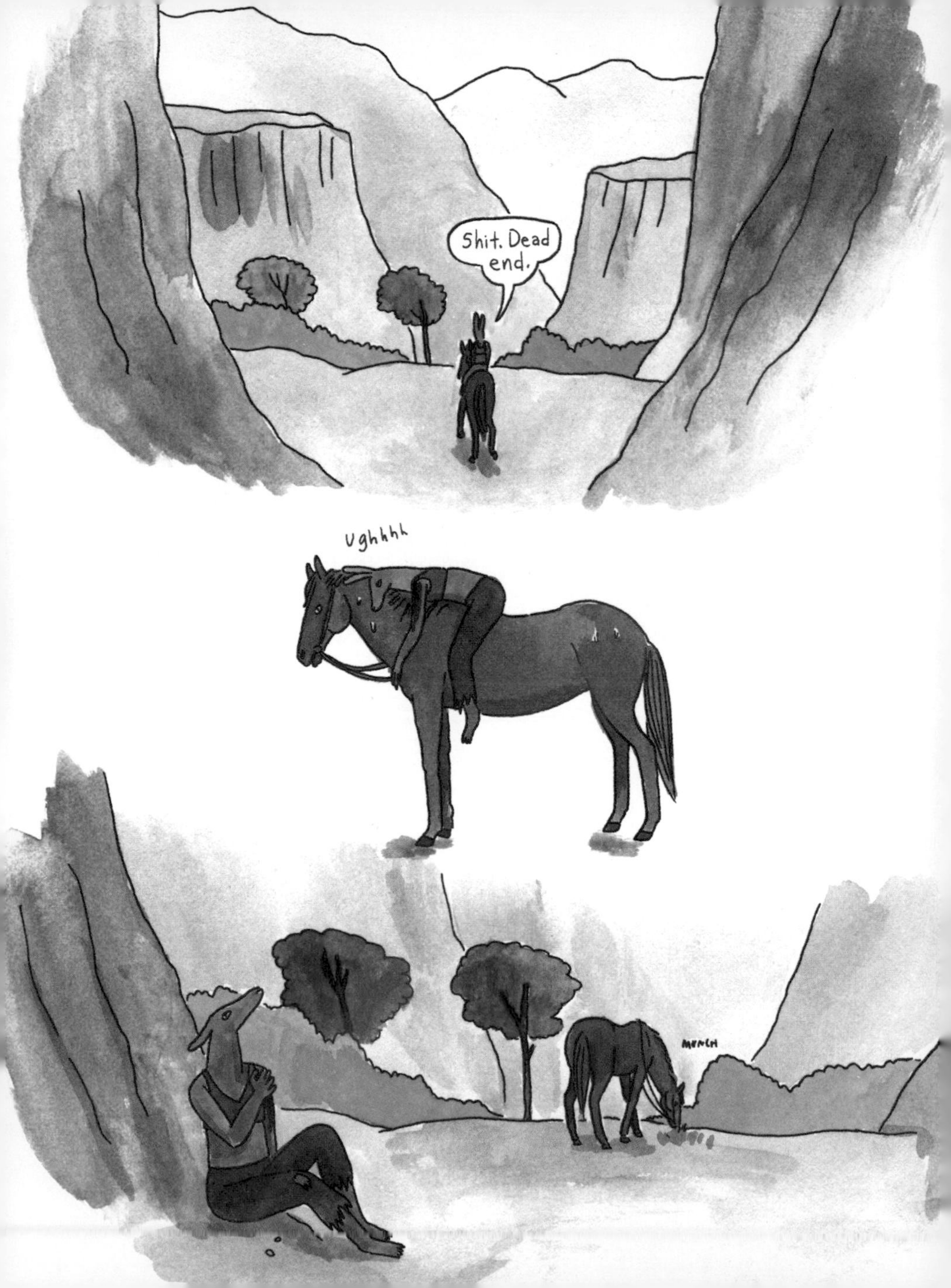

Shit. Dead end.
Ughhhh
MUNCH

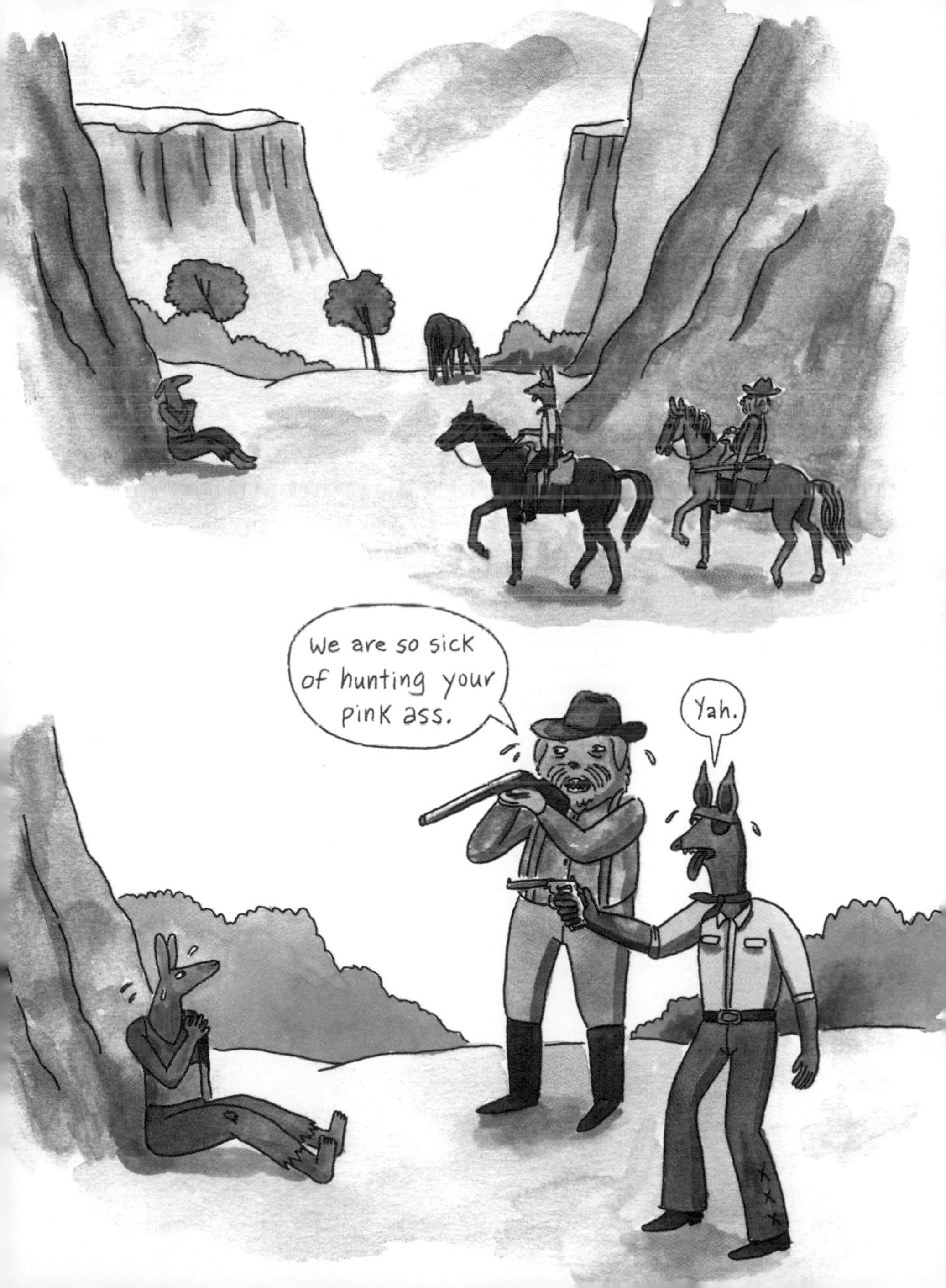
We are so sick of hunting your pink ass.
Yah.

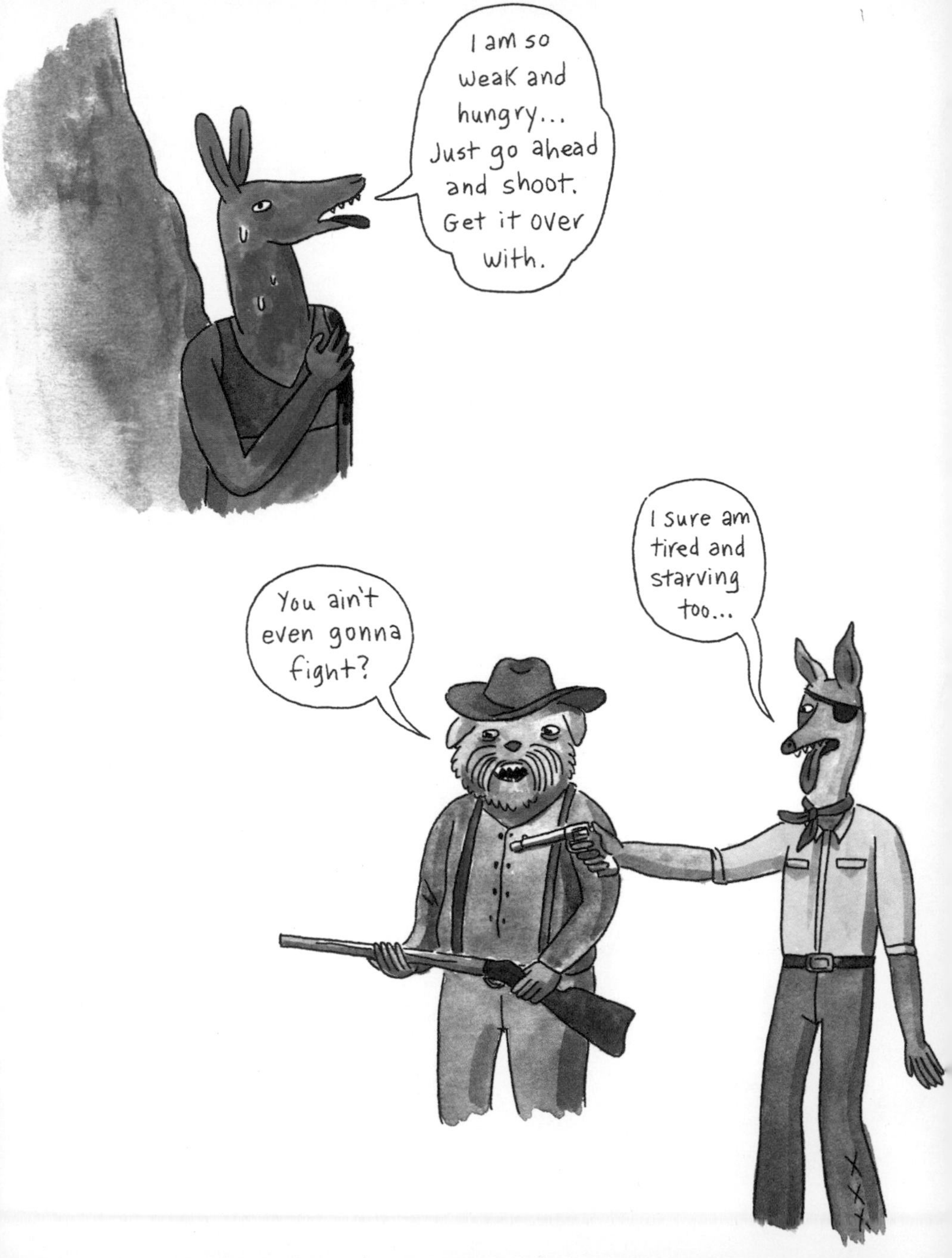
I am so weak and hungry... Just go ahead and shoot. Get it over with.
You ain't even gonna fight?
I sure am tired and starving too...

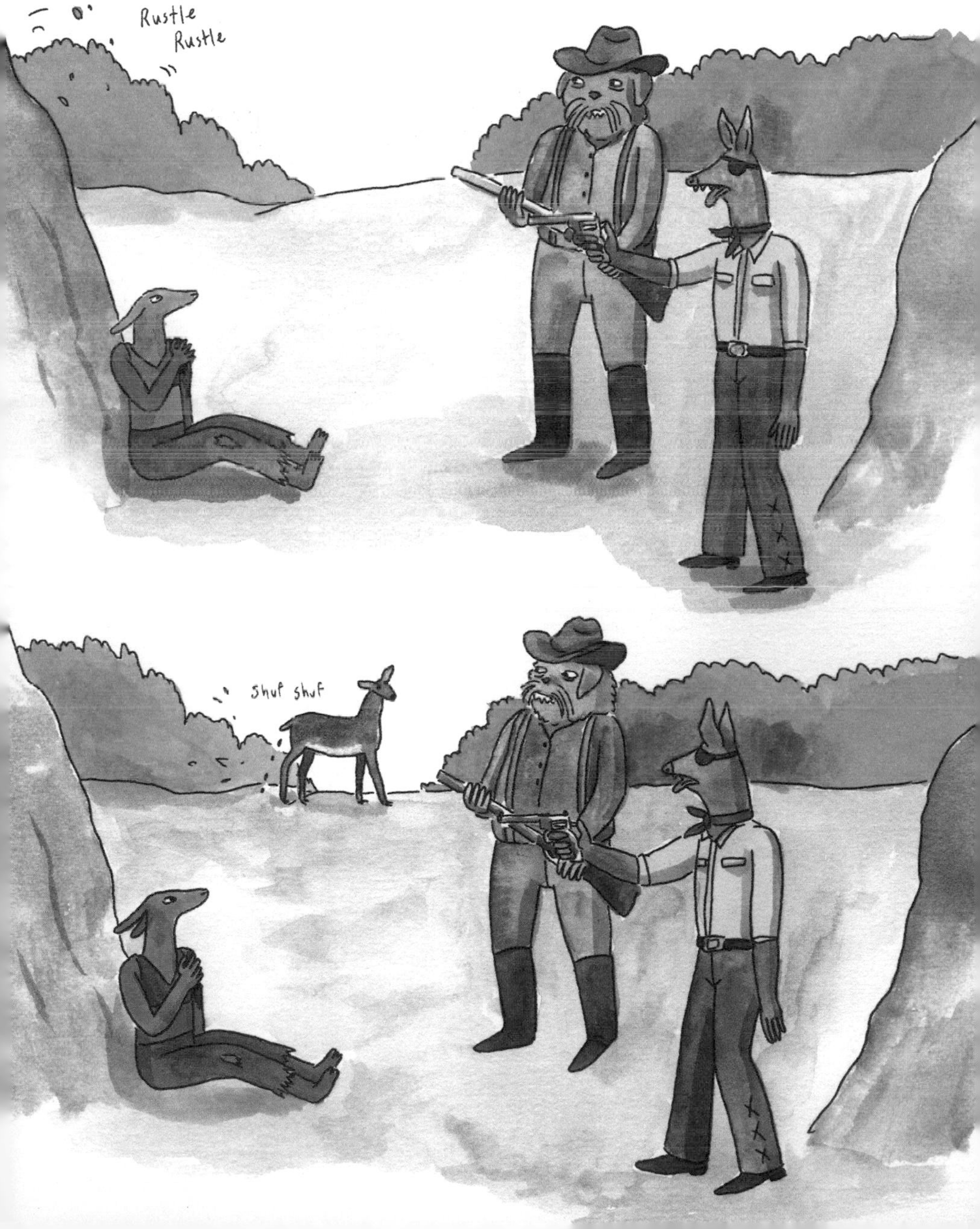
Rustle
Rustle
shuf shuf

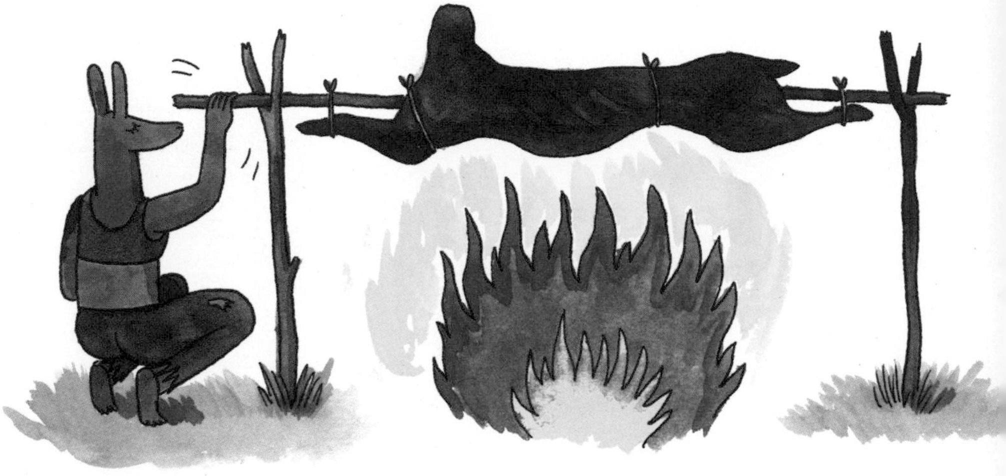

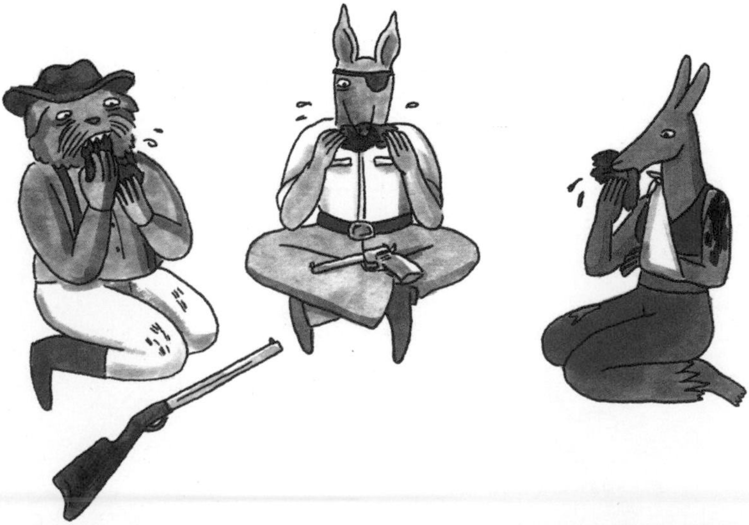

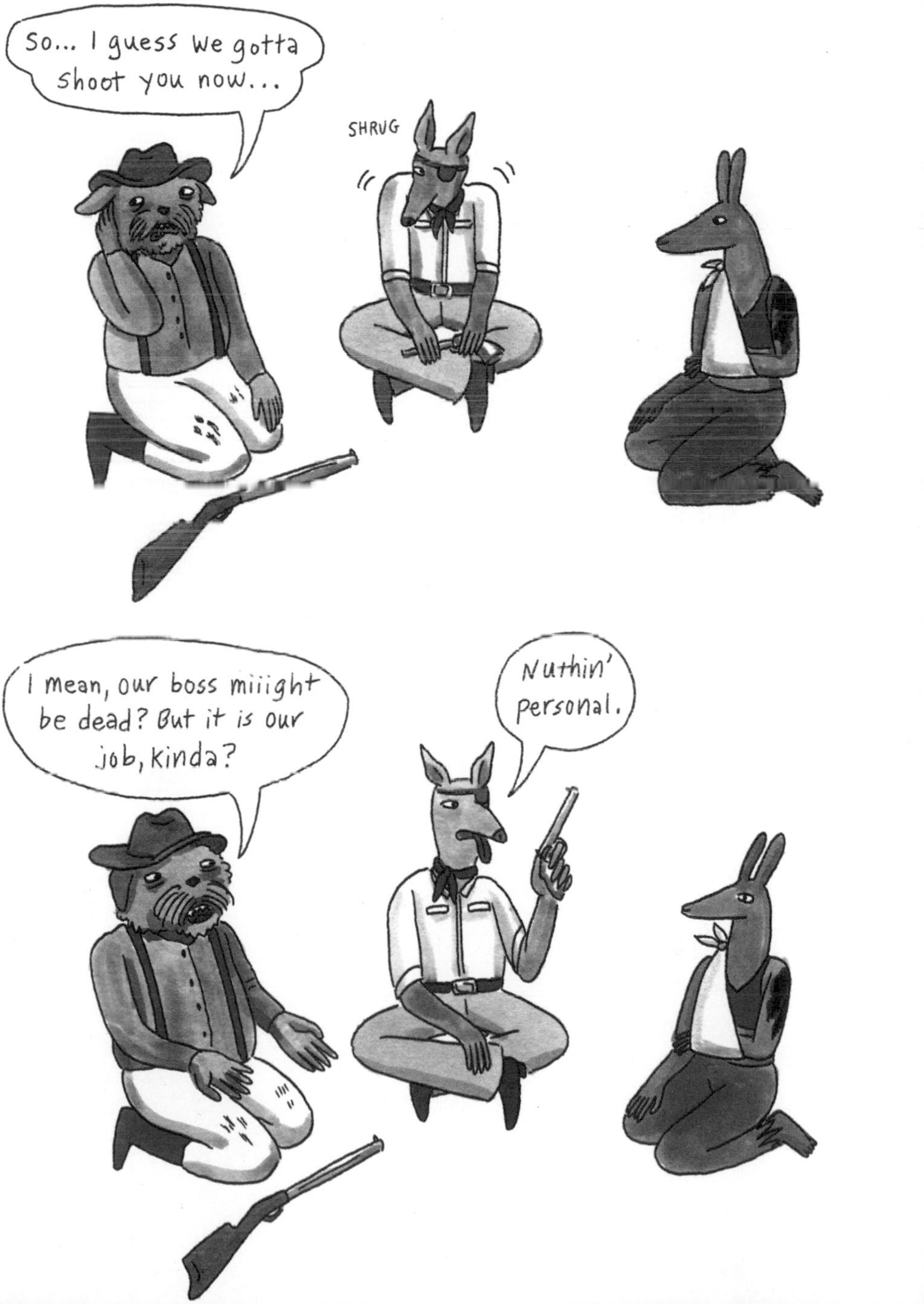
So... I guess we gotta shoot you now...
SHRUG
I mean, our boss miiight be dead? But it is our job, kinda?
Nuthin' personal.

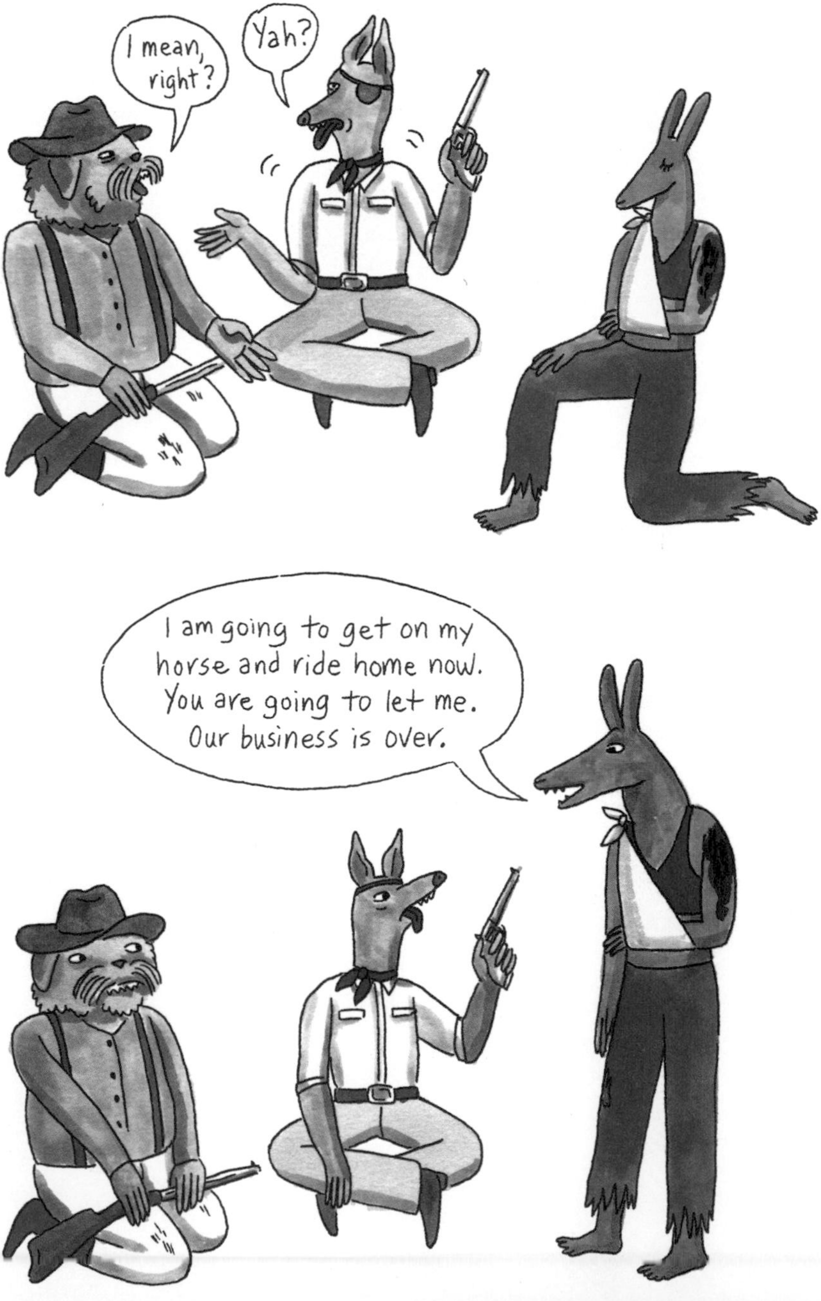
I mean, right?
Yah?
I am going to get on my horse and ride home now. You are going to let me. Our business is over.

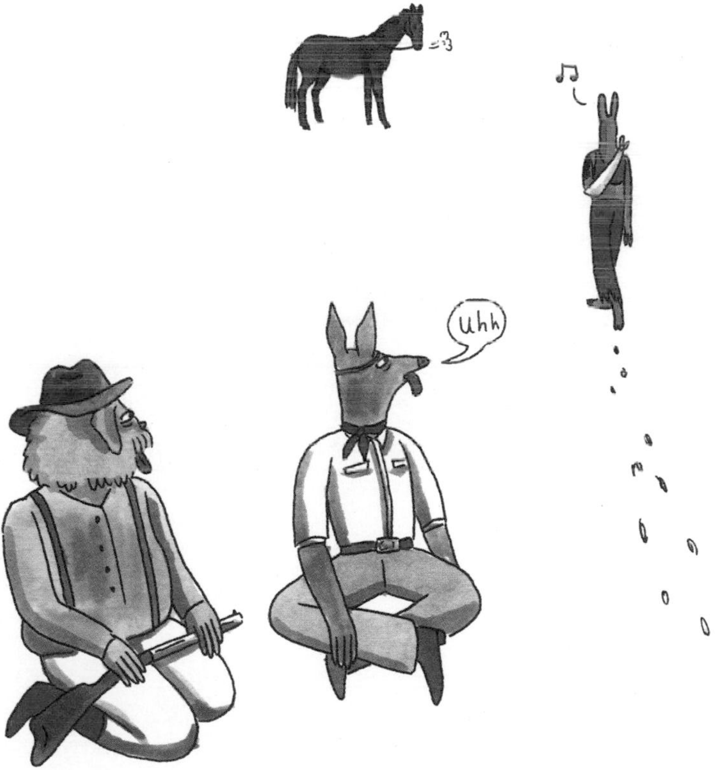
Uhh

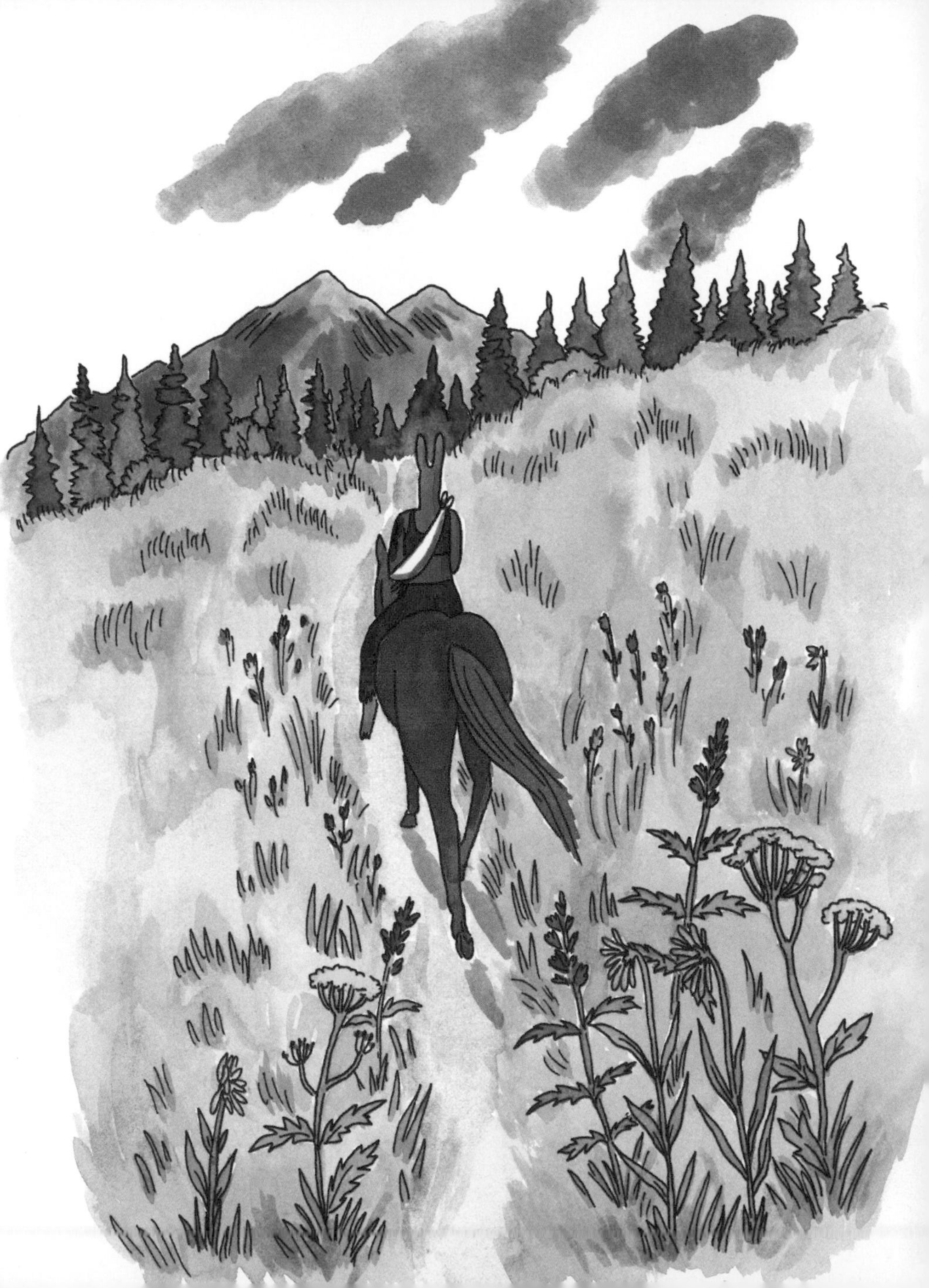

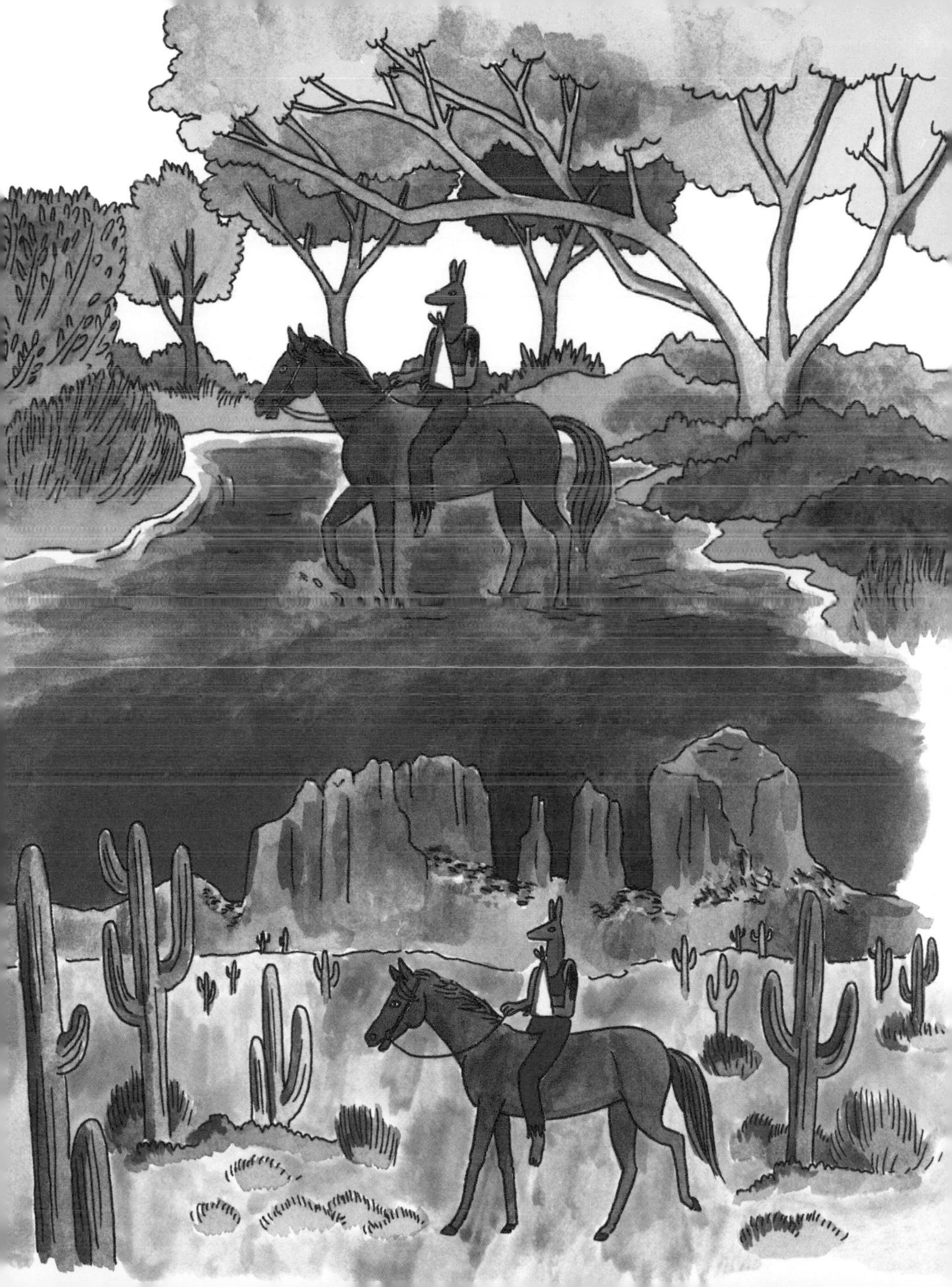

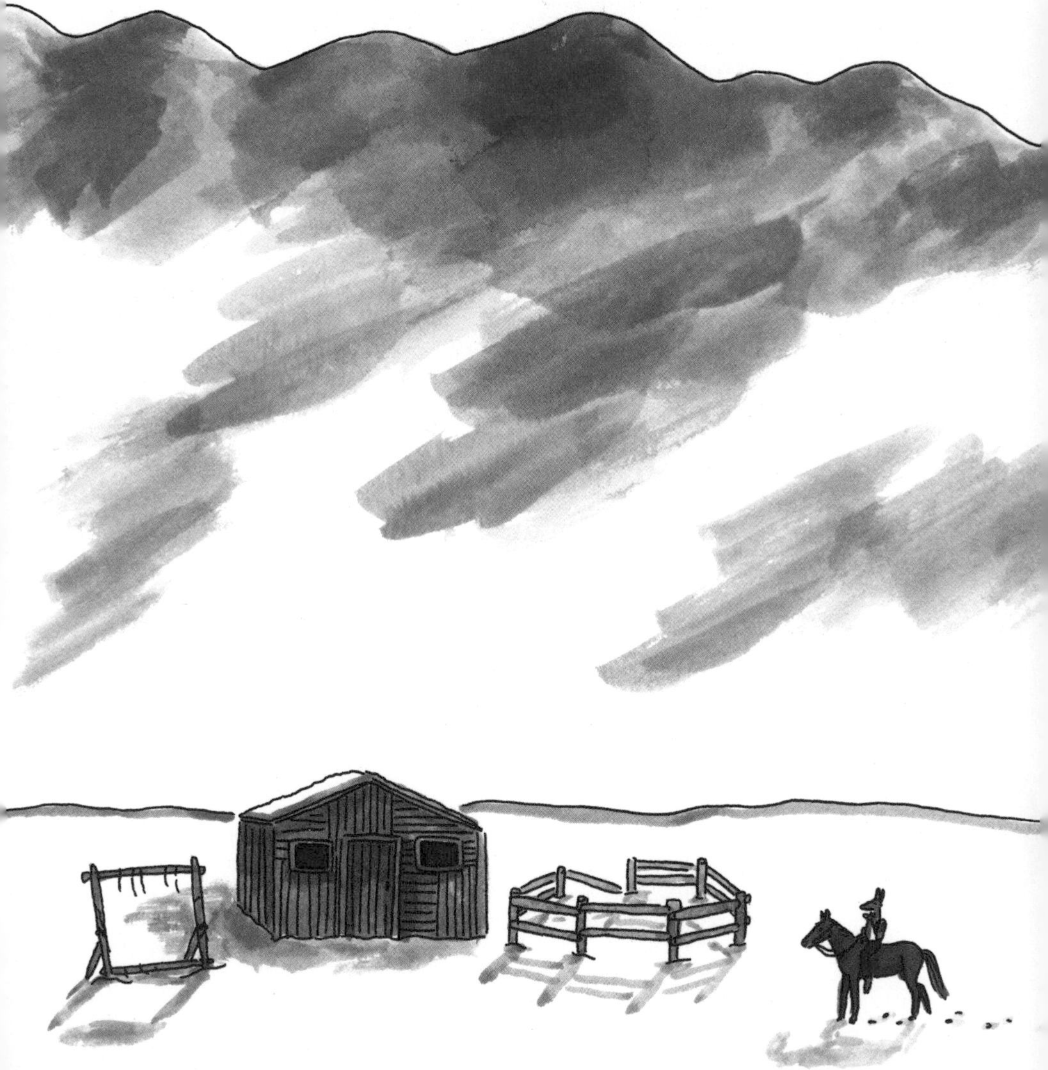

My home...

My knife
collection...

My half-finished
projects...

my stuff...

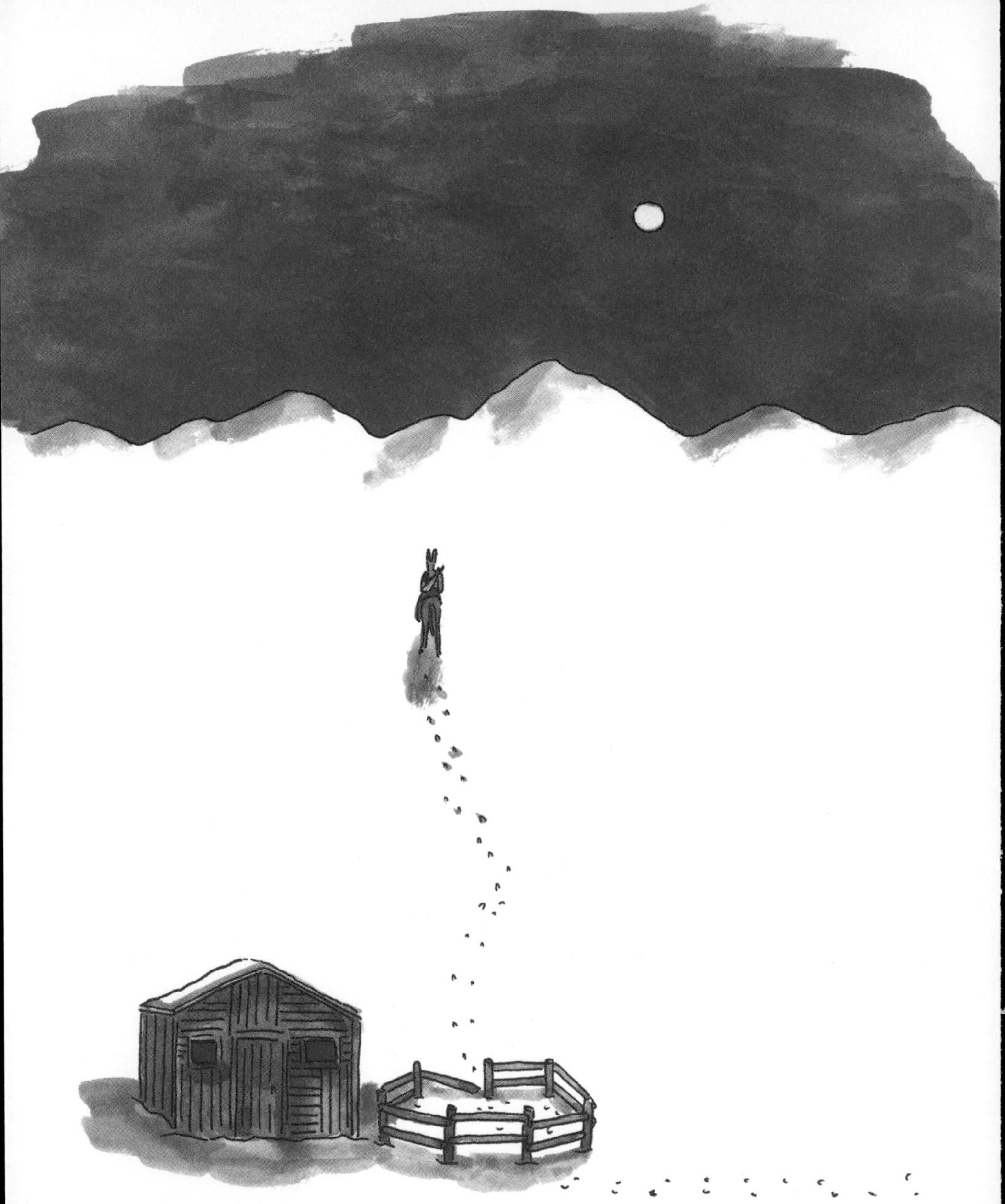

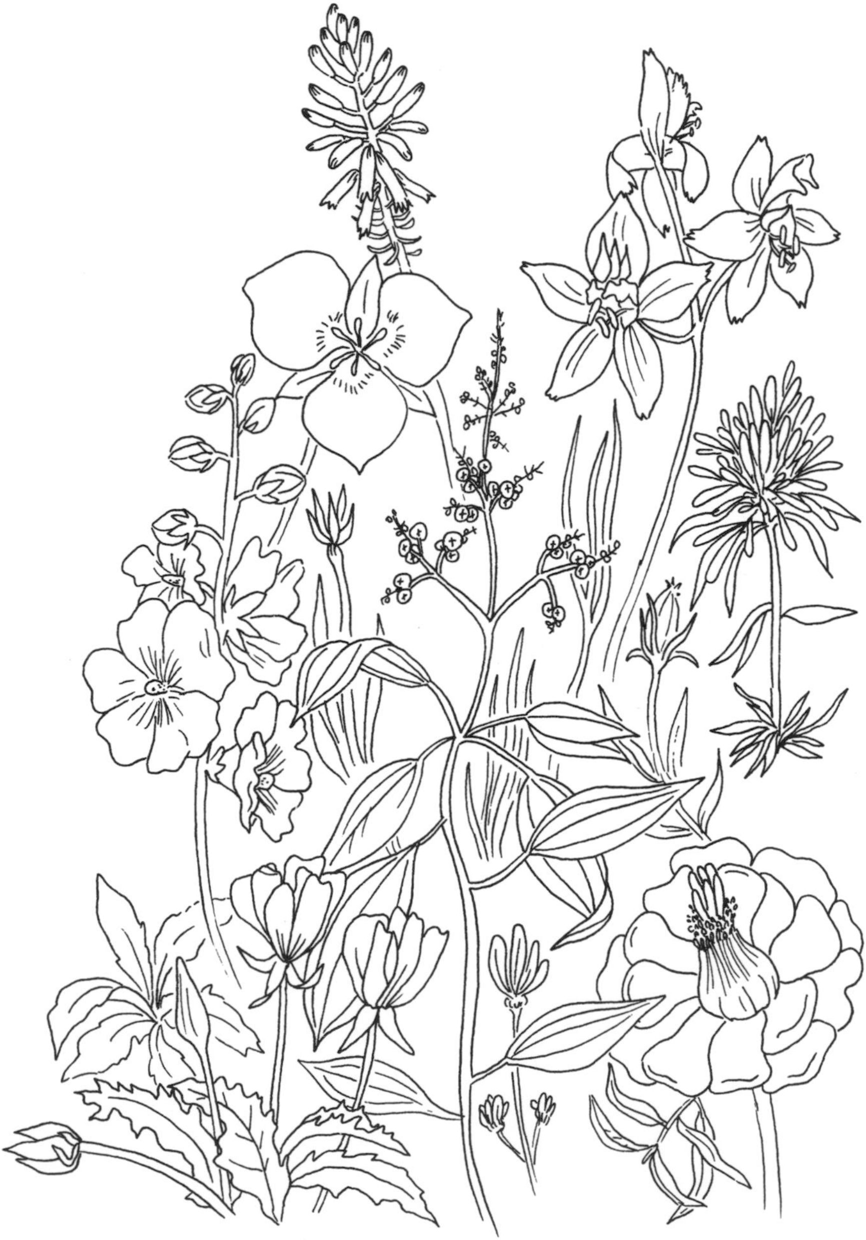

Lisa Hanawalt lives and rides in Los Angeles.

Other books by Lisa:

My Dirly Dumb Eyes
Hot Dog Taste Test

Some favorite horses Lisa has known:

Burgundy   Rebel
Sissy   Jackpot
Tony   Gus
Diamante   Risky
Valentina

COYOTE & RED in "Pony Love"

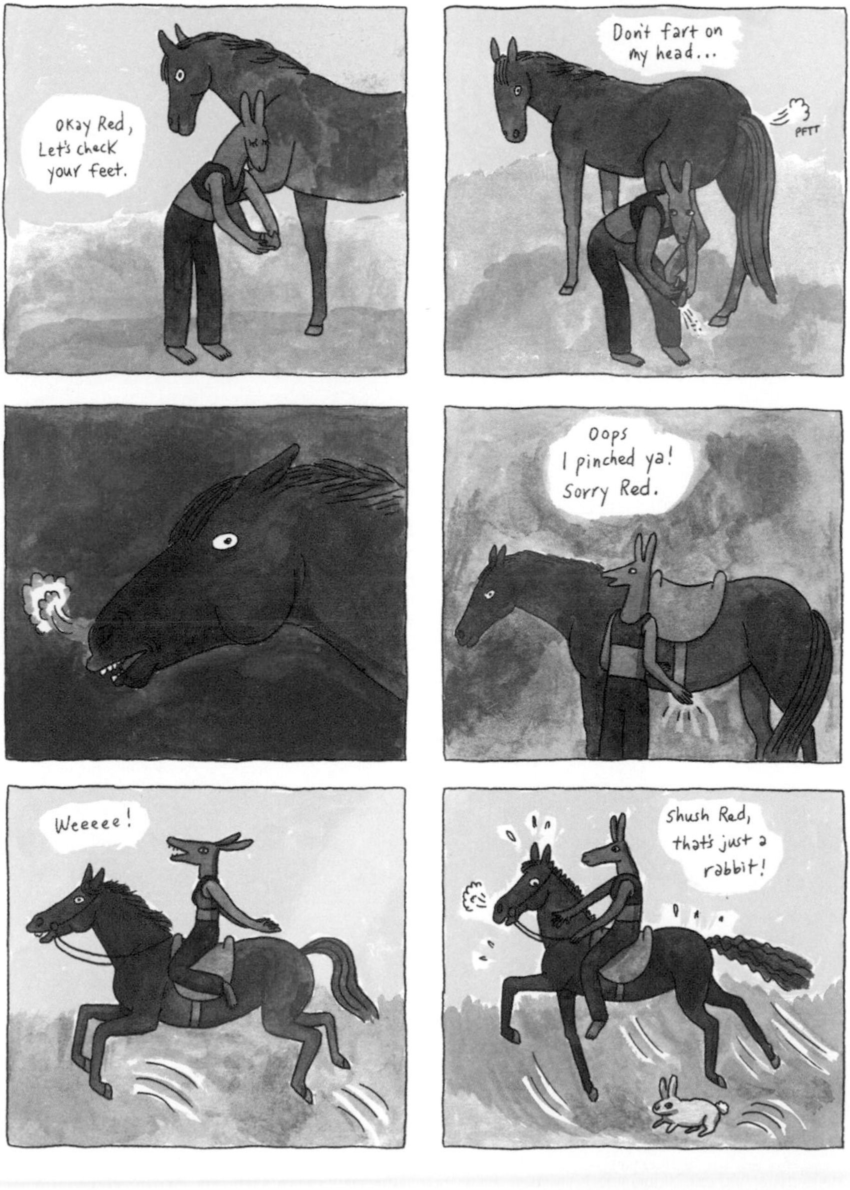
Okay Red,
Let's check
your feet.
Don't fart on
my head...
PFTT
Oops
I pinched ya!
Sorry Red.
Weeeee!
Shush Red,
that's just a
rabbit!

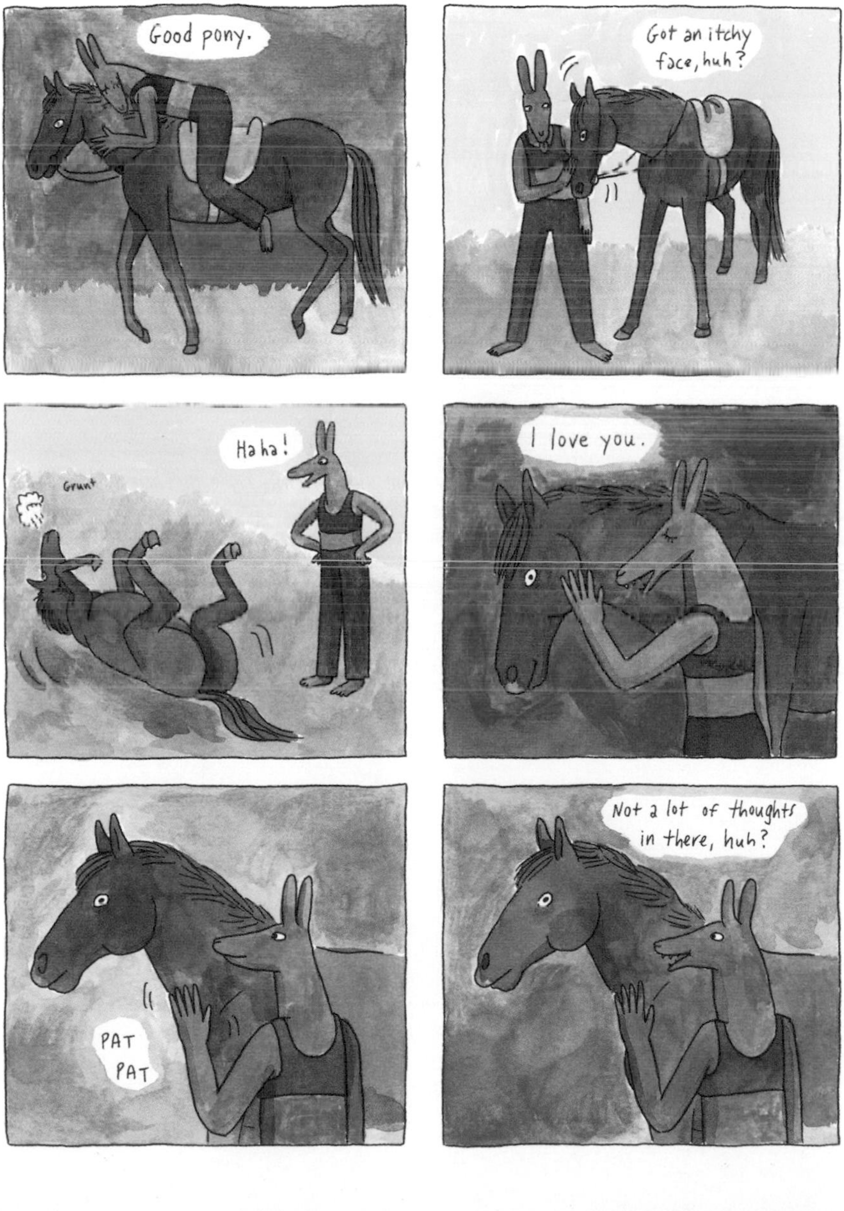
Good pony.
Got an itchy face, huh?
Grunt
Haha!
I love you.
PAT PAT
Not a lot of thoughts in there, huh?

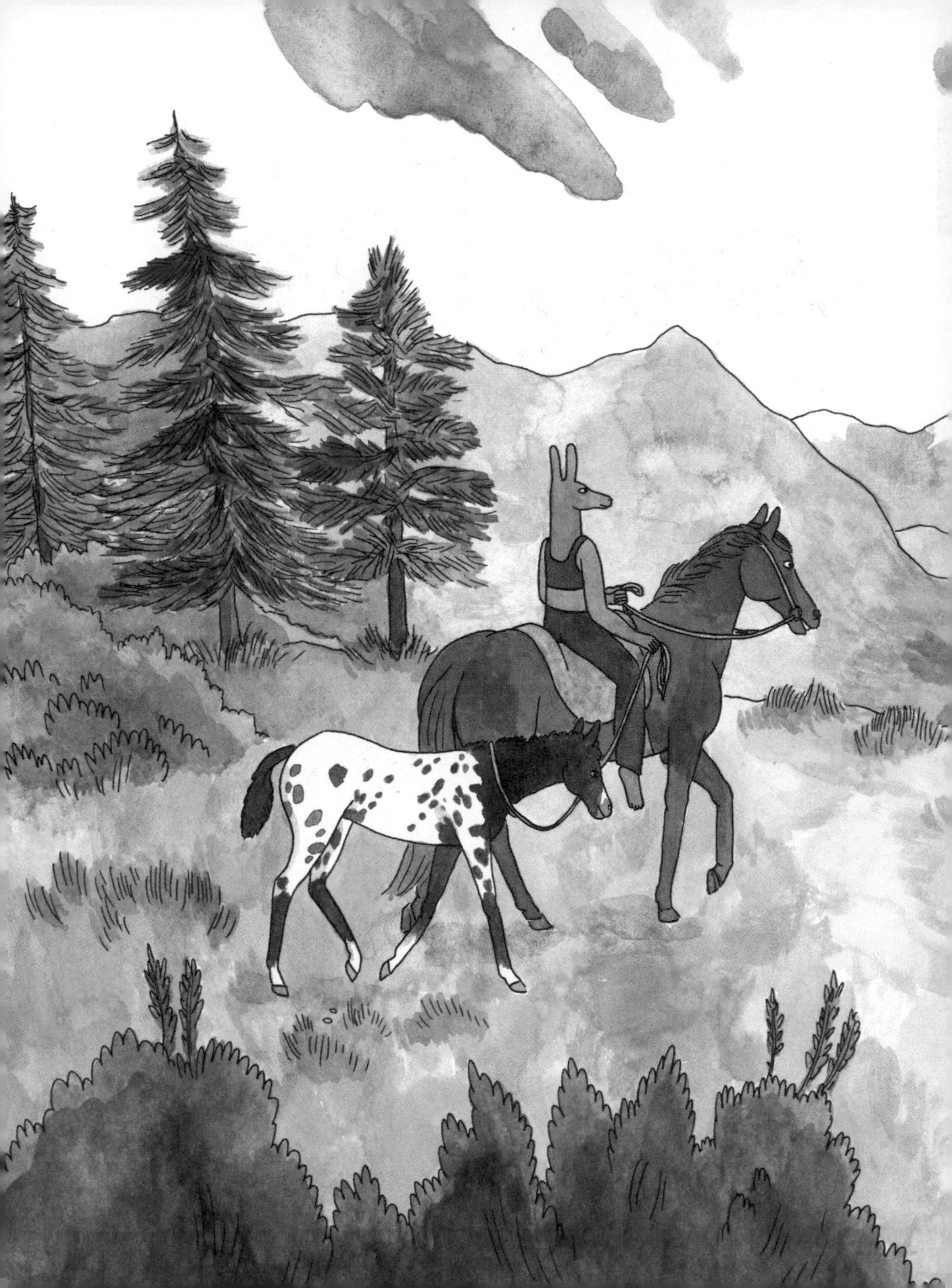